WHITEHALL AND THE LABOUR PROBLEM IN
LATE-VICTORIAN AND EDWARDIAN BRITAIN

Whitehall and the Labour Problem in Late-Victorian and Edwardian Britain

A Study in Official Statistics and Social Control

ROGER DAVIDSON

CROOM HELM
London ● Sydney
Dover, New Hampshire

©1985 Roger Davidson
Croom Helm Ltd, Provident House, Burrell Row,
Beckenham, Kent BR3 1AT

Croom Helm Australia Pty Ltd, First Floor,
139 King Street, Sydney, NSW 2001, Australia

British Library Cataloguing in Publication Data

Davidson, Roger
    Whitehall and the labour problem in late-Victorian and
    Edwardian Britain: a study in official statistics and
    social control.
    1. Great Britain—Social policy—History
    2. Great Britain—Politics and government
    —1837-1901   3. Great Britain—Politics and
    government—1901-1936
    I. Title
    361.6'1'0941   HN385
    ISBN 0-7099-0832-6

Croom Helm, 51 Washington Street,
Dover, New Hampshire, 03820 USA

Library of Congress Cataloging in Publication Data

Davidson, Roger.
    Whitehall and the labour problem in late-Victorian and
Edwardian Britain.

    Bibliography: p.
    Includes index.
    1. Labor and laboring classes — Great Britain — Statistical
services — History. 2. Labor supply — Great Britain —
Statistical services — History. 3. Great Britain — Social policy.
4. Social control. I. Title.
HD8390.D35 1984   331'.072041   84-21424
ISBN 0-7099-0832-6

Printed and bound in Great Britain by
Biddles Ltd, Guildford and King's Lynn

CONTENTS

TABLES AND FIGURES

TABLES

FIGURES

PREFACE

This book provides a systematic analysis of the nature and role of the data base of late-Victorian and Edwardian policy-making. In particular, it focusses upon the production structure and output of official statistics relating to a range of imperfections in the labour market and industrial relations, characterised by contemporary social observers, administrators and policy-makers as the 'Labour Problem'.

The book has three main objectives. Firstly, it seeks to contribute to the recent debate over the nature and motivation of late-Victorian and Edwardian social policy. It furnishes a new perspective on the controversy as to how far developments in welfare ideas and provisions during the period were in fact a function of social control.

Its second and closely related objective is to provide a case study with which to assess the competing hypotheses advanced by social scientists as to the relationship between social statistics and policy. The main issue in contention is whether the function of empirical research in the development of welfare concepts and measures is innovative or conservative. Existing case studies have focussed primarily on the framework of industrial and governmental decision-making during recent years. This study will therefore provide a valuable historical perspective for the debate.

Thirdly, in examining the status and motivation of official statisticians and their response to their scientific and bureaucratic environment, the book will shed much-needed light on the changing role of the expert in British government growth after 1880.

Incidentally, it will also constitute an important research aid for historians. Most interpretations of late-Victorian and Edwardian social and economic trends have relied heavily (and often uncritically) upon the industrial and labour statistics published by Whitehall departments. This book incorporates a critical examination of the human resources, motivation and statistical techniques which generated that data base.

ACKNOWLEDGEMENTS

Many people have helped me in the preparation of this book. I should like to express my gratitude to the Trustees of the Houblon-Norman Fund and to the Economic and Social Research Council whose financial assistance (Grant H.R. 7262) made possible much of the original research upon which this study is based.

I am very grateful to the following for permission to use collections of manuscripts and private correspondence: Mrs. Elizabeth Clay, Mr. W.R. Collet, Mr. G.B. Greenwood, Lord Layton, Lord St Aldwyn and Captain R.D. Raikes. I am obliged also to the Controller of Her Majesty's Stationery Office for permission to use Crown-copyright material in the Public Record Office. Numerous libraries and record offices have given me their ready assistance. I owe special thanks to the authorities and staffs of Birmingham University Library, The British Library, The British Library of Political and Economic Science, Edinburgh University Library, Huddersfield Polytechnic Library, the Marshall Library Cambridge, the National Library of Scotland, Sheffield University Library, and the library of University College London. In addition, I wish to thank the General Secretary of the T.U.C. and the Council and Secretary of the Royal Statistical Society for permission to consult manuscript collections under their control.

I have obtained invaluable assistance in locating archive material from Eddie Higgs, Jill Pellew, Donald MacKenzie, Joe Melling, Richard Roberts, Noel Whiteside and Meta Zimmeck. However, I owe my greatest debt of gratitude to five people. To Oliver MacDonagh and to the late David Joslin, I owe my original inspiration to investigate the administrative and welfare history of late-Victorian and Edwardian Britain. Subsequently, both Roy Hay and Rodney Lowe have played a major role in sustaining my research, by their selfless advice and encouragement. Finally, I have to thank Margaret Williamson for making it all worthwhile.

To

Margaret

and to

Andrew and Hilary

Part One

THE   CONTEXT

Chapter 1

THE TERMS OF THE DEBATE

SOCIAL REFORM AND SOCIAL CHANGE

The rationale and significance of late-Victorian
and Edwardian welfare provisions have been
subjected by historians and social scientists to a
variety of conflicting interpretations. However,
within the debate, two broad categories of
explanation may be discerned; a 'progressive'
strand which emphasises the innovative and
benevolent intent and repercussions of social
reform, and a 'conservative' strand which views
social policy-making of the period as primarily a
function of social control.

The 'progressive' viewpoint is the more
conventional of the two and dominated the efforts
of social administrators and welfare theorists in
the 1950s and early 1960s to locate the
development of the Welfare State in its
'historical perspective'.[1] A major thrust of this
thesis was. that a pluralist social policy-making
process after 1870 had provided a powerful
mechanism for affecting social transformation;
that it reflected not simply the priorities of a
capitalist elite but also embodied the values and
interests of a range of progressive ideologies
including those of the Labour Movement. Welfare
measures, it was argued, had incorporated values
that were need-orientated and communal and
therefore fundamentally antithetical to the ethics
and institutions of capitalism. In the context
of social legislation, the law had ceased to
buttress the existing economic and political order
and had instead become an increasingly active and
articulate agent of social change. It had served
to codify sentiments of altruism, reciprocity and
social duty, effectively containing the values of

the market and securing communal responsibility
for the deprivation created by economic and social
change. As a result, welfare measures such as
Old Age Pensions, Health and Unemployment
Insurance achieved a significant redistribution in
the pattern of income and life chances.

Within this framework of analysis, late-
nineteenth and early-twentieth-century social
reform was therefore viewed as initiating
structural shifts of a qualitative kind in British
industry and society. Welfare provisions were
perceived 'not as dampening down political forces
making for further social change but rather as a
powerful ally raising aspirations, widening
reference groups, illustrating and exacerbating
the value conflicts of welfare capitalism and
providing a dynamic for further change'.[2] In
brief, such provisions were viewed as 'stepping
stones' towards Socialism.

The concept of welfare as citizenship has
also served to sustain a 'progressive' model of
the links between social policy and social
change.[3] This interpretation views late-Victorian
and Edwardian welfare reforms as an important
phase in the progressive extension of the social
rights of citizenship, complementing existing
civil and political rights. Moreover, it is
contended that such welfare citizenship initiated
a cumulative process of social change by inspiring
new levels of social awareness, aspiration and
solidarity. These, in turn, generated fresh
programmes of reconstruction which substantially
modified the incidence of economic and social
inequality.

Several recent studies of the social and
economic ideology of New Liberalism subscribe to a
similarly 'progressive' interpretation of the
development of welfare ideas and measures after
1886.[4] According to this viewpoint, social
policy reflected a systematic programme of planned
social reorganisation, despite the fact that it
was only partially implemented. Measures were
perceived, even on an official level, as part of a
total strategy towards the 'Labour Problem' - a
welfare development bloc based upon a societal and
organic perception of deprivation, of the environmental context of individual hardship, of the
structural economic determinants of social
problems such as poor housing, unemployment and
low-income destitution, and of the interdependence
of private need and public good.[5]

Furthermore, it is argued that, under the influence of biological and evolutionary theories, a static, restorative and problem-orientated notion of social reform generating *ad hoc* relief measures directed at specific evils gave way to a broader conception of social reconstruction designed to ensure by means of State intervention the most productive use of the nation's resources.[6] Social reform was not therefore just a popular, reactive strategy designed to take the intellectual wind out of the Socialist sails, nor a conservative opportunist ploy to secure social stability, but part of a dynamic process of social regeneration designed to realise both the ethical and material potential of society and the individual.[7]

According to Freeden and Emy, this ethico-scientific concept of social reform had far-reaching implications for the development of social politics and welfare ideology. It justified unprecedented intervention by the State to regulate property rights and vested interests and to equilibrate the priorities of the market with the broader imperatives of social welfare.[8] In particular, Emy contends that the economic ideology of Edwardian social reform incorporated an entirely new programmatic commitment to the 'Minimum' in remuneration and in environmental and working conditions as an exercise in redistributive justice, aiming to establish more equitable links between incentive, effort and reward within the productive process, and between rights and obligations within the community.[9] Moreover, it appears that this 'progressivism' characterised not only national debate, but also social politics within the regions.[10]

Historians adhering to an innovative interpretation of welfare measures during the period have commonly identified four main features; the adoption of a more progressive system of funding social investment, the containment of market by welfare values in the determination of social policy, the erosion of individualistic moral criteria by scientific and environmental concepts in the diagnosis and treatment of social problems, and the implementation of a less stigmatic and coercive philosophy of governmental aid.

It is contended that Liberal social policy after 1886 was accompanied by a fundamental shift in financial policy in which the conventional equation of social reform with orthodox Gladstonian retrenchment was replaced by the concept of taxation as a major instrument of social planning and reconstruction.[11] By means of progressive graduated taxation aimed at large and unearned incomes, at inherited wealth and capital gains from land ownership and speculation, social reform would be funded out of 'surplus value' without undermining the profits fund, managerial incentives and the efficiency of the British capital market. Fiscal reform was also designed to address the most significant element of crisis in social and economic development -that of distribution. A coherent programme of fiscal and welfare measures was intended to stabilise and to regenerate economic activity by promoting income redistribution and thus increasing the level of working-class consumption and the social depth of effective demand.[12]

More broadly, a progressive strategy of taxation and social expenditure was the mechanism by which New Liberalism's concept of social regeneration might be realised. Despite the defeat of the most radical aspects of Lloyd George's budgetary proposals after 1910, and the deference of Liberal fiscal policy to middle-class interests, progressive taxation was conceived as a means of ensuring the optimum use of the community's resources and a fundamental shift in the framework of social responsibility.[13] A redistributive tax system would gradually enforce the effective and equitable deployment of both human and physical assets, eliminating many specific areas of injustice within the labour and housing markets and generally promoting the social good. The fiscal ideology underpinning welfare provisions was not therefore purely confiscatory in intent, representing merely the desire of traditional radicalism to undermine the power of landed wealth. According to Freeden and Emy, financial developments, such as the People's Budget and the Development Act, reflected a broader perception of taxation as complementing a long-term process of income redistribution and social progress.[14]

These historians also stress the degree to which late-Victorian and Edwardian social policy progressively incorporated normative welfare values alien to the tenets of a free market economy. Emy provides an incisive over-view of this shift, from a perception of:

6

development upon the basis of a self-regulating system, the logic of whose premises governed the nature of social relationships and the content of legislation, to development in terms of the self-conscious pursuit of goals of social equality and social justice; from a governing respect for the productiveness of private industry to the acceptance of State expenditure upon the promotion of social efficiency and social utility; from the absolute protection of private property to a concern to utilise all resources bearing upon the public interest.[15]

The creation of wealth was therefore perceived as a social as well as industrial process, operating within an ethical framework, and the productive process had by means of State regulation to conform to the needs of social welfare and not simply to the dictates of profit maximisation and to the arbitrary criteria of market forces.[16]

It is contended that within the ideology of social reform, the traditional capitalist imperatives of competition, incentive and efficiency were clearly preserved but rendered compatible with the 'organic welfare of industry' in which the mode of production harmonised with the needs of the workforce.[17] Thus, welfare legislation, such as measures relating to health and conditions of employment designed to improve labour efficiency, was perceived less in purely economic terms of reducing production costs than in biological and ethical terms of improving the earnings potential and standard of living of the labouring classes. Similarly, according to this interpretation, the concept of the 'Minimum' was formulated with a view to ensuring a healthy and vigorous community and not just the reproduction of labour power. While even advanced radicalism conceded the centrality of the profit motive and competitive incentives to the functioning of the economy, they also had to be accommodated to the social needs of human capital within the production process.[18] Likewise, as evidenced by the Trade Boards Act and Liberal fiscal innovation, social reform dictated that considerations of social utility as well as the price mechanism should determine the process of distribution and the level of remuneration within British industry.[19]

This school of thought also focusses upon

shifts in the relative weighting of character and environment within late-Victorian and Edwardian welfare debate. For example, Woodard views the period as a vital phase in the transition from a moral, character-orientated ideology of reform to one centred upon the role of environment; from the perception of deprivation as a function of personal vice to its diagnosis and treatment as a social malady, to which the orthodox virtues of abstinence, diligence and thrift were largely irrelevant.[20] More recently, some historians have adopted a less simplistic but no less progressive interpretation of social policy-making. In contrast to Woodard, they maintain that after 1880, all groups of social reformers continued to accord high priority to the 'cultivation of character' and the traditional moral virtues of individual thrift, self-help and motivation, but that their value and viability were increasingly viewed as dependent upon the provision of a suitable economic and social environment by the State. The essence of personal morality was the enforcement of a broader ethic of social morality and responsibility involving the replacement of *ad hoc*, localised and often sectarian philanthropy by systematic statutory welfare initiatives on a national scale.[21]

Such 'progressive' shifts were, it is argued, reinforced by the contemporaneous adoption of more scientific approaches to social policy. It is claimed that despite strong anti-science sentiments in late-Victorian society and the difficulty of scientists gaining access to policy-making circles in Whitehall, scientific expertise played a significant role in eroding reactionary attitudes in many areas of concern, such as preventive medicine and elementary education.[22] It is also contended that the impact of scientific methodology upon governmental strategies towards social and economic problems induced a more rigorous appraisal of their magnitude in relation to the capabilities of existing welfare provisions, and the evolution of a more functional and co-ordinated system of social administration with the potential to generate comprehensive programmes of social amelioration.[23] More generally, according to Freeden, there was considerable ideological affinity between social radicalism and scientifically-orientated movements such as Eugenics, and certain biological theories, pre-eminently those of Weisman, served to confirm the inter-relationship between character and environment and between individual welfare and social progress, thus validating both the material and ethical value of State intervention in social and economic relationships.[24]

Furthermore, it is argued that the scientific and environmental perspective of late-Victorian and Edwardian social reform necessarily minimised its punitive aspects. Indeed, the relative lack of disciplinary conditions attached to the welfare provisions of the period is commonly regarded as the acid test of their progressive intent. Particular stress is placed upon the shift from the stigma of social relief under the Victorian Poor Law to the concept of entitlement within Edwardian welfare benefits.[25]

Emphasis is also laid upon the rejection by social policy-makers of the more coercive aspects of contemporary proposals for intervention in the labour market. The bureaucratic regimentation and social engineering advocated by the National Efficiency School was resisted as fundamentally illiberal.[26] Meanwhile, social reformers within governing circles were equally unreceptive to the hard genetic determinism of eugenic views on issues such as unemployment and low-income destitution and to the totalitarian implications of Socialist collectivism.[27] Emy and Freeden contend that contemporary criticism of the Liberal welfare reforms as initiating a 'Servile State' ignored the degree to which they sought to 'balance the imperatives of liberty and welfare'. Where compulsion was incorporated into legislation, it was, they argue, designed to secure greater social and economic freedom. Thus, compulsory insurance was justified as a means of liberating the labour force from the arbitrary dictates of market forces, while the statutory constraints upon the disposition of property and other resources emancipated society and the economy from the tyranny of minority vested interests.[28]

Above all, a 'progressive' model of social policy and social change has been sustained by the conviction that social reforms reflected, either directly or indirectly, the popular demands and aspirations of organised labour. A range of historians have subscribed to the view that welfare innovations were not simply a function of hegemony, initiated and imposed by a bourgeois elite in the interests of capitalism, but that they were 'objectively, victories for working-class values within capitalist society'.[29] The allegedly anti-capitalist ethic of welfare collectivism and its intrusion into the prerogatives of the market are interpreted as clear indications of its democratic rationale and impetus. Such an interpretation is by no means passé. Recent concern that, under the conceptual imperialism of social control, a once dominant Whig perception of social amelioration might be replaced by an equally misguided 'new orthodoxy of radical cynicism' has revived the view that late-Victorian and Edwardian reforms served interests other than those of the elite and 'accomplished more than maintaining and adapting the status quo'; that they represented not merely efforts at social engineering from above but equally the struggle of the Labour Movement to secure greater control over its social and economic environment.[30]

To a significant extent, specific case studies of social policy-making during the period have provided empirical evidence to support this thesis. Thus, Brown contends that working-class agitation orchestrated by the Social Democratic Federation, and pressure by the Labour Party within Parliament, played a vital role in eroding conventional attitudes towards the unemployed, in focussing public attention upon the magnitude of the unemployment problem and the inadequacies of existing relief schemes, and in initiating shifts in welfare policy such as the Chamberlain Circular of 1886 and the 1905 Unemployed Workmen Act.[31] Likewise, Schmiechen stresses the contribution of working-class welfare aspirations to the enactment of minimum wage legislation. He concludes that the Trade Boards Act was 'the child of London-based worker agitation' and of the labour-dominated Anti-Sweating League.[32] The evolution of a range of other provisions such as old age pensions, free school meals, and subsidised working-class housing has been subject to similar interpretation.[33]

Moreover, recent research into the welfare perspectives of the late-Victorian and Edwardian Labour Movement reveals that, in the context of social policy-making and administration, organised labour was not a passive subject of elite manipulation, but tended to adopt a positive strategy of exploiting and optimising the progressive potential of welfare measures. Thane demonstrates how labour organisations such as the S.D.F. and Trades Councils were prepared to give a qualified, critical acceptance to many social reforms as a means of advancing the Socialist cause. By capturing local agencies of welfare administration such as Poor Law Boards, School Boards and District Councils, the Labour Movement endeavoured to maximise the redistributive impact of social reform, and by means of municipalisation, to institutionalise the anti-capitalist ethos of welfare collectivism.[34] As welfare theorists have noted, this optimistic perception of reform held by contemporary labour activists proved seminal in the subsequent development of the 'progressive' strand of British welfare historiography.[35]

SOCIAL REFORM AND SOCIAL CONTROL

In contrast, in recent years, a growing body of literature has interpreted developments in welfare ideas and provisions since the late-nineteenth century as primarily a means of social control rather than social transformation.[36] Some historians and welfare theorists have closely identified late-Victorian and Edwardian social policy, especially as it related to the labour market, with the needs of a maturing economy subject to both internal and external stresses.[37] Social policy was, it is argued, primarily concerned with maintaining the efficiency and stability of the capitalist system, with the daily and generational reproduction of labour power and of capitalist relations of production. Welfare legislation was accordingly designed to regulate the physical depreciation of Britain's workforce, to increase its efficiency and receptiveness to new methods of manufacture, and to sustain industrial discipline and incentives despite drastic shifts in the technical and organisational structure of British industry. According to this interpretation, by reducing alienation and unrest, social reform also fulfilled a vital role in maintaining the degree of social stability essential to the process of capital accumulation.

However, the majority of revisionists have adopted a less functionalist, Marxist analysis of welfare developments after 1880 which focusses more heavily upon their control implications

11

within class society.[38] While the importance of
actual (or potential) working-class unrest in
precipitating legislation is conceded, and while
the cruder conspiracy theories of welfare measures
as a coherent strategy of repression exercised by
the State on behalf of a homogeneous ruling class
are generally rejected, social policy is
nonetheless interpreted as fundamentally a product
of the values and interests of dominant social
groups within capitalist society. Social reform,
it is argued, was not 'a unified national effort
to meet social needs or to eradicate social
problems in an impartial way to the benefit of all
in society' but rather 'an attempt to resolve
conflicting economic and other interests along
social class lines'.[39] In short, it performed a
vital part in 'the dynamic process by which the
status quo was sustained in a maturing capitalist
society'.

Within this framework of analysis, late-
Victorian and Edwardian welfare measures fulfilled
an essentially conservative role designed to
strengthen social solidarity and to provide 'a
shock absorber for capitalism rather than a
mechanism of radical social change'.[40] As one
among many strategies of social control, 'welfare
bribery' was designed in the short term to contain
class conflict and to furnish an antidote to the
spread of Socialism, without conceding any drastic
changes in the structure of industry and society.
In the long term, the basic rationale of social
policy was to re-accommodate the labouring classes
to the capitalist social order, by mitigating the
more acute social costs of economic growth and the
more overt exploitative features of the labour
market, by generating an apparatus of State
welfare within which the Labour Movement might be
incorporated, and by exploiting welfare rhetoric
to facilitate the conflation of essentially
capitalist imperatives such as 'efficiency' with
the 'National Interest'.[41]

Much of the research into the range of
collectivist ideologies contributing to social
policy formation in late-nineteenth and early-
twentieth-century Britain has served to validate
this 'social control' perspective on welfare
developments. For example, the welfare philosophy
of the National Efficiency Movement is revealed as
having been highly autocratic. The main
objectives of its social programme were to
increase the efficiency and discipline of the

workforce by the imposition of scientific measures, (pre-eminently the enforcement of a National Minimum), determined by an expert elite. Its perception of social problems and policy priorities was primarily determined by the competitive needs of British industry rather than a concern for the quality of social life *per se*. Social efficiency rather than social equality was its overriding aim, and in promoting welfare reforms the National Efficiency School consciously modelled its proposals on the control strategies of German collectivism.[42]

Social Imperialism displayed similar conservative and coercive traits. According to Scally, it was a defensive counter-revolutionary ideology of 'order, social hierarchy and bureaucratic control'. It viewed social reform as a function of economic and military strategy, as a means of generating a more disciplined and regimented society and imperial race with which to adjust to the systemic industrial and technological problems of a mature economy and to modern modes of production and warfare.[43] Marxist historians are further disposed to interpret its welfare programme as a manipulative device employed by the State to gain labour support for imperialist expansion undertaken in the interests of entrepreneurial capitalism.[44]

Liberal Imperialists also lacked genuine radical commitment. Their main aim was to exploit the rhetoric of nationalism and social reform to combat Socialism and to dissociate welfare issues from class politics. As Matthew has demonstrated, they subscribed to a minimalist programme of State intervention designed to streamline the economic and social system without any realignment of social classes or of wealth distribution, and without more than marginal interference in the free market economy. As with the National Efficiency Movement, Liberal Imperialism was more concerned with the economic efficiency of the labour force than with the standard of living of the working classes in general and explicitly rejected any democratic process of policy-making as a threat to social stability and to the necessary rigour and rationalisation of welfare provisions.[45]

A strategy of social control was at its most explicit in the contribution of the Eugenics Movement to late-Victorian and Edwardian welfare debate. Its social policy directly reflected the

meritocratic social theory of the professional
middle classes. As self-appointed custodians of
the racial health of the community, eugenists
subscribed to a fundamentally conservative and
totalitarian programme of social engineering
designed 'to produce a population fit and clever
enough to preserve the existing social order'. In
particular, by means of negative eugenics (the
'progressive' elimination of the unskilled and
parasitic casual residuum) they sought to regulate
the quality and reproduction of the labour force
in the interests of economic efficiency and racial
regeneration. Eugenists were therefore strongly
opposed to the environmental reforms of social
radicalism as perpetuating 'the socially dependent
army of unfit'. Given that social stratification
was determined on eugenic principles - a
functional hierarchy of inherited talent - the
movement supported an inegalitarian society,
opposing even modest reforms which might
facilitate social mobility. Meanwhile, with its
close continuity of thought with the classical
ideology of the British bourgeoisie and with
Social Darwinism, it was equally concerned to
resist welfare measures which threatened, in the
interests of social justice, to impair the
competitive ethic of free enterprise and liberal
capitalism.[46]

Even the historiography of New Liberalism has
not proved immune to the concept of social
control. Its welfare programme has been commonly
interpreted as a consensus strategy designed to
secure social discipline and harmony in a period
of class conflict and deteriorating industrial
relations, rather than as a systematic attack upon
the structural causes of working-class
deprivation.[47] As with other collectivist
ideologies of the period, New Liberalism was
arguably a fundamentally reactive rather than
innovative creed with its selective social
investment designed as the most effective antidote
to Socialism and preservative of industrial
capitalism. Despite the growing influence of
social radicalism with a broader ethical
commitment to legislative intervention and planned
social change, it is contended that throughout the
period, the values and sectional interests of
traditional middle-class, nonconformist radicalism
continued to determine the scope and incidence of
Liberal welfare initiatives.[48] Moreover, it is
argued that the economic ideology of New

Liberalism reinforced the basic conservatism of such initiatives. Failing to conceive of any radical alternative to orthodox interpretations of market operations and the price mechanism, which prevented any explicit commitment to economic collectivism, its overriding concern was to maintain the profits fund and normal capitalist incentives. State expenditure on social reform was therefore contingent upon satisfying the criteria of generating wealth or the more efficient deployment of existing wealth and factors of production, of not intruding into the labour and investment markets beyond a marginal adjustment to the mechanisms of supply and demand, and of preserving the price mechanism as the final arbiter of the social relationships of production.[49]

Recent biographies of the major architects of the Liberal welfare reforms - David Lloyd George and Winston Churchill - have served to sustain this thesis. For example, Wrigley has demonstrated the strong traditional elements such as land reform and temperance in Lloyd George's radicalism, his markedly rural perception of social problems and his apathy toward the central issues of urban industrial politics and social protest. However provocative, his fiscal and welfare programmes were primarily directed against landed wealth and were not designed to reshape the economic system or to affect any fundamental redistribution of industrial income.[50] Meanwhile, Churchill's concept of social reform clearly reflected the paternalism of an erstwhile Tory democrat. His objectives were articulated in explicitly Bismarckian terms as the suppression of revolutionary socialism, as the provision of a stable social environment (i.e. the maintenance of existing class relations), and as the creation of an efficient and docile workforce. To Churchill, social security was predicated upon the security of capital and 'legitimate' private enterprise. He was opposed to the class ideology of New Unionism, and in responding to the central struggles of the Trade Union Movement over wages, conditions of work and recognition, he valued a strategy of State welfarism as much for its disciplinary as for its ameliorative effects.[51]

The more coercive features of New Liberalism have been most clearly identified in recent studies of Edwardian policy towards the labour market. They stress the degree to which collectivism not only implied emerging social benefits but also the intensification of penalties for deviant behaviour such as vagrancy. In particular, Stedman Jones vividly illustrates the 'surgical, authoritarian, labour camp' prescriptions behind late-nineteenth and early-twentieth century 'progressive' strategies. He demonstrates how the shift in the focus of public concern from the demoralisation of the individual to the degeneration of threatening urban aggregates logically involved recourse to coercive measures designed to segregate the 'residuum' from the respectable working classes.[52] Other welfare historians also underline the punitive as distinct from the remedial aspects of Edwardian social reform; revealing the use of more scientific classifications of the 'deserving' and 'undeserving' and of more environmental diagnoses of social and economic deprivation to legitimate the forcible treatment and deployment of the unfit, and the degree to which even the most advanced social radicalism was prepared to sacrifice the welfare autonomy of the individual to autocratic controls in the interests of economic efficiency and social morality.[53]

However, it is the degree to which Liberal social policy sought to reinforce industrial discipline and the work ethic which has prompted most scepticism as to its progressive intent. Hay and Whiteside have noted the persistent link of Liberal welfare benefits not with the social rights of citizenship but with the role of the recipient in the labour market.[54] They emphasise the extent to which benefit rights under a range of measures, including workmens' compensation, old age pensions and unemployment insurance, were conditional upon the adherence of the applicant to the common norms of work discipline - regularity, sobriety and diligence. They also reveal the extent to which measures of income maintenance and decasualisation, designed to regenerate the economic independence and moral integrity of the worker, were perceived by reformers as a means of restoring his responsiveness to the work ethic. Whiteside would contend that Liberal welfare strategy became increasingly a function of labour market management involving additional governmental powers to monitor and regulate the work performances of the labour force, to rationalise patterns of industrial engagement and to penalise casual and irregular employment and

work habits which threatened to perpetuate the
existence of a degenerate and inefficient
workforce. The object of social legislation such
as the introduction of unemployment insurance was,
it is argued, less to eliminate areas of poverty
than to reinforce the work ethic among areas of
the workforce freed from the normal controls of
wage labour. Within a Marxist framework of
analysis, New Liberalism is therefore viewed as
actively involved in the promotion of social
policy which enhanced the workplace subordination
of labour. By transforming orthodox labour
market incentives and ethics into statutory
requirements, it accentuated the necessity and
discipline of wage labour which formed the
ultimate social control in capitalist society.
    The role of Whitehall in formulating late-
Victorian and Edwardian welfare measures has been
subject to a similar interpretation. For
example, Hinton has depicted the administrative
elite as the 'storm corps of the Servile State'.
He argues that the collectivism promoted by
permanent officials such as Beveridge and
Llewellyn Smith was primarily designed to
undermine the Labour Movement, and to deploy the
State apparatus in the direct service of private
capital. In particular, he contends that the
'benevolent bureaucrats of Liberalism' sought by
means of welfare controls and regulations 'to
confirm the power of the capitalists, while
subjecting the proletariat to servile conditions;
to provide the workers with "security in their
subsistence" but in return to deprive them of
their freedom to withdraw their labour and to
claim possession of the means of production'.[55]
Other historians, while rejecting such a
simplistic conspiracy theory of social policy have
nonetheless maintained a radical critique of the
motives of late-nineteenth and early-twentieth-
century social administrators. According to Hay,
they were not impartial arbiters aiming to restore
some form of equilibrium between the interests of
Capital and Labour. They shared with
politicians, employers and other members of the
ruling class a common desire to preserve
capitalism, and they perceived welfare reforms as
a preferable strategy to paternalism or repression
in attaining that end. Indeed, Hay would submit
that the central bureaucracy actively constrained
radical initiatives which threatened to generate a
genuine shift in social and economic power in

favour of Labour, that it was receptive to measures of State intervention to regiment the labour market and discipline 'the submerged', and that it consciously manipulated the level and criteria of welfare benefits so as to maintain the work ethic and to preserve the social stigma and economic sanction of 'less-eligibility'.[56]

A social control model of social reform has also characterised recent analyses of the role of the 'local State' in modern British society. It is contended that, although local authorities were rarely absorbed in fundamental debate over the basic tenets on which national social policy should be founded, such policy was strongly influenced by the conservative welfare perspectives of the rate-paying electorate and of local council oligarchies upon whom the deployment of a substantial proportion of public social expenditure ultimately rested.[57] To a significant extent, therefore, the aim and scope of social reform reflected dominant relationships within the localities; the social fears and economic imperatives of local (especially metropolitan) elites. In particular, Marxist historians would submit that the formulation of locally administered provisions, such as those relating to housing, health and education, generally represented not the real needs of the working classes but the outcome of conflict between 'fractions of capital'; between the aggregate needs of the capitalist class for the reproduction of an efficient, motivated and captive labour force and the more limited financial concerns of specific industrial or propertied interest groups.[58]

Investigations into the welfare perceptions and initiatives of industrial and professional interest groups have served further to underline the manipulative intent of late-Victorian and Edwardian social reform. Authorities such as Hay and Melling concede that social reform was not just 'a simple reflex of business interest and pressure' and that no homogeneous employer view of welfare ever prevailed. Nonetheless, they argue that after 1880 the aims and priorities of industrial and commercial interest groups exerted increasing influence on the process of social policy-making and that there was a growing identity between business ideology and the rationale of State welfare.[59] Hay has sought to identify the timing and significance of this

18

convergence. He demonstrates how, faced after 1900 by the deterioration in Britain's competitive position in world markets and in the temper of British industrial relations, employers' organisations became convinced of the cost effectiveness of welfare measures as a means of improving the efficiency of the workforce, of preserving managerial prerogatives, and of averting class conflict. He further indicates the extent to which this conviction, along with its underlying perception of social reform as a function of social and economic control, was subsequently reflected in the Liberal welfare programme, especially in so far as it related to the rationalisation of the labour market.[60] Whiteside has also revealed the degree to which State welfare provisions served merely to enforce the private welfare schemes traditionally operated by British industrialists as an integral part of management strategy designed to secure a responsive and loyal workforce.[61]

Meanwhile, the concept of social control has figured prominently in analyses of the role of the professions in the process of social reform. It is evident that after 1870, professional interests became increasingly influential in 'shaping the map of social need' and governmental responses to it. Evidence would further suggest that their contribution to welfare debate and policy was status rather than problem-orientated and primarily determined by their location within the structure of late-Victorian and Edwardian society. As MacKenzie reflects, the concept of State-regulated welfare was entirely consistent with the interests of the rising professional middle classes, offering a strategy of containing revolutionary pressure by a process of social reform while replacing a social hierarchy based on wealth by a functionally stratified society based on expertise and social skills.[62] Thus, according to Parry and Parry, the participation of professionals in social policy-making, such as that of the British Medical Association in the institution of National Health Insurance, should be interpreted as part of their 'occupational strategy' directed to the achievement and maintenance of 'upward collective social mobility' rather than to the establishment of a more progressive public health service.[63] Other studies, focussing upon the role of architects and civil service inspectorates in formulating housing and environmental reforms, suggests a similar pattern of motivation.[64]

Given their social and occupational objectives, reform-minded professionals inevitably subscribed to an autocratic brand of welfare collectivism in which the erection of systematic controls would optimise the value and status of professional expertise, and in which welfare measures would be imposed in a unilateral fashion. Indeed, some authorities, such as Titmuss, Illich and Watkins, contend that the control potential of welfare in modern British society was primarily activated by professional interest groups. In particular, they submit that, in defining social problems and needs, professional experts imposed their own values and imperatives and either ignored or actively suppressed the real welfare interests of the working classes.[65] Several, more empirical studies of the evolution of social reform after 1870 would certainly indicate that professionals, including the emerging social scientific professionals such as economists, advocated a welfare programme of 'enlightened paternalism' principally designed to render capitalism more efficient rather than less exploitative, to 'channel the energies and resentments of labour to constructive middle-class ends', and to eliminate some of the more provocative forms of injustice thrown up by the advancing economic system, without altering the basic structure of industry and society.[66]

Predictably, some of the more regressive and manipulative features of late-Victorian and Edwardian social reform have emerged in studies focussing upon the welfare attitudes of the Labour Movement. As Pelling, Thane, and Yeo have demonstrated, its response to measures of State welfare varied from scepticism to active hostility. In general, trade union organisations, friendly societies and trades councils were prepared to accept welfare concessions for the sake of the unskilled and destitute but, nonetheless, they viewed such concessions as an evasion of genuine structural reform and as a threat to labour solidarity and to the integrity of working-class associative effort. In particular, union leaders feared that social reforms might merely constrain the industrial options of organised labour and compensate for the loss of legal sanctions over rank and file militancy occasioned by the Trade Disputes Act.

They were equally concerned at the apparent intent
of policy-makers to exploit welfare measures such
as unemployment insurance in order to neutralise
traditional union prerogatives at the point of
production by the imposition of central controls
over the employment and mobility of labour, and by
the rationalisation of manpower in the interests
of the employing classes.[67]
    According to Thane and Holton, a significant
element of Marxist and Syndicalist opinion
perceived and articulated the totalitarian
implications of State welfare even more
explicitly, predicting that the apparatus of
judicial and administrative controls contingent
upon the extension of social investment would
legitimate existing social and economic
structures, institutionalise industrial discipline
and incorporate the Labour Movement into
bureaucratic State capitalism. According to
these strands of labour ideology, 'welfarism' was
merely an alternative strategy of bourgeois
economic and cultural domination, with social
reform as the mechanism of working-class
'reformation' in the interests of economic
efficiency, industrial deference, and capital
accumulation.[68]
    Moreover, in identifying the relationship
between the Labour Movement and social policy,
several historians have endorsed such views. For
example, Yeo echoes the rhetoric of many Edwardian
Socialists when he characterises State welfare
programmes as 'a scramble for Socialism - as
imperialistic as the contemporary scramble for
Africa'.[69] Their prime objective, he contends,
was to 'take Socialism's germs away from the
working-class hosts and to vaccinate the body
politic with them in harmless, even health-giving
forms'; 'to de-class the idea of Socialism and to
nationalise it'. Similarly, Melling, and to a
lesser extent Hay, would identify with contemporary left-wing perceptions of social reform
as the replacement of traditional authoritarian
paternalism by a more liberal 'incorporative
welfare system' designed principally to sublimate
industrial conflict and to reconcile the working
class, especially the key skilled, supervisory and
specialised grades of worker, to the fabric of
capitalist production and society.[70]
    Finally, recent comparative analyses of
welfare systems, seeking to interpret British
social policy within a broader context of inter-

national welfare developments, have also sustained the concept of social provisions as a surrogate system of social control. According to Rimlinger, late-nineteenth and early-twentieth century welfare initiatives were commonly motivated by a range of inter-dependent economic and social imperatives of industrial capitalism which were quintessentially conservative in intent. He maintains that their overriding objective was to develop a supplementary or secondary distributional system to compensate for the failure of the primary market mechanism to allocate the costs of industrialisation, such as unemployment and low-income destitution, in a manner consistent with social stability and economic efficiency. Social reforms, especially insurance provisions, were intended to 'cement the social fabric of industrial order' at a time when fluctuations in the international and domestic economy were subjecting the mass of the labour force (and not just marginal elements) to income insecurity. At the same time, by raising the level of human capital investment and by improving industrial relations and motivation, welfare measures would raise factor productivity and strengthen cost competitiveness in world markets.[71]

Also adopting a comparative perspective, Thane confirms the conservative thrust of pre-1914 welfare reforms, not only in industrial economies but also in predominantly agrarian societies such as New Zealand, with benefits focussed upon strategic areas of the labour force (both in terms of productive and disruptive potential) rather than upon the major areas of social deprivation.[72] Higgins reveals similar 'control' implications in identifying the highest common factors motivating international welfare trends. She contends that the pattern of social reform was essentially residual; a strategy designed to provide the bare essentials to maintain subsistence and labour productivity rather than to initiate any significant alteration in income distribution; to impose values consonant with social order and economic efficiency rather than to alter existing patterns of inequality.[73]

SOCIAL STATISTICS AND SOCIAL POLICY

Clearly, the debate over the motivation of late-Victorian and Edwardian welfare reforms and the extent to which they should be interpreted as a function of social control is a wide-ranging one. Yet, welfare historians have largely ignored what is arguably one of the more revealing indicators and influential determinants of the rationale and scope of social legislation - the informational and statistical basis of welfare debate and policy-formation. This is the more surprising in that in recent years social scientists have increasingly stressed the linkages between social statistics and social policy.

Organisational theorists such as Cherns and Rein argue that social statistics exercise a significant influence upon policy although not necessarily an overt, direct, prescriptive influence.[74] They maintain that the impact of data on policy is necessarily diffuse and oblique and the linkages difficult to isolate as 'the interplay of knowledge and ideals, political manoeuvre and intelligent problem solving is bound to be very subtle, ambiguous and complicated'.[75] Nonetheless, 'social data performs a leading part in the complex process by which society constructs its perceptions of reality, defines what its problems are and determines which goals and strategies it should adopt and what principles of intervention should guide its actions'.[76] In addition, it may perform a vital function in legitimating inertia and eliminating policy options. According to this interpretation, in the short run, social statistics are instrumental in informing and enlightening the dominant policy paradigm, while in the long run, their range of diagnostic, prognostic, selective, evaluative and educative functions may play a vital role in the re-conceptualisation of social problems and appropriate welfare responses by the State.[77] In short, such a viewpoint endorses Myrdal's aphorism that, in the context of policy making, 'facts kick'.[78]

Furthermore, it argues that the institutional structure of decision-making within British social administration is not impervious to the findings of social investigation and empirical research; that despite the generalist tradition of recruitment, a significant number of statisticians and social scientists have occupied senior posts within Whitehall and/or obtained access to policy-making circles, and that certain departments have been highly receptive to their professional expertise and to the implications of their findings.[79]

Certain conditions are identified as particularly conducive to the influence of social statistics on policy; when, for example, they reveal a clear failure of an existing governmental programme to attain publicly stated or legally codified objectives or standards, when new areas or forms of State intervention are contingent upon social investigation identifying the incidence and severity of social problems rather than legitimating particular policy options, when the value system of statisticians - of their techniques, aims and findings - is in accord with that of the establishment, and when, in periods of economic and political crisis, with an unstable policy paradigm, government seeks fresh information to help legitimate, explain and manage novel social forces and friction.[80]

However, the *nature* as distinct from the *extent* of the impact of social statistics on social policy remains a highly contentious issue. Many writers subscribe to the view, which at times borders on crude conspiracy theory, that the primary role of official statistics is a conservative one.[81] They argue that statistics function as a means of social control to maintain a stable hierarchical society and to legitimate capitalist social order, that statistics are produced as part of the administration and control of society organised around exploitative class relationships, and that 'behind a veil of neutrality they form an essential part of the process of maintaining and reproducing the dominant ideologies of capitalist society'. The collection of social data is dismissed as being the traditional response of the governmental elite to industrial crisis as a means of evading any radical transformation of social and economic theory and of validating an existing range of policy options rather than generating truly innovative policy perspectives.

It is argued that, accordingly, the scope of official investigation is invariably confined to descriptive sociography rather than an examination of structural, causative, probabilistic relationships, and that investigation focusses on 'problems' that reflect the priorities of the political and industrial elite; the need to quantify the contribution of the workforce to costs, output and consumption and to identify the social conditions and 'reforms' necessary to maximise labour productivity whilst maintaining order within an alienated class society. Furthermore, in many instances, statistical investigations are officially sanctioned as a deliberate ploy to avoid a policy response to contentious or intractable issues, either as a delaying tactic or as one designed positively to obfuscate the options available. This school of thought maintains that even the techniques and methodology adopted by official statisticians reflect the social and ideological needs of the State in capitalist society; that, for example, the lag in utilisation of measures of deviancy or 'subjective' indicators in British official statistics was a function of their overriding concern to identify and reinforce consensus. The interpretation and deployment of official statistics are viewed in a similar light. It is argued that data are 'massaged' to conform with the existing policy paradigm, that deviant information is either ignored or obscured by the manipulation of its mode of presentation and that statistical methods such as averaging are employed to obscure polarities within the economic and social system.

It is contended that the production structure of official statistics merely serves to reinforce this validating and conservative role.[82] The bulk of social and economic data is produced as a by-product of routine administration. As a result, it is shaped by an inherently conservative legal-administrative perspective. The stress is on collating material relevant to the *existing* function and remit of a particular agency; on financial accountability and the cost of *existing* social provisions. Statistics are agency-specific and problem-orientated only in so far as they relate to specific administrative functions of a given department. They are therefore introspective and *ad hoc*, descriptive accounts rather than interpretative data, and as such ill-equipped to fulfil the more innovative roles of forward-planning and policy evaluation. Moreover, statisticians are subject to the same process of bureaucratisation as other specialists within Whitehall, characterised by a growing adherence to routine and precedent, an increasing concern with career structure and occupational status, with a concomitant inflexibility towards new statistical concepts and procedures necessary to sustain an innovative role within the policy-making process.

As a result, as governmental statisticians have themselves concluded, 'it is very difficult, if not impossible, to make a really radical criticism of society' using official data 'which imprisons us in the concepts and concerns that dominate official political and economic life'.[83]

An alternative viewpoint rejects both a consensual and conspiracy theory of the relationship between empirical findings and the development of policy.[84] Kelman, for example, affirms that the various agencies sponsoring social investigation are not monolithically and systematically dedicated to the maintenance of the status quo. He protests that social statisticians are not an entrenched group within the ruling class and that they very often play the role of gadflies to the establishment; they perform a 'contentious role' whereby empirical research acts either as 'moral witness for the failures of society to honour its commitments' by revealing the disparity between governmental aims and objectives or as a 'social critic' when government has failed to establish any clear policy which can be monitored.[85]

However, such a viewpoint still tends to confine the innovative function of social statistics to that of modifying the relative weighting and coherence of existing policy options. Other writers would argue that, in the long term, their influence is more far-reaching and helps generate a fundamental reconception of welfare problems and strategies - that they have 'paradigm-challenging' effects.[86] In periods of social crisis, they surmise, Government sanctions the accumulation of additional data in an effort to validate its existing assumptions and overall social and economic objectives. Yet, invariably the data instead highlights the divergence between, on the one hand, the social problem as perceived by policy-makers and on the other, its reality and the structural relationships underlying it. Thereafter, the growing inconsistency of existing ideas and assumptions with empirical evidence progressively reconstitutes the policy paradigm. Existing welfare concepts are radically altered and policy formulated within the framework of a new social theory with an attendant alteration in the strategy of the State towards the allocation of resources.

The more prominent models of government growth advanced by administrative historians also lay stress on the innovative effects, both intended and unintended, of official statistics. For example, in MacDonagh's celebrated model of self-sustained government growth, they play a vital part as propaganda in exposing the intolerability of social evils and the social costs of an unregulated industrial economy, in mobilising public opinion in favour of reform, and in providing the justification for a progressive shift from permissive to mandatory legislation and from reliance on local and voluntary initiatives to the establishment of an effective, co-ordinated inspectorate.[87]

RESOLVING THE DEBATE

It is intended to test these conflicting hypotheses as to the motivation of social reform and the function of empirical research in the development of welfare concepts and measures by analysing the impact of the 'Labour Problem' in late-Victorian and Edwardian Britain upon the nature of official statistics and their relationship to social policy. Chapter 2 locates the study in its historical context as distinct from its theoretical and historiographical context, outlined above. It examines why the 'Labour Problem' moved to the forefront of political and public debate after 1886. It reviews the extent and causes of the most acute aspects of the 'Problem' and discusses the social and economic threat posed by such phenomena as perceived by the governing classes.

The generation and the function of labour statistics are then examined in four parts. Part Two of the book deals with the inputs. In Chapter 3, it examines the origins of the Labour Department of the Board of Trade which was to provide the institutional base for the investigation and measurement of the 'Labour Problem'. Chapter 4 then reviews the production structure of official labour statistics during the period 1886-1914. The analysis focusses in turn upon the finance and manpower accorded to labour statistics, the recruitment, pay, status and career development of the statisticians and investigators, their relationship with generalist administrators, their access to the policy-making process, and their motivation and operational philosophy.

In Part Three, attention is focussed instead upon the output or commodity structure of official labour statistics. Chapter 5 discusses the rationale behind the selection and scope of enquiries, the themes to which statistical expertise was deployed, and how and why such resource allocation shifted over time. Chapter 6 then demonstrates the severe limitations of official statistics relating to the 'Labour Problem'. It identifies the aspects and areas of the labour market that were either ignored or imperfectly investigated, and assesses the shortfall between the actual and potential data-base of late-Victorian and Edwardian government.

Part Four of the book is devoted to a systematic analysis of the range of logistical, technical and ideological factors which produced this shortfall. Chapter 7 demonstrates the persistent opposition of the Treasury to the enlargement of statistical enquiry, both as an issue of financial policy and one of routine appropriation, while Chapter 8 focusses upon the impact on labour market intelligence of the apathy, ineptitude, and at times, active hostility of other areas of social administration. Chapter 9 then considers the resistance encountered by the Labour Department from both employers and workers in its efforts to quantify the 'Labour Problem'. The degree to which the statistical techniques employed by the Department inhibited its intelligence function is discussed in Chapter 10, while Chapter 11 examines the impact of the social and economic ideology of labour officials upon the selection, scope and methodology of government enquiries into the labour market.

Finally, Part Five relates the findings of the study to the central issues raised in the present chapter. It assesses the role of statistical intelligence in social policy-making during the period 1886-1914, the degree to which it reflected and sustained a conservative rather than progressive strategy of social reform consistent with social control, and its implications not only for the terms of reference of late-Victorian and Edwardian welfare debate but also for the scope of welfare and welfare-related provisions designed to address the 'Labour Problem'.

NOTES

1. For an overview of this strand of welfare historiography, see especially, R. Mishra, *Society and Social Policy: Theoretical Perspectives on Welfare* (1977), Ch. I; V. George and P. Wilding, *Ideology and Social Welfare* (1976), Ch.4; J.H. Goldthorpe, 'The development of Social Policy in England, 1800-1914: Notes on a sociological approach to a problem in historical explanation', *Transactions of 5th World Congress of Sociology* (1962), pp. 41-2.

2. George and Wilding, *Ideology*, p. 84.

3. See especially, T.H. Marshall, *Citizenship and Social Class* (Cambridge, 1950). The influence of the concept is fully treated in Mishra, *Society and Social Policy*, Ch. 2; George and Wilding, *Ideology*, pp. 75-84.

4. See especially, M. Freeden, *The New Liberalism: An Ideology of Social Reform* (Oxford, 1978); H.V. Emy, *Liberals, Radicals and Social Politics 1892-1914* (Cambridge, 1973); P. Weiler, *The New Liberalism: Liberal Social Theory in Great Britain 1889-1914* (1982).

5. Freeden, *New Liberalism*, pp. 116-120, 166-7, 198-200.

6. Ibid., pp. 18-24.

7. Weiler, *Liberal Social Theory*, pp. 183-7; Freeden, *New Liberalism*, pp.27, 91-9.

8. Freeden, *New Liberalism*, p. 44; Emy, *Social Politics*, p.296.

9. Emy, *Social Politics*, pp. 166-7.

10. See, e.g., P.F. Clarke, *Lancashire and the New Liberalism* (Cambridge, 1971), pp. 398-9.

11. Freeden, *New Liberalism*, p. 141; B.K. Murray, *The People's Budget, 1909-10: Lloyd George and Liberal Politics* (Oxford, 1980), p. 16.

12. Murray, *The People's Budget*, pp. 23, 33-5; H.V. Emy, 'The Impact of Financial Policy on English Party Politics before 1914', *Historical Journal*, 15 (1972), pp. 104-117.

13. Freeden, *New Liberalism*, pp. 134-145; Murray, *The People's Budget*, pp. 6-7.

14. Freeden, *New Liberalism*, pp. 141-5; Emy, 'The Impact of Financial Policy', p. 104.

15. Emy, 'The Impact of Financial Policy', p. 131.

16. Freeden, *New Liberalism*, pp. 128-32.

17. Ibid., pp. 73-4, 258; Emy, *Social Politics*, pp. 107-8.

18. Freeden, *New Liberalism*, pp. 165, 241.

19. Emy, *Social Politics*, p. 295.

20. C. Woodard, 'Reality and Social Reform: The Transition from laissez-faire to the Welfare State', *Yale Law Journal*, 72 (1962-63), pp. 286-328.

21. Freeden, *New Liberalism*, pp. 171-6.

22. See, e.g., J.L. Brand, *Doctors and the State* (Baltimore, 1965), pp. 73-84, 165-89; R.J.W. Selleck, *The*

New Education (1968).

23. P. Ford, *Social Theory and Social Practice* (Shannon, 1968), Parts 2-3.

24. Freeden, *New Liberalism*, p.256; *idem*, 'Eugenics and Progressive Thought: a study in ideological affinity', *Historical Journal*, 22 (1979), p.648.

25. D. Fraser, *The Evolution of the British Welfare State* (1973), pp.162-3.

26. G.R. Searle, *The Quest for National Efficiency* (Oxford, 1971), pp.32, 102, 236, 242.

27. Freeden, *New Liberalism*, pp.29, 183, 191.

28. Ibid., pp.53-4, 232-3; Emy, *Social Politics*, pp.168, 290-2.

29. See especially, D. Thompson, 'The Welfare State', *The New Reasoner*, I (1957), pp.125-30.

30. See especially, M.J. Wiener in *Journal of Social History*, 12 (1978), pp.314-20.

31. K.D. Brown, 'Conflict in early British Welfare Policy: The Case of the Unemployed Workmen's Bill of 1905', *Journal of Modern History*, 43 (1971), pp.615-29; *idem*, 'The Labour Party and the Unemployment Question 1906-10', *Historical Journal*, 14 (1971), pp.599-616.

32. J.A. Schmiechen, 'Sweated Industries and Sweated Labour: A Study of Industrial Disorganization and Worker Attitudes', unpublished PhD thesis, University of Illinois, 1975, Ch.7.

33. See, e.g., A. Marwick, 'The Labour Party and the Welfare State in Britain 1900-48', *American Historical Review*, 73 (1967-8), pp.380-7.

34. P. Thane, 'The Working Class and State "Welfare" 1880-1914', *Labour History Bulletin*, 31 (1975), pp. 6-8.

35. George and Wilding, *Ideology*, Ch.4.

36. For a review of the development and usages of the concept of Social Control, see A.P. Donajgrodski (ed.), *Social Control in Nineteenth Century Britain*, (1977), pp.9-15; F.M.L. Thompson, 'Social Control in Victorian Britain', *Economic History Review*, 34 (1981), pp.189-208.

37. See, e.g., I. Gough, *The Political Economy of the Welfare State* (1979), Chs.3-4; J. Carrier and I. Kendall, 'Social Policy and Social Change - explanations of the development of social policy', *Journal of Social Policy*, 2 (1973), pp. 212-14; D. Wedderburn, 'Facts and Theories of the Welfare State', *The Socialist Register* (1965), pp.137-9.

38. See, e.g., J. Higgins, 'Social Control Theories of Social Policy', *Journal of Social Policy*, 9 (1980), pp. 1-23; V. George and P. Wilding, 'Social Values, Social Class and Social Policy', *Social and Economic Administration*, 6 (1972), pp. 236-46.

39. George and Wilding, 'Social Values', p. 245.

40. J. Saville, 'The Welfare State: An Historical Approach', *New Reasoner*, 3 (1957-8), pp. 5-25.

41. R. Mishra, *Society and Social Policy*, Ch. 6; George and Wilding, *Ideology*, Ch. 5.

42. Searle, *National Efficiency*, Ch. 3.

43. R.J. Scally, *The Origins of the Lloyd-George Coalition: the Politics of Social Imperialism, 1900-1918* (1975), pp.4-11, 23-5.

44. B. Semmel, *Imperialism and Social Reform: English Social Imperial Thought 1895-1914* (1960), pp.13, 234-6.

45. H.C.G. Matthew, *The Liberal Imperialists* (1973), pp. 227-64.

46. G.R. Searle, *Eugenics and Politics in Britain 1900-1914* (Leyden, 1976), Ch. 5; D. MacKenzie, 'Eugenics in Britain', *Social Studies of Science*, 6 (1976), pp. 499-532; G.R. Searle, 'Eugenics and Class' in Past and Present Society, *The Roots of Sociobiology* (1978), pp.1-26.

47. See, e.g., K. Burgess, *The Challenge of Labour: Shaping British Society 1850-1930* (1980), pp.125-33; J.R. Hay, *The Development of the British Welfare State 1880-1975 (1978)*, p. 10.

48. D.A. Hamer, *Liberal Politics in the age of Gladstone and Rosebery* (1972), pp. 321-9; H.V. Emy, *Social Politics*, p. ix.

49. Emy, *Social Politics*, pp. 106-112, 157-69.

50. C. Wrigley, *David Lloyd George and the British Labour Movement*, (Hassocks, 1976), pp. 5-8, Ch. 2.

51. A.J. Mayer, 'The Power Politician and Counterrevolutionary' in P. Stansky (ed.), *Churchill: A Profile* (1973), pp. 174-8, R. Rhodes James, *Churchill: A Study in Failure 1900-39* (1973 edition), pp. 41-7.

52. G. Stedman Jones, *Outcast London. A Study in the Relationship between Classes in Victorian Society* (Oxford, 1971), Chs. 16,18.

53. See, e.g., J. Brown, 'Social Control and the Modernisation of Social Policy, 1890-1929' in P. Thane (ed.), *The Origins of British Social Policy* (1978), pp. 126-9; J. Harris, *Unemployment and Politics* (Oxford, 1972), p. 356; Freeden, *New Liberalism*, pp. 178-81.

54. J.R. Hay, 'Government Policy towards Labour in Britain, 1900-1914: some further issues', *Scottish Labour History Journal*, 10 (1976), pp. 41-9; N. Whiteside, 'Welfare Insurance and Casual Labour: A Study of Administrative Intervention in Industrial Employment, 1906-26', *Economic History Review*, 32 (1979), pp. 507-22.

55. J. Hinton, *The First Shop Steward's Movement* (1973), pp. 30-1, 44-6.

56. J.R. Hay, 'Government Policy towards Labour', pp. 41-9.

57. N. McCord, 'Ratepayers and Social Policy' in Thane (ed.), *The Origins of British Social Policy*, p. 22.

58. J. Melling (ed.), *Housing, Social Policy and the State* (1980), pp. 1-32, 37-41.

The Terms of the Debate

59. J.R. Hay, 'Employers' Attitudes to Social Policy and the Concept of Social Control, 1900-1929' in Thane (ed.) *The Origins of British Social Policy*, pp. 107-25; J. Melling, 'British Industry and the Origins of the Welfare State', *Bulletin on Social Policy*, 8 (1981), pp. 42-8.

60. J.R. Hay, 'Employers and Social Policy in Britain: the Evolution of Welfare Legislation, 1905-14', *Social History*, 3 (1977), pp. 435-55.

61. N. Whiteside, 'Industrial Welfare and Labour Regulation in Britain at the time of the First Word War', *International Review of Social History*, 25 (1980), pp. 308-10.

62. D.A. MacKenzie, *Statistics in Britain 1865-1930: the Social Construction of Scientific Knowledge* (Edinburgh, 1981), pp. 25-8, 35-6.

63. N. Parry and J. Parry, *The Rise of the Medical Profession: A Study of Collective Social Mobility* (1976), pp. 72-86, 254-5.

64. R.M. MacLeod, 'Statesmen Undisguised', *American Historical Review*, 78 (1973), p. 1403; J.N. Tarn, *Working-Class Housing in 19th Century Britain* (1971), Ch. 4.

65. R.M. Titmuss, *Essays on the Welfare State* (1963), pp. 26-8; I. Illich, *Disabling Professions* (1977), pp. 11-39; C.K. Watkins, *Social Control* (1975), pp. 104-118.

66. See, e.g., J.L. Brand, *Doctors and the State*, (Baltimore, 1965), Chs. 11-12; D. Winch, *Economics and Policy: A Historical Study* (1969), Ch. 2.

67. H. Pelling, *Popular Politics and Society in Late Victorian Britain* (1979), Ch. 1; S. Yeo, 'Working-class association, private capital, welfare and the State in the late nineteenth and twentieth centuries' in N. Parry, M. Rustin and C. Satyamurti (eds.), *Social Work, Welfare and the State* (1979), Ch. 3; Thane, 'The Working Class and State Welfare', pp. 6-8.

68. P. Thane, 'The Working Class and State 'Welfare' in Britain 1880-1914', *Historical Journal*, 27 (1984); R.J. Holton, *British Syndicalism, 1900-14* (1976), pp. 137-8, 182, 204.

69. Yeo in Parry *et al.*, *Social Work, Welfare and the State*, p.67.

70. J. Melling, 'Industrial Strife and Business Welfare Philosophy', *Business History*, 21 (1979), p. 163; Hay, 'Government policy towards labour', pp. 41-7.

71. G.V. Rimlinger, *Welfare Policy and Industrialisation in Europe, America and Russia* (New York, 1971), Chs. 1,8; *idem*, 'The "Crisis" of the Welfare State in Historical Perspective', unpublished paper to 8th International Economic History Congress, (Budapest, 1982), pp. 2-7.

72. P. Thane, *The Foundations of the Welfare State* (1982), pp. 105-7.

73. J. Higgins, *States of Welfare: Comparative Analysis*

in Social Policy (1981), pp. 43, 107-21.

74. M. Rein, *Social Science and Public Policy* (1976), pp. 111-15; A.B. Cherns, 'Social Science and Policy' in A.B. Cherns, R. Sinclair and W.I. Jenkins, (eds.) *Social Science and Government: Policies and Problems* (1972), Ch. 2.

75. Rein, *Social Science*, p. 117.

76. Ibid., p. 124.

77. I. Levitt, 'The Use of Official Statistics', *Quantitative Sociology Newsletter*, 22 (1979), pp. 68-82.

78. Cited in M. Bulmer (ed.) *Social Policy Research* (1978), pp. 72-3.

79. L.J. Sharpe, 'Government as client for social science research' in Bulmer, *Social Policy Research*, p. 69.

80. A.B. Cherns, 'Social Science and Policy', pp. 16-17; Rein, *Social Science*, pp. 112-7; P. Hall, H. Land *et al*, *Change, Choice and Conflict in Social Policy* (1975), pp. 501-6.

81. See, e.g., M. Abrams, *Social Surveys and Social Action* (1951); P. Abrams, *Origins of British Sociology 1834-1914* (1968); J. Irvine, I. Miles and J. Evans (eds.), *Demystifying Social Statistics* (1979), Chs. 1,10; Radical Statistics, *Social Indicators: For Individual Well-Being or Social Control?* (1978).

82. See, e.g., A.D. Biderman, 'Information, Intelligence, Enlightened Public Policy: Functions and Organization of Societal Feedback', *Policy Sciences*, 1 (1970), p. 217-30.

83. J. Irvine *et al.* (eds.), *Demystifying Social Statistics*, Ch. 10.

84. See, e.g., A.B. Cherns, 'Social Sciences and Policy' and H.C. Kelman, 'The Relevance of Social Research to Social Issues' in *The Sociological Review*, Monograph 16 (Keele, 1970), pp. 53-75, 77-99.

85. Rein, *Social Science*, pp. 115-6.

86. Levitt, 'The Use of Official Statistics', pp. 68-72; Ford, *Social Theory and Social Practice*, Part 2.

87. O.Q.G.M. MacDonagh, 'The Nineteenth Century Revolution in Government: A Re-Appraisal', *Historical Journal*,1 (1958), pp. 52-67.

Chapter 2

THE LABOUR PROBLEM

THE INCIDENCE OF DEBATE

> The Labour Problem, the one problem which
> above all others, demands solution in an age
> described not without reason as "the age of
> the working man". (*Fortnightly Review*,
> 1889)[1]

In April 1880, *The Times* observed that 'among the
numerous questions which claimed attention from
Parliament and the Country, the condition of the
labouring classes' was one 'of the first in
importance'.[2] More than a decade later, its editorials were still expounding upon the 'magnitude
and urgency of the labour question'.[3] In the
interim, the 'Labour Problem' had moved to the
forefront of political and public debate. The
content of *Hansard* and of Cabinet agenda clearly
reflected this shift, as did the political
correspondence and memoirs of the period. For
example, the importance of the labour question as
an electoral issue was increasingly urged in the
correspondence received by the Liberal Chief Whip,
Sir Algernon West,[4] while Sir Henry Lucy, the Tory
parliamentary correspondent, viewing the
succession of debates and enquiries devoted to
labour affairs, was moved to record in 1890 that
the 'shadow of the working man lies dark over the
House of Commons'.[5] Discussion of the 'Labour Problem' was not,
however, the monopoly of the political elite at
Westminster and there emerged a whole genre of
social and economic journalism devoted to the
issue in the periodical and daily press of the
period. Content analysis of the leading reviews,
of the trade journals, and of *The Times* editorials

for the years 1880-93 indicates a dramatic rise in the incidence of articles on social problems relating to the labour market.(See Table 2.1)

Table 2.1:
Number of Articles on the 'Labour Problem'in Leading Periodicals and Times Editorials, 1880-93[6]

1880	30	1887	88
1881	26	1888	48
1882	22	1889	74
1883	42	1890	104
1884	36	1891	82
1885	100	1892	93
1886	78	1893	97

THE NATURE OF THE 'PROBLEM'

The 'Labour Problem' as articulated in late-Victorian and Edwardian debate was not just one problem but a range of mutually interdependent and often reinforcing problems. Contemporary concern was primarily related to three main areas of dysfunction within the labour market - the breakdown of industrial relations, the persistence of unemployment and endemic under-employment, and the incidence of low-income destitution.

Industrial Unrest

In turn, three major areas of explanation for the escalation in industrial unrest after 1880 may usefully be identified; the performance of the economy, changes in the structure and social relationships of production, and shifts in the social, economic and political ideology of the Labour Movement.

The industrial consensus which prevailed from the 1850s to the early 1870s was heavily dependent upon the prosperity of the British economy and the hegemony of British exports and enterprise in world markets. Given Britain's industrial pre-eminence, profit margins could be maintained without recourse to any long-term reduction in labour costs and growth rates could be sustained without a massive injection of capital-intensive techniques threatening the value and status of skilled labour. Instead, the pattern of domestic investment tended to be labour intensive, generating a steady growth of employment incomes and enhancing the scarcity value of skilled workers.[7]

However, after the mid-1870s, the economic climate was no longer conducive to industrial consensus. The sustained decline in commodity prices and in profit margins during the Great Depression, and the increasing competition in world markets from technically advanced rivals such as Germany and America engendered a more aggressive attitude on the part of employers towards wage costs and labour productivity. Faced by rising production costs and unfavourable shifts in factor and product markets, employers sought to reduce labour costs and to optimise their control over the deployment and remuneration of the work-force.[8]

These changes in the market environment for British industry and in the labour policy of management were duly reflected after 1875 in the erosion of wage levels in many industries (especially where wages were traditionally linked to the selling price of the product), in the increased intensity of labour utilisation, and in the heightened insecurity even for the privileged minority of trade unionists.[9] The general upward trend in the number and occupational distribution of strikes after 1870, and in particular, the explosion of militancy in the late 1880s and early 1890s, testified to the resulting alienation of Labour.[10] Moreover, economic trends after the 1880s continued to polarise industrial relations. The downturn in the rate of economic growth, the continuing low rates of yield on domestic investment with stagnant or falling productivity after 1900, the consequent stagnation or decline of real wages and the increasing disparity between the economic fortunes of wealth-holders and wage-earners, served further to discredit the concept of an identity of interest between Capital and Labour.[11]

The conciliatory tone of mid-Victorian industrial relations was also eroded after 1870 by shifts in the production structure of British industry. The efforts of employers to lower production costs and increase productivity invariably involved greater mechanisation and

rationalisation of the work process, necessitating
new working arrangements and a changed pattern of
authority and power in the workplace.   Within
manufacturing, there was a steady increase in the
size of plant, in the amount of capital per worker
and in the level of industrial concentration,
which rendered work more tightly controlled and
supervised.   Increasingly, management sought to
reassert control over the speed and conditions of
production.[12]   As a result, the privileged
position of skilled workers was severely
undermined.   Technical innovation, the adoption
of labour-saving investment, and labour dilution
threatened traditional skills in a range of trades
such as engineering and construction.   The degree
of autonomy and authority of craft unionists
within the Victorian labour process was progressively weakened by new forms of manning,
shift-work and incentive payments, as were their
semi-normative concepts of a 'just wage' and a
'normal working day'.[13]   The increasing focus of
industrial unrest after 1880 upon issues such as
manning requirements, demarcation, apprenticeship
ratios and other work-related questions, duly
reflected the heightened sense of workplace
alienation and status insecurity of the skilled
workforce.[14]   The growing realisation that they
could no longer ensure their scarcity value within
the local labour market by means of restrictive
practices created distrust of the traditional
ideology and machinery of industrial consensus.
Consequently, in the last quarter of the
nineteenth century, new traditions of local
militancy and grassroots discontent emerged which
threatened to fragment any attempt by trade union
leaders to sustain conciliatory tactics.[15]
     The emergence after 1870 of a 'New', more
militant unionism amongst the semi-skilled and
unskilled labour force was also related in part to
shifts in the mode of British industrial production.   Changes in technology and labour
utilisation had precipitated a new group of semi-
skilled workers.   This group was isolated from
the exclusive practices and attitudes of existing
skilled unions and it lacked their established
bargaining position within the workplace that had
functioned to some degree as a point of trans-
mission for consensus values.[16]   Faced in the
1880s with drastic increases in the level of work
intensity and job insecurity, semi-skilled workers
advanced a more militant conception of trades

unionism as an all-grades movement cutting across
established occupational and even industrial
divisions.[17] Meanwhile, the increasing rationalisation and inter-dependence of the urban labour
market facilitated the organisation of significant
areas of the unskilled workforce and their first
celebrated challenge to the economic and social
conditions which appeared 'to condemn them to
perpetual "marginalism"'.[18]

The escalation in industrial unrest after
1880 also reflected fundamental shifts in the
economic and social ideology of the Labour
Movement.[19] There were marked discontinuities in
the economic philosophy of organised Labour. It
is unlikely that the leaders of mid-Victorian
unionism had ever accepted *in toto* the economic
determinism of the wages fund, yet they clearly
perceived the mechanisms of the market economy as
fundamentally compatible with the interests of
Labour. They did not conceive of wage
determination as primarily a function of social
need but as a market calculation of labour's
utility - a reflection of its ingenuity, industry,
and above all, skill. Union leaders were
therefore prepared to bargain in terms of the
conventional market criteria of wage negotiation
(viz. the state of the market, the selling price
of the product, or the competitive needs of the
district) as manifested in the operation of the
system of conciliation and arbitration boards
throughout British industry.[20] The older craft
unions continued to accept in the 1860s and 1870s
the virtues of the 'individualistic norm' of
thrift and co-operation with the employers, and
their perception of the industrial process as one
in which wage claims were essentially trade-
specific issues and substantially dependent upon
industrial conditions outwith union control served
to reinforce their disinclination to participate
in any general programme of labour militancy.[21]

In contrast, by the early 1890s there had
emerged an explicit conflict:

> between the orthodox theory of production
> which stressed saving and the sanctity of
> capital, managerial freedom of production,
> labour-as-cost and flexible wage-rates, and
> the trade union repudiation, based on
> experience, of the assumptions of perfect
> competition and their ensuing demand for
> minima of wages, hours and working conditions

to be imposed by legislation upon the market, not only for their own good but as an essential condition of the market's own progress.[22]

As the proceedings of the Royal Commission on Labour bore witness, the economic assumptions that had underpinned the consensus tactics of mid-Victorian unionism had lost their credibility.[23] Faced by the competitive downward forcing of wage costs after 1880 and the status erosion consequent upon innovations in the technical and organisational structure of British industry, even skilled unionists ceased to view the mechanism of the market economy and purely market criteria of wage determination as consistent with the just reward and income security of Labour.[24] Recent experience of collective bargaining and progressive theories of the labour market alike appeared to demonstrate that working conditions and the share of wages in National Income could not improve without concerted confrontation with prevailing industrial norms.[25]

However, after 1880, Trade Unionism's rejection of the concept of Labour as a commodity whose significance did not extend beyond its function in the labour market, and its critique of the labour process, were rarely articulated in purely economic terms. Alienation from the market economy was increasingly expressed as but one facet of a broader social and political protest.

During the period 1850-75, 'Labourism' had dominated working-class social and political philosophy. With its stress upon the unity of Capital and Labour, and its overriding assumption that fair dealing was obtainable, it had exercised a persistent constraint upon the scope and objectives of the Trade Union Movement, and, despite its stubborn insistence on bargaining rights at the point of production, served to moderate the prevailing temper of industrial relations. The Trade Union Movement had been highly elitist and dominated by middle-class values. Despite its token recourse to the rhetoric of working-class solidarity, it had focussed primarily on the fears and aspirations of the more skilled and strategically placed workers within the workforce.[26] In particular, the ideology of self-improvement, with its stress on individual thrift, respectability and social mobility, had militated against a conception of the common interests of Labour as a whole and consequently impaired the ability of the union movement to articulate a genuine class analysis of the social relations of production.[27]

This consensus philosophy had been reinforced by the cultural and intellectual environment of mid-Victorian unionism. Within the community, patterns of working-class associative effort, of leisure and consumption, of housing and religious affiliation, had served to emphasise the lack of class solidarity.[28] Meanwhile, Labour was markedly lacking in any rigorous intellectual critique of the existing social structure. Working-class radicalism, inspired by writers such as Carlyle and Ruskin, subscribed only to 'a limited and partial critique not of society as a whole but of individual segments of the social order'.[29] It advanced no coherent attack either upon the structure of capitalist society in general or upon the exploitative features of the labour market in particular. This rather 'complacent acceptance of the fundamentals of bourgeois society' was duly reflected in the incorporation of organised trade unionism within the radical wing of the Liberal Party, the diversion of its aggression away from industrial and financial oligarchies and towards the traditional landed elite, and its reluctance to politicise its social and economic grievances within an independent political movement.[30]

As Lovell rightly cautions, the shift in the ideology and machinery of British trades unionism after 1880 and the discontinuities between Old and New Unionism should not be exaggerated, nor should undue significance be attached to the impact of ideology *per se* in determining the incidence of industrial unrest.[31] Nonetheless, it is evident that during the 1880s and early 1890s the grip of 'Labourism' upon working-class social and political ideology was relaxed. 'Labourist' assumptions with respect to the benefits of class collaboration and to the potential for social amelioration within the existing social structure lost credibility in the more hostile industrial environment and insecure labour market of the 1880s. A doctrine of industrial harmony appeared, in reality, to sacrifice working-class living standards and social advancement on the altars of private property and the free market, while values such as self-help lost relevance to a workforce whose status and income were constantly eroded by social and economic forces beyond its control.[32]

New Unionism served to provide a more relevant diagnosis of the labour market and agenda for industrial action. As Clegg, Fox and Thompson have demonstrated, it was far from a homogeneous movement but its operational philosophy can fairly be characterised as militant.[33] In its pattern of recruitment and tactics, it sought to appeal in *class* terms to all grades of workers and to escalate industrial confrontation from *ad hoc* issues at the point of production to a broader attack on the structure of social and industrial power and the cluster of industrial and legal elites which shaped it.[34] Increasingly, after the mid-1880s, within labour militancy, the defence of traditional skills was allied with the basic struggle of the semi-skilled and unskilled workforce to obtain a living wage and some form of countervailing power against the *diktat* of management. 'By the 1890s, the principles of the new and general unionism and of class solidarity had obtained at least verbal acquiescence from most union leaders.'[35]

Cultural factors reinforced this class-orientation of industrial unrest. The social ecology of the late-Victorian city produced a socially segregated pattern of urban growth. The pattern varied, depending on the nature of local transportation systems, housing and labour markets, but generally working-class communities acquired greater stability, homogeneity and cultural autonomy. Accordingly, the forms of cultural mediation which had adapted Labour to its economic situation during the mid-Victorian period were gradually eroded.[36]

Meanwhile, the transition in the social politics of British trades unionism after 1886 in part caused and in part reflected the deterioration in industrial relations. Despite the strength and tenacity of the labourist tradition, industrial politics increasingly polarised along class lines. The transformation of Conservatism into the broader-based politics of industrial and commercial property as well as that of the landed interest was paralleled by new forms of working-class politics that sought directly to challenge rather than to mediate Labour's relationship with the existing distribution of power and wealth in society. The new generation of labour leaders were more sceptical of the benefits of a Lib-Lab alliance and receptive to the Socialist propaganda of groups such as the S.D.F. A significant minority of trade unionists were converted to the Socialist concept of unionism as a means not merely to optimise wages and working conditions but also to modify the structure of industry and society.[37] Moreover, in combating the changing scale of capitalism, many older craft unions were prepared to identify with socialistic strategies of industrial militancy and independent working-class political activism in an effort to resist the further erosion of their position in the labour market and the community.[38]

Unemployment and Under-Employment

In so far as late-Victorian industrial unrest was a function of social and economic insecurity within the market economy, it tended to reflect variations in the level of employment. Thus, contemporaneously with the rising incidence of strikes and lockouts after 1880, the problem of unemployment and under-employment began to emerge as a distinctly new theme of social anxiety.

Despite the serious inadequacies of the available data, it is evident that the 1880s witnessed a significant rise in the level of British unemployment.[39] That the term 'unemployed' was first recorded in the *Oxford Dictionary* in 1882 and 'unemployment' in 1888 was not merely fortuitous. The years 1884-7 were probably the worst continuous sequence from the stand-point of unemployment of any throughout the era 1790-1914.[40] 'For no other recorded period before 1921 did the level of unemployment stay above 7.5 per cent for four successive years.'[41] In the worst year, 1886, unemployment averaged 10.2 per cent. Leading the list were the engineering, metal-working and shipbuilding unions with 13.5 per cent unemployment.[42] However, evidence submitted to the Royal Commission on the Depression of Trade and Industry would suggest that rates were substantially higher in trades and localities associated with the staple export industries. For example, over 22 per cent of the Boilermakers and Iron-shipbuilders Union drew out of work benefit in 1886 while marine engineering on the Clyde registered unemployment rates of around 36 per cent.[43] The depression of the 1880s was more prolonged and hit a far broader spectrum of occupations than the previous slumps of 1866 and 1879. Even the 'light' industries witnessed a severe rise in unemployment from 2 per cent in 1882 to over 10 per cent in 1886, and relatively sheltered trades such as building construction registered equally high levels of distress in certain districts, such as Liverpool.[44] Moreover, the labour market remained depressed in 1888 and was subjected to a further period of slump from 1892-5.

The intensity of British unemployment during the 1880s closely reflected the falling rate of growth of industrial output. The upswing of the business cycle in the early 1880s was below average intensity, with prices of British manufactures not having effected a full recovery from their collapse in the 1870s and with a decelerating rate of growth of industrial production.[45] Thereafter, industrial output fell by 10 per cent over the period 1884-7, the growth rate of industrial production for the period 1883-9 dipping further to 1.7 per cent per annum, a recession sustained by every major industry except textiles.

A wide range of explanations for this recession in British manufacturing in the 1880s has been advanced by economic historians, but an emerging consensus would attribute a key role to the low rate of growth of manufactured exports,[46] due in part to import substitution by Britain's overseas customers, in part to the intensification of German competition in world markets, but primarily to the sharp fall in the growth of world trade in manufactures consequent upon shifts in the terms of international trade. As a result, the growth rate of British industrial production was severely inhibited and the consequent competition for restricted trade, in depressing the price level at a faster rate than the fall in costs, rendered the economy unprofitable. This in turn engendered a low level of domestic investment. Moreover, it appears probable that the depression in manufacturing caused the downturn in construction which further constrained the rate of domestic capital formation and the aggregate demand for labour. The fact that the size of the labour force was growing faster than ever in the 1880s, despite a deceleration in population growth rates and a sharp rise in the level of emigration, served merely to accentuate this disequilibrium.

The Labour Problem

A variety of factors magnified the economic, social and ideological impact of unemployment. Firstly, 'the conjuncture of rising real wages with widespread unemployment stressed the economic and social distinction between those who were regularly and those irregularly employed, and for the first time the unemployed were perceived as a distinct class whose problems were different from those of the working classes as a whole.'[47] Secondly, even though the purchasing power of wages was rising, the prolonged depression after 1883 tended to undermine the capacity of both organised and unorganised workmen to retain their independence whilst unemployed. Despite the extent of institutionalised thrift, the level of personal and mutual saving proved inadequate to cope with the protracted unemployment of the mid-1880s, and among certain sections of the workforce this erosion of private resources was exacerbated by the contemporaneous efforts of Whitehall to impose greater stringency and uniformity on the administration of poor relief.[48] Thirdly, as recent studies of the local labour market within late-Victorian and Edwardian Britain have demonstrated, the fortunes of staple industries such as heavy engineering, shipbuilding and iron and steel, often determined both the prosperity of the local community and the buoyancy of demand for labour throughout the region. The negative employment and income multiplier effects of unemployment within such industries upon the local or regional economy were therefore particularly high.[49] Finally, it must be stressed that the problems of unemployment and under-employment within the late-nineteenth century labour market were intimately linked. Hence, periods of industrial depression could readily undermine the precarious equilibrium of the casual labour market and the 'sensitively tuned economic and credit system' upon which it was based, and as the works of Stedman Jones and Treble have vividly demonstrated, it was just such a 'conjunctural crisis' which characterised Britain's major cities during the 1880s.[50]

Although the problem of under-employment loomed larger in the industrial life of the East End than elsewhere in Britain, each major industrial centre possessed a chronic glut of male and female unskilled labour within a wide spectrum of occupations.[51] Broadly speaking, the existence and persistence of a casual labour problem can be attributed to two main factors; to shifts in the industrial structure of inner-city perimeter areas, and to self-reinforcing rigidities within the casual labour market itself.[52]

By the 1880s, the process of de-industrialisation was far advanced in a number of metropolitan areas such as London, Manchester and Liverpool, with a consequent de-stabilisation of the pattern of employment. Some traditional manufactures in semi-processed or capital goods had either been eliminated by the long-term impact of the industrial revolution or been forced by rising wages and rents to migrate to more cost-effective provincial locations where the economies of aggregation foregone were more than offset by the reduced burden of overhead costs. In addition, many finishing trades had also responded to the rise of a mass-consumer market and the competitive demands of new technology by shifting to areas with fewer physical and cost constraints so as to adopt large-scale factory methods of production. There remained a cluster of predominantly labour-intensive, consumer goods industries which maintained a precarious existence by adopting ruthless economies in labour costs and rent, by expanding home work and by the vertical disintegration of production (i.e. 'sweating'). With their characteristically low input of fixed capital, their small scale of production, their ease of entry *and of exit*, their fragile margin of profitability, and their heavy dependence on fluctuations in consumer demand, such trades provided little stability of employment. In particular, their seasonality of production greatly inflated the size of the surplus labour force by necessitating a labour supply in excess of normal needs to meet seasonally recurrent peaks in output. Furthermore, as Stedman Jones emphasises, irregularity of employment in these trades had adverse lateral effects on the labour market in general:

> Where the seasonal pattern of employment was unpredictable, the work force in casualised limbo supplemented short periods of employment by invading an already overfilled general unskilled labour market. Where the seasonal pattern was regular and predictable, the dovetailing of occupations merely increased the pressure on the lowest and

45

least skilled strata of the labour market.[53]

Rigidities within the casual labour market rendered the problem of under-employment chronic. Lack of mobility between primary and secondary labour markets starved the under-employed of reliable information on alternative employment opportunities. Such workers were caught in a self-perpetuating circle by the nature of casual employment, the essence of which was that the work offered was insufficient to provide a regular livelihood but sufficient to prevent workers straying permanently into other occupations. It demanded not only their geographical proximity to work in order to be in localised contact with recruiting agents but also that of their wives whose incomes were essential to maintain families above the poverty line.

This need for supplementary female earnings served to redouble the immobility of the casual labourer. In addition, the family-income structure of the casual labour market, by mitigating the effects of intermittent or low-paid employment upon male earnings, discouraged a radical reassessment by male workers of their employment position. Low wages also excluded casual workers from employment outwith the inner industrial perimeter area by denying them access to new transport and alternative housing facilities. The immobility of the under-employed was reinforced by the extent to which their family budgets were dependent on local credit systems to survive seasonal and cyclical fluctuations in earnings. Finally, as Anderson has argued, the absence of inter-occupational mobility amongst the under-employed was not only determined by the structure of the casual labour market but was also a function of 'pre-labour market disadvantages, especially in areas of education and skill'.

During the 1880s, a combination of both long-term and short-term economic developments served to escalate the casual labour problem in Britain to crisis proportions. There was, contemporaneous with a growing influx of workers to the casual labour market, a severe contraction in demand for unskilled labour. The cyclical depression of the mid-1880s greatly accentuated an already endemic condition of under-employment in inner-city areas due to structural decay and the vertical disintegration of production. A series of exceptionally severe winters (1879-81, 1886-7,

1891) seriously retarded the demand for seasonal
labour, while the concurrent recession in the
building trade effectively eliminated the most
likely source of alternative male employment. The
consequent influx of wives and daughters onto a
falling labour market in order to sustain family
income merely aggravated the glut of casual
workers. Meanwhile, the ranks of the urban
under-employed were swelled by the addition of
permanent workers ousted from regular occupations
due to shifts in the structure of production (e.g.
dockworkers affected by the mechanisation of the
distribution sector) or to cyclical trade
depression (e.g. engineering labourers and
agricultural workers). Although the magnitude of
its displacement effects are debatable, the
dramatic rise in Jewish immigration acted, at
least in London, as an additional de-stabilising
factor. Above all, while the size of the urban
workforce peaked in the 1880s, and would
subsequently be absorbed by the expansion of the
tertiary sector, the pace of structural change
within urban manufacturing remained insufficient
to absorb the growing labour surplus.

Low-Income Destitution

Poverty studies would suggest that irregularity of
earnings due to unemployment and under-employment
constituted a prime cause of low-income
destitution in late-Victorian society.[54] There
is no reliable time series of poverty rates for
the period, but on the evidence of contemporary
surveys, such as those undertaken by Booth and
Rowntree, it clearly existed on a massive scale.
It is estimated that, depending on variations in
the structure and buoyancy of local labour
markets, the percentage of the urban population
lacking the means of subsistence in the 1880s
ranged from 15 to 35 per cent.[55] Moreover, the
Booth enquiry disclosed that some 55 per cent of
London poverty in the lowest classes A and B and
68 per cent in classes C and D could be attributed
to inadequate or irregular earnings.[56] Given
that the London economy was especially deficient
in well-paid employment and factory work and was
uniquely dependent on casual labour and low-
productivity domestic industry, it is possible
that Booth's data inflated the significance of
low-income destitution.[57] Yet Rowntree's later
analysis of primary poverty in York yielded a

47

roughly comparable figure of 52 per cent and there is no reason to believe that such findings were anomalous with the pattern of destitution elsewhere. 'Low and irregular pay remained the principal route to primary poverty in towns of markedly different socio-economic structures.'[58]

In many areas of the late-Victorian labour market, poverty arose because the wage-earner, even in regular employment, was inadequately remunerated. Such poverty was most clearly entrenched amongst the unskilled. There existed a whole range of unskilled work in which meagreness of wage left no margin between income and necessary expenditure - occupations characterised not only by ease of entry, but also by a relative lack of unionisation and established bargaining procedures, and in many instances by a high female participation ratio.

Labouring, especially in the shipbuilding, engineering and iron manufacturing trades, constituted the major area of male employment in which regular earnings failed to provide a subsistence wage. Treble maintains that 'there was little hope of families of this element of the workforce, even when the head of the household was fully engaged, escaping the grip of primary poverty'. The lower echelons of the retailing sector, with their ease of access to any section of the able-bodied workforce and dependence on the poorest sections of the market, were also characterised by exceptionally low earnings. A sizeable group of small dealers and traders maintained a precarious existence, often with incomes that were incapable of ensuring adequate food and housing. In addition, transport workers such as plate-layers and surfacemen with little bargaining power and confronted by dictatorial management structures, were notoriously badly paid, and they could rarely rise above the poverty line without supplementary income from other members of the household. Finally, female employment in general was inadequately remunerated. Starvation wages were common in the retailing and service industries (for example, shop assistants, waitresses and laundry-workers) and also in a range of factory-type or factory-based jobs (for example, in the Birmingham metal work or Manchester India-rubber trades), where women found it progressively more difficult to contribute in a meaningful fashion to the budgets of families never far removed from a state of primary poverty.

However, the main focus of low-income destitution in the 1880's was the casual labour market. The social and economic forces producing endemic under-employment served also to generate widespread poverty. Immobility within the urban workforce effectively isolated unskilled workers within a secondary labour market with low and irregular pay. The economic decline of inner-city areas rendered this growing but immobile unskilled workforce acutely vulnerable to exploitation and generated a low-wage economy in Britain's urban centres. Low-income destitution became increasingly self-perpetuating within such areas after 1880. On the one hand, the availability of cheap labour created a demand for it and on the other, the demand for cheap casual labour promoted its supply. The form and irregularity of earnings also perpetuated low-income destitution. Daily payment, which fluctuated arbitrarily, further increased the real cost of living of the labourer. The meagreness and uncertainty of earnings discouraged saving of any sort, and this in turn reduced the credit-rating of the casual labourer and hence inflated the charges imposed by creditors (especially the landlord). Meanwhile, as Sutcliffe has demonstrated, not only did the inflation in inner-city housing costs after 1880 severely erode wages depressed by an urban labour surplus, but this 'scissors effect' was also rendered more acute by the highly regressive incidence of housing costs, with the poorest families in the unskilled and under-employed workforce paying the most inflated rents. Thus, the very poverty of the casual imposed upon him additional expenses which the more prosperous workers managed to escape. Furthermore, the destitution of the casual workforce reduced the physical efficiency and the educational and vocational skills of its children, thus denying them also access to more secure and well-paid employment, and producing a seemingly self-sustaining culture of poverty.

Within the secondary labour market, the most notorious area of low-income destitution lay within the sweated outwork and home work trades such as the London clothing and Midland light-metal trades. The social and economic conditions generated by the 'sweating system' figured prominently in contemporary debate over the 'Labour Problem'. The production structure of the system was geared to minimising overheads and wage costs and to optimising the ease of disinvestment. Insecurity of employment with truly starvation wages and 'searing distress' was therefore the inevitable lot of workers within the system, with their families subjected to acute and persistent social deprivation.

Evidence would suggest that the 1880s witnessed the most dramatic period of expansion in the sweated trades. In contrast to national trends in the organisation of industry and the labour market, a number of regional and local economies witnessed the decentralisation, and on occasions the actual defactorisation of production. This anomalous pattern of industrial evolution was produced by the historical conjuncture of shifts in technology, in the supply of labour, in consumer demand, and in the pattern of late-Victorian urban growth. Manufacturers, confronted by the physical and cost constraints of inner-city areas, sought to exploit the revolution in Victorian demand for ready-made, mass produced consumer goods and the availability of a cheap, captive and docile labour force of under-employed, female and immigrant workers. At the same time, the advent of new technology (for example, the sewing machine in the clothing and shoemaking trades) enabled the sub-division and sub-contraction of the labour process and thereby the proliferation of small-workshop and home work production. However, although technical innovation initially strengthened the domestic system of production in certain trades, it also inexorably increased the cost-competitiveness of provincial factory production. Even at its peak, therefore, the inner-city domestic system was fighting a losing battle within the market, leading to endemic under-employment and the ruthless suppression of wage rates, (as, for example, in the shirt-finishing and chain-making trades). 'From the 1880s, the 'sweating'masters were engaged in a struggle for survival against an encroaching factory system, and amongst the first casualties were the wages and employment prospects of their workforce.'

Meanwhile, although designed to equalise the working conditions of labour, the Factory and Workshop Act of 1875 may have actively reinforced the centrifugal movement within certain labour markets, especially within London. It is arguable that the sporadic and uneven incidence of statutory inspection encouraged the growth of the most depressed sector of the labour market; its effect being to drive trade into the lower channels of production, thus eroding workforce solidarity and perpetuating the low-income destitution which remained the hallmark of 'sweated' labour.[59]

CRISIS PERCEPTIONS

The mere existence of adverse conditions, however acute, within the late-Victorian labour market does not fully explain the emergence of a 'Labour Problem' after 1880. As Tallman and McGree observe: 'Social conditions do not, in themselves, provide either a necessary or sufficient condition for a social problem.'[60] Depending on their theoretical standpoint, sociologists have identified a wide range of criteria defining a social issue as 'problematic'; that it should, for example, engender conflict and anxiety and a reappraisal of policy options and priorities by questioning the existing structure of industry and society; that it should mobilise public opinion and violate prevailing normative perceptions of the 'healthy' functioning of society; that it should reveal areas of social disorganisation and question the credibility of existing strategies of social control; that it should inhibit the proper process of socialisation, thereby endangering social norms and both moral and economic imperatives; that the issue should pose a sufficient threat to consensus as to motivate the government to institutionalise it as a means of defining and legitimating the 'problem'; that it should involve injustice and deprivation to a degree deemed intolerable by an influential section of society; and above all, that it should be perceived by the governing classes as a fundamental threat to the social and economic values and institutions upon which their hegemony is based.[61]

A content analysis of the leading reviews, trade journals and establishment press for the period after 1880 reveals that the issues of industrial conflict, unemployment, casual labour, and low-income destitution fully met these criteria.

The Labour Problem

Social Instability

Although, in 1880, G.P. Bevan advised the Royal Statistical Society that striking had become a disease and a very grave disease in the body social',[62] the establishment press was disposed to view industrial relations in the early 1880s with complacent optimism. Reporting on the Trades Union Congress in 1881, *The Times* reflected that:

> The thunderous element is altogether absent. There is nothing alarming, nothing revolutionary ... Working men, it may be presumed, are waking to the consciousness that not only their social interests, but their political instincts and sympathies, are the same as those of other men.[63]

The following year, its verdict was even more reassuring, the editor stressing the absence of 'anything very revolutionary or confiscatory' from the proceedings, and concluding that 'British industry at present must have attained the peace and placidity of a happy family';[64] a view endorsed by John Morley in the *Fortnightly Review*.[65] As late as 1883, *The Times* was able to sustain its favourable perception of British labour relations:

> Trade unionists have little or none of the wild fancies and subversive schemes and idle rhetoric which are too commonly the stock-in-trade with their French and German fellows. There is no trace now of a deep-rooted antagonism to the capitalist class as such, no belief whatever in a millenium to follow from a general over-throw of the existing institutions of the country ... When we remember how vast the power is which they wield already, we may well rejoice at the moderate use they seem prepared to make of it.[66]

However, such euphoria proved short-lived. With the subsequent escalation in strikes and lockouts and the emergence of a new and more militant trades unionism, industrial relations become a major area of social crisis, threatening not merely property rights and managerial prerogatives but 'the very fabric of society'. By 1890, *The Times* was convinced that 'never had the conflict between Capital and Labour been more distinctly marked or more disastrous in its results' and warned its readers of the full extent of the threat:

> The aim of the New Unionism is nothing less than the wholesale appropriation of the property of employers ... We doubt whether the public at large, or even the mass of employers, have yet fully realised the nature and scope of the assault that is preparing upon industrial property and social prosperity.[67]

Such sentiments were echoed in a wide range of contemporary periodical and polemical literature. They incorporated several strands of 'crisis perception'. Firstly, they reflected a general concern at the breakdown of mid-Victorian social and industrial consensus. As the *Quarterly Review* lamented:

> The present condition of Capital and Labour approaches that of Civil War. The hostile sentiment is but thinly disguised even in the soberest utterances of the old unions, while among the younger, more democratic organizations of labour, uncompromising war with capital, even to the extreme of violence and sanguinary revolution is openly and frequently assured ... Two nations are in our midst: the social fabric is divided against itself.[68]

Secondly, such sentiments revealed a growing conviction amongst the propertied classes that there had occurred a major shift in the ideology of labour unrest; that although still concerned ostensibly with narrow economistic issues, militancy now constituted, largely through the machinations of a small minority of professional agitators and Socialist idealogues, a more fundamental challenge to the structure of industrial power, to the social relations of production, and to the viability of free enterprise. The views of Edmund Vincent, articulated in 1891, typify this conviction:

> [The policy of New Unionism] is that of the daughter of the horse-leech, it is a policy of continual importunity. The new Union cares not whether men are ill or well paid,

it is ever ready with a fresh demand. Concession does but whet its appetite; it claims for labour the whole of the profits made by labour and capital combined; it aims to be the absolute dictator of the conditions of toil; to say who shall work and how much he shall receive ... The principle which underlies the militant Union is the principle of socialism. In the first place, the individual is subordinated to the class; in the second place, the class desires to obtain the whole of the profits which are derived from capital and labour combined. In other words, it desires to confiscate capital.[69]

Thirdly, the tactics of New Unionism such as mass and secondary picketing were viewed as a discrete problem in that they threatened to undermine the rule of law and freedom of contract within the labour market. Journalists and social commentators made constant reference to the 'violence and organised tyranny' of New Unionism; to its adoption of the subversive and revolutionary tactics of Irish Nationalism and Continental Socialism, to its intimidation of industrialists and local authorities, and to the 'blatant disregard' by its leadership - described by the *Quarterly Review* as 'our national Mafia' - for the laws relating to conspiracy, trade combination, and the protection of property.[70] Disillusionment at the more 'anti-social' characteristics of New Unionism was the more acute in that, during the 1860s and 1870s, the governing classes had increasingly viewed trades unionism as having an important civilising function to play in inculcating the values of thrift, self-help and class harmony and engendering patterns of workforce behaviour consistent with social stability.[71] The degree of concern at its failure to fulfil such a function was clearly reflected in the range and virulence of the legal and military sanctions urged upon Whitehall and Westminster after the mid-1880s not only by right-wing extremists and 'defence' associations but also by a wide spectrum of industrialists and civic leaders, as a means of repressing the 'new forms of corporate tyranny' employed by trade unionists in industrial disputes.[72] The rise in the level of British unemployment during the 1880s was also viewed in middle and upper-class circles with growing disquiet. In

1882, *The Times* described unemployment as 'a social problem always pressing in this country and liable at times to become dangerous'.[73] By 1888, it constituted according to the same authority, 'the fundamental problem of modern society, in comparison with which almost every question in politics seems diminutive'.[74]

The issue of unemployment gave cause for concern on a number of counts. An overriding fear in the early and mid-1880s was that the distress of the 'genuine unemployed' would become confused with the 'real threat' of the 'dangerous classes', and that in treating a vital issue of law and order as merely a problem of social administration, local and central government authorities would compromise social stability and the security of urban property.[75] The establishment press was adamant that disturbances such as the Trafalgar Square Riots of 1886 did not signify any social revolt by the real unemployed, but the attempt by a small group of Socialist agitators to exploit their distress as a smokescreen behind which to mobilise the criminal classes so as to intimidate civic authorities into conceding left-wing demands. Reviewing the so-called 'unemployed riots' of 1886-7, *The Times* concluded:

> We entirely refuse to believe that the riots were the work of bona fide unemployed workmen ... Such men have too much self-respect to make themselves the companions and accomplices of roughs, rowdies and ranting revolutionaries. The rioters are the professional beggars, the petty pilferers and thieves, the disreputable drunkards who may always be seen loafing about the streets ... These are the classes which regularly give ear to Socialist spouters of the baser sort when they rave against the richer classes ... but they are not working men and they are only unemployed because honest and regular employment of any kind is hateful to them.[76]

However, as high levels of unemployment persisted in the late 1880s and early 1890s, there was increasing concern that even the deserving unemployed would become increasingly receptive to Socialist dogma and 'bitten', as the *Contemporary Review* expressed it, 'by the political tarantula yclept social democracy'; that in the eyes of the

artisan classes, radical critique of existing
social values and institutions would gain
credibility.[77] Even *The Times* adopted a less
phlegmatic attitude towards the unemployed,
reflecting that 'want of work is very apt to make
honest men impatient and even indignant with the
social order which seems to help them so
little.'[78] To Canon Barnett, the founder of
Toynbee Hall, 'the danger at hand' was not so much
'abnormal distress' as class antagonism:

> A degraded class creates an oppressive class,
> and the end is a revolution which means 'the
> death of the first-born' ... The state of
> things is dangerous. The unemployed may be
> driven by the police out of the
> thoroughfares, they may have no place in
> poor-law returns, but their existence cannot
> be denied, and if their ignorance and their
> sense of injustice are allowed to increase,
> they may some day appear, to overturn ... the
> very foundations of our trade and
> greatness.[79]

The fact that social agitation surrounding the
unemployment issue was invariably orchestrated by
the leaders of the New Unionism served to give
added conviction to his message.

This fear of social polarisation and
incipient revolt characterised a wide range of
contemporary appraisals of the unemployment
problem, from those advanced by orthodox
Liberalism to the diagnoses furnished by emerging
ideologies such as Social Imperialism. It was
accentuated by an additional concern that
unemployment, and especially cyclical
unemployment, in generating distress in the ranks
of the regular labour force, would blur the
distinction between the respectable working
classes and the residuum; that under the stress of
exceptional unemployment, artisans would identify
with the 'submerged' under-employed groups beneath
them, especially as they shared, albeit to a
lesser degree, the same problems of insanitary
housing, overcrowding, and high rents.[80] As
Stedman Jones has vividly demonstrated, for the
governing classes of the 1880s there therefore
existed the dangerous possibility 'that the
respectable working class', faced by protracted
unemployment, might 'throw in its lot with the
casual poor'.[81] As a result, the residuum would

become politicised and its mass deployed by
Socialist agitators against the State.
Conversely, the respectable working classes would
become 'contaminated' and 'demoralised' by contact
with the casual residuum, and increasingly
resistant to the work ethic and to industrial and
social discipline.

The existence of acute unemployment therefore
threatened the traditional distinction between the
deserving and the undeserving which remained the
central tenet of middle-class social philosophy
and which underpinned the whole fabric of
Victorian social control designed to sustain the
virtues of labour, thrift and self-help within the
workforce.[82] On the one hand, as *The Spectator*
warned, there was a danger that the identification
of the unemployed with Socialist agitation and
with the cost to ratepayers of civic disorder
would alienate philanthropists from the deserving
unemployed and thereby erode the traditional role
of charity in preserving an urban deference
community.[83] On the other hand, as *The Times* was
at pains to point out, having witnessed the rapid
inflation of the Mansion House Relief Fund after
each phase of unemployed disturbances, there was
an equal danger that, in their concern to buy off
the social menace of the unemployed, civic
authorities would succumb to indiscriminate
charity and breach the chastity belt of welfare
morality - the principle of less eligibility; thus
'fortifying the undeserving in their evil habits
and often overlooking the deserving altogether'.[84]

In threatening traditional, individualistic
moral distinctions between the deserving and
undeserving, unemployment also posed a serious
threat to the existing social policy paradigm
because it questioned the adequacy of self-help in
sustaining the economic viability of the artisan
classes. *The Times* was insistent that Government
should not be stampeded into the adoption of
collectivist measures:

> When distress is rife, and when everybody is
> casting about for its remedy, the tendency is
> to regard the State as a great milchcow. It
> ought to be strenuously resisted however. No
> State mechanism can replace the need of
> thrift and providence, and besides the direct
> mischief it does, it indirectly saps the
> vitality of the social organism by
> discouraging voluntary effort.[85]

However, other areas of the press, especially those expounding the views of Social Imperialism, were inclined to the view that coercive and interventionist legislation was necessary as a means of segregating the residuum from the labour market proper and that it was legitimate to harness collectivism to enforce 'traditional moral judgements and expectations'.[86] The unemployment problem of the 1880s therefore generated welfare issues that were, in subsequent decades, to prove the focus of major contention within British social politics.

From the viewpoint of the British governing classes, the most serious social threat posed by the 'Labour Problem' in the 1880s was the existence of a large, chronically poor, casual residuum within the urban labour force; a destitute residuum which, on the evidence of contemporary investigations, appeared to represent a substantial and growing proportion of the working class. As Stedman Jones has argued:

> The predominant reaction to this rediscovery of poverty in the early 1880s was not so much guilt but fear ... Discussions of the condition of the poor which in the 1870s had been confined to experts within the pages of specialised journals now become the subject of urgent general debate. From 1883 onwards [with the publication of *The Bitter Cry of Outcast London*] the quarterly journals and the press were full of warnings of the necessity of immediate reform to ward off the impending revolutionary threat.[87]

Such social fear was centred primarily around 'Outcast London' and was mainly articulated in the London-based press, but such was the position of London at the time in setting the terms of reference for opinion elsewhere in Britain that metropolitan anxieties coloured the response of civic authorities and social commentators to the problems of under-employment and low-income destitution throughout the country.[88]

In part, their fear was expressed as one of spontaneous social revolt engendered by destitution and the failure of existing institutions and controls to socialise the casual poor. The *Fortnightly Review* struck a note typical of this genre when it cautioned its readers in 1883 that 'the warning of Danton must be heeded. If you suffer the poor to grow up as animals, they may chance to become wild beasts and rend you.'[89] A contributor to the *Contemporary Review* expressed similar sentiments in 1885 when he predicted that:

> The time is approaching when this seething mass of human misery will shake the social fabric, unless we grapple more earnestly with it than we have yet done ... The proletariat may strangle us unless we teach it the same virtues which have elevated the other classes of society.[90]

However, a second and more general crisis perception was that the casual poor would become increasingly receptive to revolutionary ideologies and provide the 'naked proletariat' with which class warfare might be waged. This strand of concern was perhaps most colourfully articulated by Samuel Smith, the philanthropist, in the *Nineteenth Century*. 'Our country', he declared:

> is still comparatively free from Communism and Nihilism and similar destructive movements, but who can tell how long this will continue? We have a festering mass of human wretchedness in all our great towns, which is the natural hotbed of such anarchical movements; all the great continental countries are full of this explosive material. Can we depend upon our country keeping free from the infection, when we have far more poverty in our midst than the neighbouring European nations ...
> The time has come when the neglect of these social questions will exact a terrible vengeance on the wealthier classes ... If we do not drain away the foul sewage that stagnates at the base of our social fabric, we inevitably prepare terrible disasters for our descendants. In these days of popular rights and unlimited license of speech and pen, it is never safe to count upon immunity because the 'dumb, driven cattle' have not made a mighty noise. It is far better to anticipate the thunderbolt by drawing off the electric fluid. It is foolish to wait until the volcano is in motion before we legislate.[91]

The Labour Problem

A third area of concern was that, as with unemployment, the existence of endemic and chronic low-income destitution would increase the credibility of Socialist and 'confiscatory' ideologies amongst the respectable working classes and alienate the labour force from the social relationships of production. There was widespread uncertainty as to the mood of the respectable working classes when faced by the prospect of immiseration. Poverty was viewed by the establishment press as a contentious issue which might generate divisive and class-orientated debate over the equity of the existing social structure and distribution of National Income, and over the opportunity cost to Labour of social consensus.[92] As the *Spectator* lamented in 1885, poverty was 'breeding conflict and social turbulence'. 'Socialism', it concluded, 'was really partisanship for the poor'.[93]

In particular, concern at the popularity of Henry George's *Progress and Poverty* ran like a *leit motiv* through the social journalism of the 1880s. For example, in the *Fortnightly Review,* Joseph Chamberlain argued that the acceptance which Henry George's proposals had found amongst the working class was 'full of significance and warning':

> The needs of the poor are gradually finding expression ... If something be not done quickly to meet the growing necessities of the case we may live to see theories as wild and methods as unjust as those suggested by the American economist adopted as the creed of no inconsiderable portion of the electorate.[94]

In similar vein, *The Times* labour correspondent complained in 1889 of the condition of the poor being exploited by the disciples of George and by the S.D.F. as 'a pretext for pushing confiscatory theories and indulging a class antipathy'.[95] His repeated protestations that no real poverty crisis existed served merely to reflect the degree of anxiety expressed elsewhere in the press.

The existence of a ghetto of destitute, under-employed, casual labour within Britain's inner-city areas after 1880 was also perceived as a threat to existing mechanisms of social control based on traditional patterns of deference and paternalism.[96] Poverty was increasingly viewed as an aggregative problem of 'urban degeneration' - a process whereby structural features of the social and economic environment of the urban poor produced a self-sustaining pool of degenerate labour whose existence demoralised the respectable working classes and distorted the labour market. In confronting 'urban degeneration', traditional controls (which centred on the individualistic efforts of organised philanthropy to moralise the casual poor and on a narrow concern to protect the ratepayer from the expense of pauperism and to secure a labour market unhampered by competition from charity) appeared increasingly inadequate, and there was growing apprehension that this inadequacy would precipitate a confrontation between poverty groups and the local State.[97]

Economic Retardation

Far from sustaining a view of economic crisis, economic historians have in recent years adopted an increasingly optimistic view of the performance of the late-Victorian British economy.[98] They stress its continued commercial and industrial vigour and, in particular, its pivotal role in international trade and investment. Revisionists view the failure of the economy after 1870 to sustain earlier rates of growth of output as the predictable growth profile of a maturing economy in the process of diversification and consider the notion of drastic retardation as illusory. Furthermore, they conclude that other industrial economies such as Germany and the U.S.A. experienced similar downturns in their growth performance during the period and that conventional texts have exaggerated the shortfall between Britain's economic performance and that of its major competitors. Although some authorities have argued for an inelasticity in factor inputs (specifically capital) operating to constrain the late-Victorian economy,[99] this has not seriously modified the optimistic stance of revisionists, especially as their calculations appear to indicate only a marginal lag in the rate of growth of Britain's total factor productivity relative to the rates prevailing in Germany and America.[100] Likewise, econometric analysis of contemporary technological and investment strategies has served to discredit the traditional view of a crisis in the calibre of British enterprise and entrepreneurship.[101]

Nor does recent research identify any areas of crisis within the various strands of late-Victorian demand. While the level of domestic investment as a proportion of Gross Domestic Product was lower in Britain than in several other industrialised economies, the disparity, it is argued, was primarily focussed on building rather than manufacturing investment.[102] With hindsight, deficiencies in the cost, commodity and market structures of British exports are readily apparent but writers such as McCloskey would deny that, judged by realistic historical criteria, their performance 'failed' or constituted a significant brake on British economic growth, while Britain's greater propensity to import has been interpreted as a rational response to shifts in the availability of international resources and in Britain's comparative advantage. More generally, the level and pattern of British domestic consumption is not regarded as 'deviant' nor as a key retardative factor in her economic performance after 1870.[103]

More specifically, recent interpretations of British economic growth in the late-nineteenth century have not attributed its deceleration to any significant extent to either quantitative or qualitative aspects of the labour market. Although McCloskey has contended that an inelastic supply of labour constrained economic growth after 1870, the consensus of academic opinion is that the evidence of emigration, unemployment and under-employment, and recent estimates of labour inputs for the period render such a thesis untenable.[104] Furthermore, the cliometricians have also resisted the contention that deficiencies in the quality of Britain's labour force, stemming primarily from the educational system, inhibited its growth performance. Some authorities argue that the reluctance of industrial management and of government fully to recognise the utility of applied science, and to finance its diffusion, was a rational policy from a short and even medium-term economic standpoint and did not adversely affect the level of labour productivity.[105] More generally, Floud considers that, although Britain clearly lagged behind in providing higher education in science and technology, there is substantial evidence of improvements both in the simple literacy and in the technical training of the labour force after 1870 and that, as an early-starter, Britain did

not require such a dramatic shift in educational
investment as its competitors in order to maintain
the quality of its human capital. Indeed,
Matthews *et al* would contend that improvements in
the quality of labour inputs during the period had
a significant impact on the rate of growth of
total factor inputs.[106]
  The cliometric school has adopted a similarly
phlegmatic attitude to the downturn in labour
productivity after 1870 despite the fact that, as
Crouzet has noted, there is a 'clear fall in the
growth rate of this variable; a fall which
continued uninterrupted, bordering on a collapse
and ended in a negative rate at the beginning of
the twentieth century'.[107] Thus, Floud seeks to
devalue the significance of this downturn, arguing
that the variance between the estimated rates of
labour productivity in Britain and her major
competitors was relatively narrow given the large
margin of error to which such estimates are
subject, and that the drastic fall in labour
productivity after 1900 was not a peculiar British
failure but a phenomenon shared by the German and
American economies.[108]
  Yet, however optimistic the findings of
modern economic historians may prove to be, the
fact remains that a significant spectrum of
contemporary middle and upper-class opinion
perceived the late-Victorian economy as under-
going a crisis and identified it with the 'Labour
Problem', particularly with the deterioration in
industrial relations. There was a general fear
that labour unrest would compromise the efficiency
of the economy in an increasingly competitive
world market. This fear incorporated a range of
crisis perceptions of which several major strands
may usefully be identified.
  Firstly, it was feared that in disrupting the
continuity of production, industrial conflict
would dissipate Britain's economic potential and
industrial enterprise and furnish the opportunity
for her rivals to invade both her overseas and
domestic markets. *The Times* editorial of 21
December 1889 was a typical expression of this
anxiety:

> Strikes and lockouts are essentially a
> barbarous and most costly method of
> squandering those economical resources which
> are the life-blood of an industrial
> community. They expend in what may be called

internal friction energy which ought to be
employed in doing useful work, especially in
combating external competition... There is
not much margin for the unproductive
expenditure of energy in the form of strikes,
lockouts and other modes of conflict. If we
are to hold our own, we must close up our
ranks and gird ourself for the industrial
conflict with our neighbours. If we fall to
fighting among ourselves, our rivals will
gradually secure the markets in which we have
hitherto been supreme.[109]

The *Economist* voiced a similar concern throughout
the 1880s and early 1890s. In its view,
industrial stoppages were 'a luxury' which the
'British economy could ill-afford':

We have rivals to contend with who, if they
do not possess superior energy, have
nevertheless the most modern English
machinery and the advantage of location and
high tariffs with which to fight us. A
prolonged fight between masters and men, even
though it may have good reasons to back it,
gives a handle to all these competitors, and
often enables them to obtain a footing they
might otherwise not have obtained on markets
that we are wont to regard as our own
exclusively.[110]

Secondly, it was widely and persistently
argued that, by artificially inflating the level
of wage earnings, trade unionism was crippling the
cost effectiveness of British industry; that its
refusal to treat labour as a commodity whose price
should fluctuate freely in accordance with the
level of economic activity, final product prices,
and the competitive needs of industry, had eroded
the viability of manufacturing enterprise and its
ability to compete in world markets. As a
contributor to the *Nineteenth Century* in 1883
warned, excessive wage costs of production were
'insinuating, eating like a canker at the vitals
of our industries' and operatives were in danger
of finding 'that they had sucked out the yoke and
left nothing but the shell'.[111] Particular
concern was expressed at the 'reverberatory
effects' of wage disputes in the primary sector
(especially in the volatile coalmining industry)
upon the production costs and market performance

of the capital goods sector of the economy.[112]
Although the Majority Report of the Royal
Commission on the Depression of Trade and Industry
exonerated trade unionism from blame, many
witnesses before the Commission firmly located the
cause both of protracted recession and the loss of
commercial hegemony to Germany and America in the
militancy and restrictive practices of British
organised labour.[113] Indeed, the Minority Report
was unequivocal in its view:

> That the general maintenance of the rate of
> wages, accompanied by the necessity of a
> diminished and irregular production from a
> given fixed investment, has operated to
> increase the cost of manufacture, and so to
> weaken our manufacturers in the race of
> international competition.[114]

The impact of labour unrest and of trade
union restrictive practices upon the level of
productivity and the rate of technical innovation
in British industry was yet a further cause for
concern amongst the late-Victorian political and
industrial elite. It was widely argued that trade
union interference with the mode and rate of
production, and specifically with the recruitment,
remuneration and deployment of labour, would
progressively lower the cost competitiveness of
British industry and the motivation and work ethic
of its workforce.[115] Unfavourable comparisons
were repeatedly made by economic commentators
between the 'inflexible and combatative' attitude
of British workers towards business efficiency and
the 'resilience and cost consciousness' of German
and American labour.[116] As a result, as the Royal
Commission· on the Depression of Trade and Industry
cautioned in 1886, foreign manufacturers could
'enjoy greater economies of production in being
able to work plant and machinery more intensively'
while British enterprise suffered from 'diminished
output on a given basis of fixed expenses'.[117]
The resistance of skilled labour in Britain
to the adoption of new standardised techniques of
mass production was viewed as an equally serious
threat to national efficiency. *The Times* lamented
in 1886 that: 'It is no use to mince words. The
unions are engaged in a gigantic conspiracy to
hinder and retard the development of labour-saving
appliances in this country.[118] The *Economist*
concurred that the rise of a more militant trade

unionism had markedly increased the opportunity cost to employers of innovation. As it observed in 1889, 'a stoppage is worth risking only where gains from the new technique are certain to be considerable, and in the interests of good labour relations, changes which would otherwise have been advantageous, are not made'.[119] According to the *Quarterly Review*, the inability of British manufacturers to reduce piece rates to the extent warranted by the increased productivity due to labour-saving machinery rendered the adoption of such machinery less attractive, as did their inability to manipulate rates as a means of capital-saving by speeding up the production process.[120] More generally, it was feared that the intrusion of the 'Labour Problem' into the operation of private enterprise and the free market would seriously impair the quality of British entrepreneurship by constraining the ability of industrialists to innovate in accordance with shifts in technology and in the market for final products.

An associated anxiety voiced by many economic commentators of the period related to the possible effects of reduced profit margins and entrepreneurial scope upon managerial incentives. Reflecting on the relationship of wage disputes to commercial depression in 1883, *The Times* observed that:

> We do not pretend to affirm that there is nowhere a margin of profit which might be more equally distributed, but simply that the tendency of the time is to swallow up all such partial reserves and to bring the trade of the country to a point at which it offers a bare return to those engaged in it.[121]

In its evaluation of Britain's economic relapse, the Minority Report of the Royal Commission on the Depression of Trade and Industry developed a similar argument:

> It is however right to point out that the share of the total rewards of production which now falls to labour is larger, and the share which falls to capital much less than in times past; and this is obviously a process which cannot be continued beyond a certain point, now very nearly, if not quite attained. A time may come when capital,

ability and enterprise will no longer find in this country sufficient inducement to go on extending the work of production, and if the employer is driven out of the field, the labourer will necessarily suffer with him.[122]

Likewise, the *Fortnightly Review*, in reviewing contemporary diagnoses of the industrial situation, concluded in 1889 that 'the most worrying feature of the 'Labour Problem' [was] the apparent diminution in the reward of capital and management'.[123] Other journals focussed their concern not only upon the erosion by wage demands of the profits fund but also the inability of British entrepreneurs confronted by inflexible factor costs to adapt to shifts in the market environment. Thus *The Economist* warned in 1893 that:

> The men may argue that wages should be a fixed charge, like a royalty rent or a wayleave payment, but employers must have some element of cost, more or less elastic in character, which they can adjust to the fluctuations of the market, and wages is the only item that they can so control in any effectual degree, besides being the principal one. In the absence of such flexibility the ability of British industrialists to sustain a vigorous market strategy in the future will be severely handicapped.[124]

The likely impact of such constraints upon business confidence and the level of investment constituted a further major strand of concern. The fear that the 'Labour Problem' was choking off domestic manufacturing investment and driving capital abroad was expressed in a wide range of press articles and other contemporary literature. Thus, the *Fortnightly Review* considered that the breakdown in industrial relations and the attendant spread of Socialist rhetoric had 'spread a general feeling of distrust and insecurity among the wealthier classes, and by contributing to arrest the investment of capital at home and driving it abroad for employment had visibly retarded the return of prosperity'.[125] 'Depression', it affirmed in a subsequent article, 'is in a great measure attributable to the unreasonable demands of the working classes causing capitalists to hold aloof from investments

The Labour Problem

in industrial undertakings';[126] while the
Quarterly Review lamented that:

> At present capital is grievously diverted
> from our own working class because of their
> unfaithfulness and folly. Why should three
> hundred millions be sent out to Australia, as
> much more to South America and twice as much
> elsewhere, if quiet men of capital could use
> their funds in payment of trust-worthy
> workmen here at home.[127]

The Times agreed that the rise of labour unrest
meant that 'the field for the employment of
capital in this country' was becoming 'seriously
restricted'.[128] Meanwhile the *Nineteenth Century*
considered that strikes had:

> Struck such a severe blow at the foundations
> of British industry that we may well feel
> alarmed for the stability of the
> superstructure. Capital, if increasingly
> exposed to such risks, will feel so insecure
> that it will be repelled from industries that
> are attended by constant but unmeasurable
> losses at home and migrate abroad where
> greater safety is assured, even if the
> chances of high profits are less apparent.[129]

Many official and unofficial inquiries
relating to the economy and the labour market
shared such apprehensions. For example, much of
the evidence to the Royal Commission on the
Depression of Trade and Industry posited a
relationship between the incidence of industrial
unrest and the downturn in domestic capital
formation, and this was duly reflected in its
Minority Report.[130] Likewise, the Royal
Commission on Labour subsequently reported in 1894
that 'by ill-timed and excessive demands, as well
as by placing employers under apprehension of
those, strikes discouraged enterprise and further
investment of capital in this country'.[131]
Finally, from the viewpoint of the late-
Victorian governing classes, the ideology of New
Unionism posed a fundamental threat to a whole
range of assumptions and priorities which had
underpinned the political economy of mid-Victorian
government. It threatened by means of industial
militancy and collectivist legislation to fracture
the relationship between wages and prices, to

substitute social for market criteria in the determination of factor costs, and to subordinate savings and the profits fund to the subsistence needs of labour and the dictates of working-class consumption.[132] According to *The Times* the 'visionary schemes and iconoclastic theories' of the 'new militancy' proposed to restructure relationships both at the point of production and at an aggregate level of industrial organisation, and to confiscate as 'surplus value' the return due to capital and entrepreneurship.[133] They also threatened to subsume traditional economic incentives based upon profit, efficiency and risk within 'novel' societal objectives while creating a wedge of State regulations with which to undermine the autonomy of factor and commodity markets. In short, as *The Economist* warned in 1886:

> The community [was] called upon to defend itself in a battle of ideas between good and bad political economy and the survival of British industry within an increasingly hostile international market environment [was] at stake. A host of destructive fallacies which [sought] to degrade sound economic principles [had to] be resisted, and in confronting the Labour Question public opinion and policy-makers [had to] discriminate between a legitimate concern for social reform and the pernicious and rabid vapouring of Socialist economics.[134]

NOTES

1. D.F. Schloss, 'The Labour Problem', *Fortnightly Review*, 46 (1889), p. 437.

2. *The Times*, 24 April 1880.

3. Ibid., 24 Feb. 1891.

4. D. Sommer, *Haldane of Cloan, His Life and Times 1856-1928* (1960), p. 88.

5. Sir Henry Lucy, *A Diary of the Salisbury Parliament: 1886-1892* (1892), p. 355.

6. Compiled from *The Times*, *The Economist*, *Contemporary Review*, *Edinburgh Review*, *Fortnightly Review*, *Nineteenth Century*, *Quarterly Review*, *Spectator*.

7. K. Burgess, *The Challenge of Labour* (1980), pp. 13-15; R.A. Church, *The Great Victorian Boom 1850-73* (1975), pp. 71-3; S.G. Checkland, *The Rise of Industrial Society in England 1815-85* (1964), p. 232; K. Burgess, *The Origins of British Industrial Relations* (1975), p. 25.

8. W.R. Garside and H.F. Gospel, 'Employers and Managers: Their Organizational Structure and Changing Industrial Strategies' in C.J. Wrigley (ed.), *A History of British Industrial Relations 1875-1914* (1982), pp. 106-7.

9. Burgess, *Challenge of Labour*, pp. 44, 48; E.J. Hobsbawm, *Labouring Men* (1971), pp. 350-6; J.H. Porter, 'Wage Bargaining under Conciliation Agreements, 1860-1914', *Economic History Review*, XXIII (1970), pp. 465-6.

10. J.E. Cronin, 'Strikes 1870-1914' in Wrigley, *British Industrial Relations*, pp. 81-2.

11. See, e.g., S. Meacham, '"The Sense of an Impending Clash": English Working-Class Unrest before the First World War', *American Historical Review*, 77 (1972), pp. 1343-64.

12. Burgess, *Origins*, pp. 60-4; Wrigley (ed.) *British Industrial Relations*, pp. 64, 83-4.

13. Meacham, 'Working-Class Unrest', pp. 1357-8; J. Lovell, *British Trade Unions 1875-1933* (1977), p. 28; G. Crossick, *An Artisan Elite in Victorian Society* (1978), p. 248. However, for a contrary interpretation, see C. More, *Skill and the English Working Class, 1870-1914* (1980), Ch.9.

14. J.E. Cronin, *Industrial Conflict in Modern Britain* (1979), p. 93.

15. Van Gore, 'Rank-and-File Dissent' in Wrigley, *British Industrial Relations*, pp. 64-5; R. Price, *Masters, Unions and Men* (Cambridge, 1980), pp. 241-6.

16. Hobsbawm, *Labouring Men*, pp. 326-7; Burgess, *Challenge of Labour*, pp. 52-4.

17. E.H. Hunt, *British Labour History 1815-1914* (1981), pp. 305-6.

18. H.V. Emy, *Liberals, Radicals and Social Politics 1892-1914* (Cambridge, 1973), p. 29.

19. Ibid., pp. 18-30.

20. Ibid., p. 23; Porter, 'Wage Bargaining', pp. 470-1;

The Labour Problem

Lovell, *British Trade Unions*, p. 13; Burgess, *Challenge of Labour*, pp. 19-20.

21. Emy, *Social Politics*, pp. 23-4.

22. Ibid., p. 36.

23. T.G. Spyers, *The Labour Question: A Digest of the Evidence to the Royal Commission on Labour* (1894), p.52.

24. See especially, Emy, *Social Politics*, pp.20-2.

25. H. Lynd, *England in the Eighteen-Eighties*, (Oxford, 1945), p. 292; A.E.P. Duffy, 'New Unionism in Britain 1889-90: A Re-appraisal', *Economic History Review*, XIV (1961-2), pp. 306-19.

26. R. Gray, *The Aristocracy of Labour in Nineteenth-Century Britain, c.1850-1914* (1981), Ch. 6.

27. Burgess, *Challenge of Labour*, p.19.

28. P. Joyce, *Work, Society and Politics: The Culture of the Factory in later Victorian England* (Brighton, 1980), Ch. 3; Gray, *The Aristocracy of Labour*, pp. 35-44.

29. J. Saville, 'The Ideology of Labourism' in R. Benewick, R.N. Berki and B. Parekh (eds.), *Knowledge and Belief in Politics: The Problem of Ideology* (1973), pp. 215, 222-4.

30. Ibid., p. 215; Burgess, *Challenge of Labour*, p. 38.

31. Lovell, *British Trade Unions*, pp. 20-4.

32. Duffy, 'New Unionism', pp. 315-19; Emy, *Social Politics*, pp. 23-4.

33. H.A. Clegg, A. Fox and A.F. Thompson, *A History of British Trade Unions since 1889, vol. 1. 1889-1910*, (Oxford, 1964), pp. 87-96.

34. G. Anderson, 'Some Aspects of the Labour Market in Britain' in Wrigley, *British Industrial Relations*, p. 14.

35. Cronin, *Industrial Conflict*, p. 96.

36. Cronin in Wrigley, *British Industrial Relations*, pp. 83-5.

37. H. Pelling, *A History of British Trade Unionism* (1963), Ch. 6.

38. Lovell, *British Trade Unions*, pp. 27-8.

39. W.W. Rostow, 'Cycles in the British Economy: 1790-1914' in D.H. Aldcroft and P. Fearon (eds.), *British Economic Fluctuations 1790-1939* (1972), p. 88; S.B. Saul, *The Myth of the Great Depression 1873-1896* (1969), p. 30.

40. W.W. Rostow, 'Cycles in the British Economy', p. 89.

41. Saul, *Great Depression*, p. 31.

42. W.A. Lewis, *Growth and Fluctuations 1870-1913* (1978), p. 53.

43. Burgess, *Challenge of Labour*, pp. 48-9; Lynd, *England in the Eighteen-Eighties*, pp. 55-7.

44. G. Stedman Jones, *Outcast London*, (Oxford, 1971), p. 281; Lynd, *England in the Eighteen-Eighties*, p. 56; Burgess, *Challenge of Labour*, p. 49.

45. The following analysis is based upon Lewis, *Growth and Fluctuations*, pp. 50-1.

71

46. Lewis, *Growth and Fluctuations*, p. 55 cites the following United Kingdom growth rates (%) of manufactured exports:

1853-72	3.7	1882-89	1.9
1872-82	2.2	1889-99	0.4

47. J. Harris, *Unemployment and Politics: A Study in English Social Policy 1886-1914* (Oxford, 1972), pp. 51-2.

48. Ibid., p. 53.

49. See, e.g., J.H. Treble, 'Unemployment and Unemployment Policies in Glasgow 1890-1905' in P. Thane (ed.), *The Origins of British Social Policy* (1978), pp. 147-72.

50. Stedman Jones, *Outcast London*, Ch. 16; J.H. Treble, *Urban Poverty in Britain 1830-1914* (1979), Ch. 2.

51. Treble, *Urban Poverty*, p. 54.

52. Unless otherwise stated, the following analysis is based on Stedman Jones, *Outcast London*, Chs. 2, 5, 7; Treble, *Urban Poverty*, Ch. 2; G. Anderson in Wrigley, *British Industrial Relations*, pp. 1-19; A. Sutcliffe, 'In Search of the Urban Variable: Britain in the later Nineteenth Century' in D. Fraser and A. Sutcliffe (eds.), *The Pursuit of Urban History (1983)*, pp. 234-63.

53. Stedman Jones, *Outcast London*, p. 43.

54. M. Rose, *The Relief of Poverty 1834-1914* (1972), p. 17.

55. Hunt, *Labour History*, p.119; H. Perkin, *The Origins of Modern English Society 1780-1880* (1971), p. 423.

56. Rose, *Relief of Poverty*, p. 18.

57. Hunt, *Labour History*, pp. 118-19.

58. Treble, *Urban Poverty*, p. 16. Unless otherwise stated, the following analysis is based upon Treble, *Urban Poverty*, Ch. 1; Hunt, *Labour History*, Ch. 4; G. Anderson, 'Aspects of the Labour Market'; Stedman Jones, *Outcast London*, Ch. 4.

59. J.A. Schmiechen, 'State Reform and the Local Economy: An Aspect of Industrialisation in Late Victorian and Edwardian London', *Economic History Review*, 28 (1975), pp. 413-28.

60. I. Tallman and R. McGree, 'Definition of a Social Problem' in E.O. Smigel (ed.), *Handbook on the Study of Social Problems* (Chicago, 1971), p. 41.

61. See, e.g., Ibid., Ch. 2; M. Spector and J.I. Kitsuse, 'Social Problems: A Re-Formulation' in K. Henry (ed.), *Social Problems: Institutional and Interpersonal Perspectives* (Glenview, 1978), Part 1, Ch. 1; P. Halmos, 'The Concept of Social Problem' in Open University, *Introduction to Welfare: Iron Fist and Velvet Glove*, (Milton Keynes, 1978), Unit 1; E.M. Lemert, *Human Deviance, Social Problems and Social Control* (New Jersey, 1972), pp. 3-25.

62. G.P. Bevan, 'The Strikes of the Past Ten Years', *Journal of the Royal Statistical Society*,93 (1880),pp. 35-54.

63. *The Times*, 13 Sept. 1881.
64. *The Times*, 16 Sept. 1882.
65. J. Morley, 'Home and Foreign Affairs', *Fortnightly Review*, 31 (1882), p. 675.
66. *The Times*, 15 Sept. 1883.
67. Ibid., 6 Jan. 1890; 2 Sept. 1890.
68. 'The Conflict between Capital and Labour', *Quarterly Review*, 173 (1891), p. 253.
69. Cited in A. Briggs and J. Saville (eds.) *Essays in Labour History* (1960), pp. 321-2.
70. Ibid., pp. 320-1, 340; *The Times*, 11 Sept. 1893.
71. C. Wrigley, 'The Government and Industrial Relations' in Wrigley, *British Industrial Relations*, pp. 136-7.
72. See especially, J. Saville, 'Trade Unions and Free Labour: The Background to the Taff Vale Decision' in Briggs and Saville, *Labour History*, Ch. 9.
73. *The Times*, 7 April 1882.
74. Ibid., 2 Feb. 1888.
75. See, e.g., Ibid., 15 Oct. 1887; 'Law and License', *Fortnightly Review*, 39 (1886), p. 298.
76. Ibid., 17 Feb. 1886.
77. B. Burleigh, 'The Unemployed', *Contemporary Review*, 52 (1887), pp. 770-80.
78. *The Times*, 19 Oct. 1887.
79. S.A. Barnett, 'A Scheme for the Unemployed', *Nineteenth Century*, 24 (1888), p. 754.
80. Stedman Jones, *Outcast London*, pp. 284-5.
81. Ibid., p. 285, Ch. 16 *passim*.
82. E.P. Hennock, 'Poverty and Social Theory in England: The experience of the eighteen-eighties', *Social History*, 1 (1976), p. 78; R. Vorspan, 'Vagrancy and the New Poor Law in late-Victorian and Edwardian England', *English Historical Review*, XCII (1977), pp. 80-1.
83. *Spectator*, 6 & 13 Nov. 1886.
84. *The Times*, 17 Feb. 1886.
85. Ibid.
86. Stedman Jones, *Outcast London*, pp. 312-13.
87. Ibid., p. 290.
88. Hennock, 'Poverty and Social Theory', p. 68.
89. 'The Radical Programme', *Fortnightly Review*, 34 (1883), p. 596.
90. Cited in Stedman Jones, *Outcast London*, p. 291.
91. S. Smith, 'Social Reform', *Nineteenth Century*, 13 (1883), pp. 897, 911-12.
92. See, e.g., 'Socialism in England', *Quarterly Review*, 156 (1883), p. 358; E. Hopkins, 'Social Wreckage', *Contemporary Review*, 44 (1883), p. 96; F.W. Bockett, 'The People and their Friends', *Fortnightly Review*, 39 (1886), pp. 307-9.
93. *Spectator*, 31 Jan. 1885.
94. J. Chamberlain, 'Labourers and Artisans Dwellings',

Fortnightly Review, CCIV (1883), pp. 761-2.

95. *The Times*, 4 April 1889.

96. See especially, Stedman Jones, *Outcast London*, Part 3.

97. Ibid.; B.B. Gilbert, *The Evolution of National Insurance in Great Britain* (1973), pp. 21-58.

98. For an overview of recent literature, see R. Floud and D.N. McCloskey (eds.), *The Economic History of Britain since 1700: Vol. 2, 1860 to the 1970s* (1981), Chs. 1-7; Francois Crouzet, *The Victorian Economy* (1982), Ch. 12.

99. See, e.g., D.N. McCloskey, 'Did Victorian Britain fail?', *Economic History Review*, 23 (1970), pp. 446-59.

100. Floud and McCloskey, *Economic History of Britain*, p. 22.

101. L. Sandberg and D.N. McCloskey, 'From damnation to redemption: judgements on the late-Victorian entrepreneur', *Explorations in Economic History*, 9 (1971), pp. 89-108.

102. Floud and McCloskey, *Economic History of Britain*, p. 16.

103. D.N. McCloskey, 'Britain's loss from foreign industrialization: a provisional estimate', *Explorations in Economic History*, 8 (1970-1), pp. 141-52; Floud and McCloskey, *Economic History of Britain*, pp. 18-19.

104. McCloskey, 'Did Victorian Britain Fail?', p. 455; D.H. Aldcroft, 'McCloskey on Victorian Growth: A Comment', *Economic History Review*, 27 (1974), pp. 272-3; Crouzet, *Victorian Economy*, p. 389.

105. See, e.g., P.L. Robertson, 'Technical education in the British shipbuilding and marine-engineering industries, 1863-1914', *Economic History Review*, 27 (1974), pp. 222-35.

106. Floud and McCloskey, *Economic History of Britain*, pp. 13, 106; R.C.O. Matthews, C.H. Feinstein and J.C. Odling-Smee, *British Economic Growth 1856-1973*, (Oxford, 1982), Ch. 4.

107. Crouzet, *Victorian Economy*, p. 387.

108. Floud and McCloskey, *Economic History of Britain*, p. 22.

109. *The Times*, 21 Dec. 1889.

110. *The Economist*, 1 April 1893.

111. A.W. Finlayson, 'Falling Trade and Factory Legislation', *Nineteenth Century*, 13 (1883), p. 977.

112. See, e.g., *The Times*, 17 Oct. 1888; *Fortnightly Review*, 53 (1893), pp. 302-3.

113. *R.C. on Depression of Trade and Industry, Final Report and Digest of Evidence*, PP 1886 (C.4893) XXIII, pp. xx-xxi; 109-27.

114. Ibid., p. xliii.

115. See, e.g., M. Pattison, 'Industrial Shortcomings: An Address', *Fortnightly Review*, 28 (1880), p. 739; 'English Trade and Foreign Competition', *Quarterly Review*, 152 (1881), pp. 278-81; *Spectator*, 27 March 1886, pp. 411-12.

116. See, e.g., *The Economist*, 24 April 1880; *Economist Monthly Trade Supplement*, 15 Aug. 1885.

117. PP 1886 (C.4893) XXIII, p. lix.

118. *The Times*, 14 Sept. 1886.

119. *The Economist*, 11 July 1889.

120. 'Some Lessons of Prosperity and Depression', *Quarterly Review*, 166 (1888), pp. 79-80.

121. *The Times*, 28 Dec. 1883.

122. PP 1886 (C.4893) XXIII, p. lx.

123. D.F. Schloss, 'The Labour Problem', *Fortnightly Review*, 46 (1889), p. 439.

124. *The Economist*, 25 Nov. 1893.

125. *Fortnightly Review*, 39 (1886), p. 588.

126. 'The Present Depression of Trade', *Fortnightly Review*, 53 (1893), pp. 303-4.

127. 'A Plea for Liberty', *Quarterly Review*, 172 (1891), p. 514.

128. *The Times*, 15 Jan. 1890.

129. I.S. Jeans, 'The Coal Crisis and the Paralysis of British Industry', *Nineteenth Century*, 34 (1893), p. 791.

130. PP 1886 (C.4893) XXIII, p. lx.

131. *R.C. on Labour, Fifth and Final Report*, PP 1894 (C.7421) XXXV, p. 33.

132. Lynd, *England in the Eighteen-Eighties*, pp. 77,93-4; Emy, *Social Politics*, p. 36.

133. *The Times*, 24 Sept. 1891.

134. *The Economist*, 11 Sept. 1886.

Part Two

THE   INPUTS

Chapter 3

THE ORIGINS OF THE LABOUR DEPARTMENT

THE CAMPAIGN FOR LABOUR STATISTICS

The most tangible response of late-Victorian
government to the 'Labour Problem' was the
refinement of the machinery of civil
intelligence, by the creation of a Labour
Statistical Bureau in 1886 and its subsequent
extension into a separate Labour Department in
1893. As an insight into the dynamics of
Victorian government growth, the origins of the
Labour Department present an interesting case
study. They had no clear relationship with any
one coherent body of thought or doctrine. Nor did
they conform to any pattern of self-generating
bureaucratic growth. The isolated efforts of
individualist reformers, the collectivism of
radical and socialist ideologies, the persistence
of national and international statistical pressure
groups, the incentives of foreign example and
competition, of domestic economic insecurity and
industrial unrest, the caprice of electoral
tactics and political ambition, and the nature of
administrative response, all combined to determine
the character of the new department. Yet,
underlying this fusion, a number of broadly
chronological phases of development can be
detected, the first of which was the growth of
demand for the establishment of a Bureau of Labour
Statistics.

Before 1886, the only official statistical
sources available for an objective appraisal of
the condition of Labour in Britain were deficient,
chaotic, and unmanageable.[1] They largely lay in
the evidence before Royal Commissions and Select
Committees, the annual reports of departmental
inspectorates, and the mass of publications issued

relating to trade. To disentangle significant
data that was both continuous and comparable was
virtually impossible. Social commentators and
policy-makers lacked any authoritative or
representative data on labour remuneration,
unionisation, industrial militancy, working-class
consumption and income patterns, unemployment, and
a range of related factors affecting the social
relationships and economic efficiency of British
industrial production.[2] Royal Commissions may
have been effective media for the exposé of
specific social evils but they were unsuited to
the demands of monitoring the overall welfare of
the working classes.

As the 'Labour Problem' moved to the
forefront of late-Victorian public debate, this
shortfall in official statistics became
increasingly intolerable. In particular, it
motivated two closely-related strands of political
and scientific opinion; firstly, a sizeable group
of middle-class trade union sympathisers and
traditional radicals who saw in the educative
effects of the provision of adequate labour
statistics the means both of working-class self-
improvement and of the restoration of mid-
Victorian industrial consensus without recourse to
counter-productive measures of State intervention;
and secondly, an influential London-based elite of
social investigators and official statisticians
concerned to measure the degree and cost of social
wastage, which was centred upon the Royal
Statistical Society and imbued with its
ameliorative philosophy of empirical research.[3]

The first recorded representations to the
government for the provision of labour statistics
were those of the Positivist, George Howell, in
1869 as a member of the T.U.C. Parliamentary
Committee.[4] His initial efforts brought no
response, the more so as the labour
representatives sitting in Parliament after 1874
proved apathetic to the issue.[5] Howell was
therefore compelled to renew the attack in a
forceful article in the *Beehive* in 1876:

> The vast and daily increasing importance of
> all movements connected with labour, and
> especially the legislative tendency of very
> many of these movements, point conclusively
> to the necessity of a Bureau of Statistics of
> Labour, where the statesman, philanthropist,
> author, journalist, or citizen, can at all

times obtain authentic information and
reliable statistics when attempting to deal
with some of the many problems connected
therewith.[6]

However, as economic depression intensified
and persisted into the 1880s accompanied by social
hardship and unrest, individual initiative was
soon swallowed up in broader institutional
offensives and the question of labour statistics
became subsumed within the broader campaign for
the general reform of official economic and social
statistics. Two vigorous memoranda from the Board
of Trade outlining the major defects in the labour
and commercial intelligence available to the
government led the Treasury to appoint an Official
Statistics Committee in 1879.[7] Although its
report fully endorsed the Board's critique, its
recommendations for structural reform were
tentative and confused.[8]

The Royal Statistical Society, backed by
officials of the Board of Trade with which it had
close traditional affiliations,[9] therefore
launched a new offensive in its Jubilee Year of
1885. The President, Sir Rawson Rawson, set the
tone in his opening address to the Jubilee
Conference when he suggested that the occasion
should be used to press the government to initiate
a thoroughgoing reappraisal of its social and
industrial statistics in line with measures
previously adopted in America and a range of
European countries.[10] The Royal Statistical
Society further reinforced the international
significance of their campaign when, again at the
Jubilee Session, the International Statistical
Institute was inaugurated 'to call attention of
governments to matters capable of solution by
statistical observation'.[11] With the Royal
Commission on the Depression of Trade and Industry
groping vainly through its task in the background,
J.S. Jeans, the industrial journalist, summed up
the mood of the time when he remarked that:

It has now come to this; that a high degree
of civilization and a high and adequate
standard of efficiency in regard to the
collection of statistical data respecting
matters of public concern, may almost be
regarded as convertible terms.[12]

Meanwhile, earlier in the year, the Royal

Statistical Society had organised the Industrial Remuneration Conference, designed to identify the causes of the breakdown in industrial relations and the merits and demerits of possible remedies. The Conference was to prove a major landmark in the development of the Labour Department. Four of its leading participants were later to preside over the Department's inception at the Board of Trade.[13] More immediately, its proceedings, riddled with ineffectual debate, were a telling picture of the sheer lack of a statistical basis for objective discussion.[14] They also highlighted the importance attached in contemporary debate to accurate industrial statistics as a precondition of any effective system of collective bargaining. As Sir Thomas Brassey observed in the opening speech: 'Statistics with reference to the state of trade and the remuneration and supply of labour are indispensable to form sound judgements as to the relative claims of capital and labour', and this was a theme reiterated throughout the proceedings.[15] When therefore, on 2 March 1886, following the Liberal electoral victory, Charles Bradlaugh proposed to the House of Commons that immediate steps should be taken 'to ensure in this country the full and accurate collection of labour statistics', the Industrial Remuneration Conference had done much to prepare a receptive audience. In the subsequent debate, his resolution was adopted on behalf of the Board of Trade and what had been a struggle for official recognition became one for administrative viability.

It should be explained why the responsibility for a labour bureau was given to the Board of Trade as opposed to other departments possessing extensive administrative commitments to Labour. As a result of its mid-Victorian transformation from merely an advisory committee on trade policy into a board of industry, the Board of Trade had acquired several labour functions.[16] Under the Merchant Shipping Acts, the Mercantile Marine Department was charged with the regulation of the employment, pay, food, accommodation, and safety of seamen.[17] Meanwhile, a concern for public safety had increasingly involved the Railway Department in matters affecting the hours and working conditions of railwaymen.[18] In addition, under the Cheap Trains Act, it was empowered to ensure the adequate provision of cheap trains for the working classes. Finally, the Board of Trade undertook a number of miscellaneous duties relating, either directly or indirectly, to Labour. These included the protection of emigrant workers from exploitation by the implementation of the Passenger Acts, the supervision of works' rules entailed under the Employers' Liability Act, and the enforcement of anti-truck regulations in the hosiery trade and of legislation designed to facilitate the recovery of wages in bankruptcy proceedings.[19]

Nevertheless, on the grounds of its share of labour administration alone, the Board of Trade had a relatively weak claim to a labour bureau in 1886. The Railway and Marine Departments dealt with Labour only as an incidental part of their general duties and the Board had no direct concern with conditions of employment, trade unionism, industrial remuneration, or allied questions affecting the working classes as a whole.[20] In contrast, the Local Government Board was heavily involved with the problems of pauperism and the destitute unemployed, with the protection of health in factories and workshops and with matters relating to the housing of the working classes.[21] Meanwhile, the Home Office was charged with the administration of a vast conglomeration of laws relating to the hours, wages, and conditions of employment, including the Factory and Workshop Acts, Truck Acts, and the Employers' Liability Act. It was also responsible for legislation involving not simply the material interests but the social and legal status of the working man, such as the Masters and Workmen Acts and Trade Union Acts. Finally, it was concerned with industrial relations and unemployment in so far as they were treated as problems of public order rather than social distress.[22] By 1886, the Home Office was therefore considered as being the most important department concerned with labour administration and it would not have been unreasonable to suppose that it would ultimately develop into the single and supreme labour authority.

However, it was not administrative functions that the early advocates of a labour bureau envisaged. They viewed its duties as primarily statistical, and it was in statistics that the Board of Trade was paramount. As early as 1832, a Statistical Department had been established at the Board under the supervision of G.R. Porter to provide the necessary data for effective government administration and reform in an indus-

trialising society.[23] Thereafter, as the adviser
on trade and industry, the Board had accumulated a
mass of information, much of which was published
in the form of statistical abstracts. By 1886, *de
facto*, it represented the Central Statistical
Department of the country.[24] Above all, despite
the fact that several departments such as the Home
Office and Local Government Board handled labour
statistics incidentally in the course of compiling
routine reports, in the compilation of 'public' as
opposed to 'working administrative statistics' the
Board of Trade possessed unique experience that
was vital to the implementation of Bradlaugh's
Motion. As Robert Giffen, the distinguished head
of the Commercial Department, observed in 1889,
the Board of Trade 'is conspicuous as a department
which publishes statistics for statistical
purposes alone, the statistics not being required
for daily administration'.[25]

An equally important factor in the allocation
of the Labour Bureau was the presence at the Board
of Trade of Giffen and A.J. Mundella.[26] Giffen was
the foremost government statistician of the day
and a leading advocate of the need for more
extensive and systematic industrial data.[27] He
also believed that the formal centralisation of
all statistical work at the Board of Trade was
essential for efficient and economical government
and had clearly indicated these views to
Bradlaugh.[28] Mundella's attitude towards the
projected Labour Bureau was even more decisive.
As President of the Board of Trade, he was anxious
to confirm his reputation as a leading protagonist
for Labour's interests in Parliament, and regarded
his main function within the Cabinet as forwarding
radical measures.[29] He had taken a keen interest
in the development of labour bureaux abroad and
had as early as 1870 advised Wendell Philipps, the
American social reformer, on the best use of the
Massachusetts Bureau.[30] At the same time, as a
member of the Royal Statistical Society, he had
been closely involved in the campaign for improved
British labour statistics.[31] As a leading
advocate of arbitration as a solution to
industrial conflict, he welcomed especially the
prospect of reliable and readily available
information to which both employers and employed
could appeal.[32] When Bradlaugh proposed the
formation of a Labour Bureau in March 1886,
Mundella had already entered into negotiations
with the Treasury over the expenditure involved

and under Giffen's supervision, labour statistics were duly attached to the duties of the Commercial Department of the Board of Trade.

THE LABOUR BUREAU

The programme of the new Labour Bureau was announced in a Parliamentary return on 22 September 1886.[33] Its objectives were: firstly, to chart the 'progress' of wage earnings since 1830 using existing wage statistics published in Blue Books and reputable unofficial sources; secondly, to provide regular and full returns on wages, including information on hours of work, the level of unemployment, and the proportion of workers at each wage rate; thirdly, to publish information of 'immediate practical use' on matters relating to the condition of the working classes, especially labour costs of production, and trends in working-class savings and the cost of living; finally, to provide comparable data on labour conditions abroad.

Those who had campaigned for a Bureau of Labour Statistics were, on the whole, well satisfied with these terms of reference. Bradlaugh would have wished for more information on capital, industrial profits, and working-class budgets, and on the health and living conditions of Labour, but he freely admitted that the Board of Trade had undertaken more than he had antici-pated at the outset.[34] However, the struggle for adequate labour statistics had only just begun, for the performance of the Labour Bureau over the next five years fell well below his expectations.

At first sight, the output of the Bureau between 1886 and 1891 appears impressive. It duly synthesised existing wage data, undertook a census of current wage rates, and issued reports and returns on hours of work, the short-time movement, profit-sharing, working-class expenditure, foreign immigration, and the relationship of wages to costs of production. In addition, 'under the pressure of opinion outside and in Parliament', the Bureau began to investigate labour questions from a more comprehensive standpoint and to issue reports of a largely non-statistical character. These included several influential investigations into 'sweating' and regular surveys of the trade union movement and industrial unrest. Finally, brief notices on various labour topics were inserted in the *Board of Trade Journal* including short periodical reports on the state of the labour market.

However, a closer appraisal by social commentators and statisticians of these publications revealed grave deficiencies, in their compilation, in their coverage, and in their timing.[35] A number of the Labour Bureau's reports, including that on the relationship of wages to production costs which was potentially of immense importance to contemporary economic discussion, were 'fragmentary and incomplete', relying *faux de mieux* upon a collation of pre-existing data. More seriously, where the Board of Trade did undertake original research into labour questions, the results were often meagre and unreliable. As no provision was made for investigation by agents on the spot, the Department had to rely for information mainly upon answers to circularised enquiry forms. An overwhelming proportion of these questionaires were either never returned or completed in such a way as to be valueless. Consequently, many reports, including those on wages, working-class expenditure and industrial disputes, were based upon extremely selective evidence. In some instances, the Bureau was forced to supplement its information from newspaper cuttings and trade union reports, which did little to strengthen the confidence of social statisticians in its findings. The monthly statement on the condition of the labour market was equally deficient. It ignored the mass of the unskilled labour force together with a large number of skilled workers who did not belong to a trade union. Nor did it reveal any information on the condition of the seasonal and casual labour markets. The provision of foreign labour statistics was similarly lacking in rigour.

Perhaps the most serious weakness of the reports issued by the Labour Bureau was the notorious delay in their publication. Some, such as the Census of Wages and the Reports on Trade Unions, took three years to produce, by which time they could scarcely be said to have retained any 'immediate practical value'. The original intention that the Labour Bureau would facilitate the settlement of industrial disputes by the provision of reliable, up-to-date statistics was therefore frustrated and the programme outlined to Parliament in September 1886 remained largely unfulfilled.

The Origins of the Labour Department

The inability of the Labour Bureau to effect its original objectives stemmed to a significant extent from the triumph of economy. The Permanent Secretary to the Treasury, Sir Reginald Welby, viewed the Bureau as a 'potentially extravagant departure for the Board' and one which would prove 'dangerously expansive' unless 'its tendency was checked'.[36] With the exception of John Burnett, the Labour Correspondent, no addition was made to the number of superior officers of the Board. Even with his appointment, the Treasury proved singularly obstructive, intimating that the duties involved could quite adequately have been performed by an assistant clerk and proposing that Burnett might 'be paid so much per day as required'.[37] The Treasury were anxious not only to regulate the growth of establishment but also to withhold special status for labour statistical work for fear of the proliferation of specialist posts outwith the normal channels of Civil Service recruitment. As Welby observed of Burnett's appointment:

> We are all agreed that the appointment is not really necessary at all, and therefore the more exceptional and temporary we can keep it, the better. It would be an abuse of the language to call such an appointment 'professional'.[38]

In 1891, the Treasury adopted a similar stance towards the recruitment of a labour statistician, insisting that the post be filled by a redundant Superintendent of Publications at the Patent Office.[39]
Robert Giffen was already involved in a long-standing battle with the Treasury over the funding of commercial intelligence and threatened to resign unless the Labour Bureau was properly staffed 'and made visibly what it ought to be'.[40] Reporting to Parliament on the Bureau's progress in December 1888, he ignored the normal rules of official propriety and made no attempt to disguise his opinion that the Treasury had crippled the Bureau's ability to fulfil its statutory remit.[41] Meanwhile, in their evidence to the Royal Commission on Civil Establishments, both Giffen and Thomas Farrer, the Permanent Secretary, singled out the Bureau as a prime example of where the abuse of Treasury control had destroyed 'any equation between economy and efficiency'.[42]

However, such representations won few concessions and by late 1892 there were still only four junior clerks under the direction of Burnett devoted exclusively to labour statistics, and even they were entirely unversed in the technicalities of working-class industrial and political organisation.[43] As a result, the burden of supervising investigations and of interpreting their findings continued to fall on officials having other important commitments within the Commercial Department; a situation exacerbated by the amount of time both Giffen and Burnett were forced to devote to giving evidence before official enquiries on a range of issues relating to the 'Labour Problem'.[44] Some comparative figures of government expenditure are instructive. Whereas only an estimated £1,935 was expended on the provision of labour statistics in Britain in 1891-2, the initial budget of the newly established French Labour Department amounted to £7,000. The outgoings of the American Bureau of Labour in the same year exceeded £35,000.[45]

Nevertheless, in all probability, Giffen could have resisted the Treasury had either his political chiefs or public opinion displayed any strong commitment to the Labour Bureau. Such a commitment was singularly lacking in Mundella's successors. There is no evidence that his immediate successor, Lord Stanley (1886-8), contributed anything to the discussion of either commercial or labour policy. He has been characterised as embodying 'the virtues of the squirarchy', as a representative man of Tory orthodoxy; 'home-loving and uxorious' with an absorbing interest in the management of the Derby Estates rather than in politics.[46] Hicks Beach was a President (1888-92) of much greater political stature and had had previous experience of social administration at the Poor Law Board and Home Office. However, his social and economic philosophy was constrained by an overriding concern for economy and for the need to prevent social expenditure or fiscal reform distorting the cost structure of British industry. He was hostile to all radical proposals for State intervention, perceiving social issues in relation to property and rural society rather than as problems generated by the urban labour market.[47]

The Board of Trade's Parliamentary Secretaries were similarly disinterested in labour affairs. Henry de Worms' interests lay chiefly in scientific and diplomatic history,[48] and although the Earl of Onslow was to pursue a fairly distinguished career in colonial administration, his main assets in 1888 were that he was 'a keen sportsman and a good whip' and 'in all respects a good representative of the country gentleman'.[49] His successor, Balfour of Burleigh, was a Tory 'of that firm unbending order which is perhaps only to be met with in Scotland'. He had little time for Mundella's Bureau and concentrated on the administration of strictly commercial affairs along with his abiding interests in local government and the Church of Scotland.[50]

It was not simply the personal prejudices of the Board's political chiefs that starved Giffen of allies in his fight for an efficient Labour Bureau. By the late 1880's, 'the themes of popular appeal and social reform' were increasingly 'at a discount' in Conservative counsels.[51] The Home Rule split had added many Whigs and commercial liberals to the Conservative Party upon whose support the government's majority depended, and who brought with them a deep distaste for the expansion of State intervention for the welfare of the working classes and hostility to organised labour.[52] Radicals reasoned in vain with Stanley and Hicks Beach that the Labour Bureau could be properly funded at 'the cost of one torpedo',[53] for the Conservatives regarded an appeal to national solidarity and imperialism as a more effective means of sustaining social cohesion and electoral support than social measures such as the provision of labour statistics.[54]

They were confirmed in this belief by the fact that the bulk of the Labour Movement appeared either apathetic or actively hostile to the Labour Bureau. The T.U.C. passed several bland resolutions in favour of the Bureau's establishment but its debates were markedly silent on the issue of labour statistics.[55] It is evident that, compared with other labour issues such as the legal status of trade unions, employers' liability, hours and conditions of work, or the provision of working-class magistrates and factory inspectors, labour statistics were of little consequence to the average working man. At best, they were regarded as tangential to the major objectives of the Labour Movement, such as the reform of trade union law and the reduction of unemployment, which, it was argued, required a separate Ministry of Labour devoted specifically

to the needs of the labouring classes. Some
labour aristocrats in the older unions welcomed
the provision of improved labour intelligence as
facilitating the peaceful settlement of
disputes,[56] but many leaders of the New Unionism
and much of the Labour Press were hostile to the
Labour Bureau, viewing its objectives with intense
suspicion. It was argued that while trade
unionists were starved of information on
production costs, industrial stocks and profit
margins, employers were provided by the Bureau
with data on comparative wage rates and trade
union finances, which merely served further to
strengthen their bargaining position. Official
labour statistics would, it was feared, actually
retard the ability of Labour to modify the
distribution of national income and the social
relationships of production.[57]

Such fears were not without justification.
Labour statistics *were* conceived by many of the
Bureau's advocates as a means of social control;
designed to scotch the new labour militancy and to
contain it within the conservative framework of
traditional collective bargaining. To Bradlaugh,
for example, its main function was to sustain
British individualism and the existing social
consensus against the bogeys of 'Russian Nihilism
and German Socialism' by revealing the identity of
interests between Capital and Labour.[58] He
anticipated that labour statistics would act as an
automatic solvent of industrial conflict by
helping 'union leaders to pacify workers in
depressions' and by giving 'the moral sanction of
public opinion to employers when the latter felt
bound to resist some unjustifiable wage claim'.
Labour statistics were not, therefore, generally
perceived as providing the raw material of State
collectivism. On the contrary, they were viewed
by many politicians and social scientists as the
'first condition of self-help'; the means by which
to maintain the stability of existing liberal
capitalist institutions by identifying and
correcting the major deficiencies of the labour
market with the minimum of legislative interference. Professor Foxwell, a leading economist,
best summed up the prevailing sentiment when he
observed that:

No part of the public expenditure is so truly
remunerative as that which is spent in
enquiry. It results in a greater economy of

> legislation as well as an increase in the
> efficiency of legislation. If the State,
> instead of trying in a clumsy way to remove
> abuses, would content itself with publishing
> the facts, public opinion would often deal
> with them far more effectively. This is a
> case where, by the thorough performance of
> one of its functions, the State would be
> relieved of a great deal of work in other
> directions.[59]

Such an attitude was clearly at odds with the
interventionist philosophy of the New Unionism and
held little appeal for a Labour Movement
increasingly committed to social collectivism.

Moreover, Labour leaders had little
confidence in a Labour Bureau that was
administered by the Board of Trade. They
considered that a department whose primary
function it was to represent the interests of
industry and commerce would prove ineffective in
fowarding the claims of Labour.[60] Besides, the
permanent officials of the Board of Trade were
renowned for their hostility to State intervention
and welfare legislation. Indeed, it was very
often in spite of their views that the Board had
acquired its labour functions.[61] Thomas Farrer,
who had as Permanent Secretary from 1866-86
dominated the Board and many of its political
chiefs, was a 'high priest' of classical Liberal
policy and proved a major obstacle to the reform
of seamen's wages and working conditions.[62] His
resignation in May 1886 was popularly ascribed to
his distaste for Mundella's radical views on
social reform in general and his establishment of
a Labour Bureau in particular.[63] Furthermore, it
was widely known in Labour circles that Robert
Giffen shared Farrer's social philosophy. Given
Giffen's advocacy of classical political economy
and his ill-disguised contempt for progressive
Liberalism and Socialism, it was considered
unlikely that the Labour Bureau would make any
constructive contribution to the betterment of the
economic status of Labour. His deployment of
official statistics in support of a series of
optimistic pronouncements on the 'progress of the
working classes' and on the need for wages to
fluctuate freely according to market forces, and
his consequent opposition to welfare legislation,
served to reinforce this view.[64] As Baumann, the
Lib-Lab M.P. for Camberwell, observed in 1889,

Labour regarded Giffen as 'a statistical machine'
with 'no knowledge of or sympathy with the
condition of the working men of this country'.[65]
    Thus, Giffen could not rely upon either the
commitment of his political chiefs or the force of
Labour opinion to counter Treasury control, and
between 1886 and 1892 the Labour Bureau fell an
easy victim to the forces of economy.

THE EMERGENCE OF THE LABOUR DEPARTMENT

Yet, a year later the Bureau had been transformed
into a separate Labour Department with a
substantial establishment of investigators and
statisticians. The transition was largely
prompted by the political manoeuvres surrounding
the General Election of 1892, for the efforts of
both parties to bid for working-class support
resulted in a number of proposals relating to the
reform of labour administration. In the case of
the Liberals, this was especially true as a
'popular front' of advanced radical groups
temporarily united to fill the vacuum in party
ideology left by the Home Rule split.[66]
    Although Labour had remained apathetic to the
issue of labour statistics, both Tory democrats
and Liberal radicals were well aware that the
general reform of labour administration was a
matter of some importance in Labour circles. A
leading article in the *Workman's Times* underlined
the prevailing discontent with the inadequacy and
confusion of existing machinery:

> The question of a separate Ministry of Labour
> will be taken up ... as one of the test
> questions of the election by the working
> electorate. Labour is inadequately
> represented in the administrative machine.
> The War Departments ignore it and in the
> opinion of the pacific departments, Labour is
> completely subservient to the interests of
> land, commerce, and finance. Consequently,
> it gets wedged in here, and pigeon-holed
> there, and inspected somewhere else. Its
> health is kept in one length of red tape, its
> statistics are kept, or supposed to be kept
> in another, whilst the Minister round the
> corner has a department in the cellar which
> will see that the Factory and Mining Laws are
> duly observed ... Labour candidate or no

Labour candidate, whoever stands will have to pledge himself to a Ministry of Labour if he wants the workman's vote.[67]

There was, however, little consensus of opinion as to what functions such a Ministry of Labour would perform beyond a vague belief that it 'would do more for the working man'. More moderate unionists looked to an extension of labour statistics as a means of promoting industrial conciliation and believed that the proper co-ordination of administrative functions relating to labour would ensure a more stringent application of existing labour legislation. The more militant and Socialist elements viewed its role instead as essentially innovative, involving the State provision of labour exchanges and employment, the regulation of sweating and alien immigration, and the systematic elevation of the social, economic, and legal status of the workforce.[68] The reorganisation of labour administration was therefore a sufficiently ambiguous proposal to have a broad electoral appeal.

Despite the fact that the Conservative Party was becoming more and more 'a union of propertied interests, embattled against organised labour' and Socialism,[69] several Tory Democrats led by Sir John Gorst, together with a number of Tory M.P.s representing urban constituencies, urged the establishment of a Ministry of Labour on the government as a means of maintaining a share of the working-class vote in the coming election. In early 1892, they introduced a Department of Labour Bill designed to co-ordinate under one minister all pre-existing statistical and administrative duties.[70] The Department was to provide comprehensive information on Capital as well as Labour, to constitute a National Arbitration Board, to control technical education, and to examine the viability of State-assisted old age pensions and of any other 'means of promoting Labour's material, intellectual, and moral prosperity'. However, the majority of the Conservative Cabinet were either apathetic or hostile to the Bill. The Home Secretary declined to consider it as a serious proposition,[71] while at the Board of Trade, Hicks Beach's views were firmly coloured by a hostile memorandum from Robert Giffen.[72]

Giffen's objections were fourfold. Firstly, he maintained that there was little evidence that the general body of workmen desired the establishment of a Ministry of Labour. Secondly, he suspected that many of those advocating such a Ministry contemplated collectivist functions such as the provision of employment-measures which Giffen refused to entertain. Thirdly, he did not consider that an 'equivalent advantage' would accrue to offset the administrative disruption involved in transferring all labour functions from the Home Office, Local Government Board, Board of Trade and Registry of Friendly Societies to a new ministry. In particular, he questioned whether it would in fact be practicable or indeed desirable to separate off all labour questions from commercial and industrial considerations to which they were often intimately related. Finally, he objected that 'it would raise again the old question as to a Central Statistical Department which *de facto* exist[ed] at the Board of Trade but which would be *pro tanto* impaired to the public inconvenience by the transference of labour statistics to another department'. Not surprisingly, the Bill failed to gain a Second Reading.

Meanwhile, the Liberals had not been idle over the issue. Led by James Dalziel, the young advanced radical M.P. for Kirkcaldy, they tried unsuccessfully in May to move a Commons' Resolution to call attention to the need for a 'Department of Labour, with a Minister responsible to Parliament', and similar proposals appeared in the election manifestoes of many of the more progressive Liberals such as Arthur Acland and Sydney Buxton.[73] A.J. Mundella considered that it was unnecessary to establish a new ministry, but in early June, prior to the General Election, he urged on Gladstone the importance of extending the Labour Bureau of the Board of Trade and of concentrating in the 'one department all matters relating to and affecting labour'.[74] He argued that, although this would involve the Board in functions other than the provision of labour statistics, it would be entirely in accordance with other duties respecting railway and mercantile labour currently being attached to the Board. Moreover, it would, he claimed, remove from the Home Office labour duties that had been administered 'very inefficiently and insufficiently' by an Inspectorate appointed by Tory jobbery.

Nevertheless, after their party's victory at the election, the Liberal Progressives pressed instead for a separate Ministry of Labour and

Technical Education under Arthur Acland.[75] They
felt that Mundella's 'labour propositions' were
outdated and unoriginal.[76] But Gladstone, with
his avowed hatred for radical ideas, was dis-
inclined to accept their proposals.[77] In an
attempt to forestall deadlock, Richard Haldane,
sensitive to the need to secure 'the confidence of
the nascent body of opinion in the constituencies
which care[d] little for any Irish policy' and
concentrated 'itself on social questions', urged
that Acland, who possessed the confidence of
Labour, be given a new post of Vice-President of
the Board of Trade in charge of a proper Labour
Department.[78] Acland viewed the prospect of
developing the Labour Bureau with enthusiasm, but
he insisted that, if Labour's interests were to be
adequately represented in government policy-
making, such a post should carry with it Cabinet
status.[79] As an additional Minister of Labour was
unacceptable to the Liberal 'old guard', he
proposed that he should supervise labour
administration from the Chancellorship of the
Duchy of Lancaster, but this alternative was also
rejected. Instead, he was offered the President-
ship of the Board of Trade. In Acland's opinion,
no adequate reform and extension of labour
administration was possible so long as the Labour
Bureau remained a subordinate branch of a
commercial department. Moreover, for reasons of
health, he felt himself unable to shoulder the
manifold responsibilities of the Board of Trade.[80]
On 14 August 1892, he opted instead for the
Education Department; Mundella accepted the Board
of Trade, and subsequently Thomas Burt was offered
the Assistant Secretaryship on the vague assurance
from Gladstone that 'the development of the labour
bureau and the prosecution of the interests
connected with it' would 'engage the attention of
the Government and open a long and broad
perspective'.[81]

Between August 1892 and the formation of the
Labour Department in January 1893, the future of
labour administration remained in the melting pot
of public debate. In particular, witnesses before
the Royal Commission on Labour, appointed in 1891
to investigate the deterioration in British
industrial relations, submitted a variety of
proposals.[82] Some argued that the Board of Trade
should be transformed by the addition of a Board
of Labour into a Board of Industry. Other
witnesses, who favoured significant extensions of

State intervention, desired the creation of a
Ministry of Labour distinct from the Board of
Trade. A formidable array of functions were
advocated for any future Labour Department; that
it should provide frequent and comprehensive
labour statistics including forecasts of trade
fluctuations, co-ordinate the activities of local
labour registries by acting as a general clearing
house for labour, administer the laws relating to
mines and factories, and arbitrate in trade
disputes. Perhaps the most arresting evidence was
that of Elgin Gould of the United States Labour
Department when he warned that, if Britain failed
to establish a properly staffed Labour bureau with
skilled investigators, she would 'be alone amongst
the principal nations'.[83]

The Webbs were also making their contribution
to the debate. Since 1890, they had been
advocating the co-ordination of all labour
functions in one department, partly in the
interests of administrative efficiency, but more
especially as a launching pad for socialistic
legislation,[84] and in September 1892, at Haldane's
request, they wrote a memorandum for Henry
Asquith, the Home Secretary, on the transformation
of the Factory and Mines Department into a
Ministry of Labour.[85] Also circulating in
government circles were the proofs of a paper by
David Schloss, another Fabian and a member of the
Booth enquiry, analysing in detail the weaknesses
of the existing Labour Bureau and advancing a
programme of reorganisation.[86] In particular, he
emphasised the need both for local labour correspondents who could collect information at first
hand and for a team of skilled investigators and
administrators at the Board of Trade who were
experienced social statisticians and 'experts
acquainted with labour questions'.[87]

Thus, ostensibly, when in late 1892 Mundella
and Burt came to consider what measures they
should adopt, they were faced with a wide range of
options. However, political and administrative
considerations effectively closed most of them.
Politically, the paucity of the parliamentary
majority, the continued preoccupation with Home
Rule, and the policy of evasion to social reform
of the 'old gang',[88] meant that any new departure
had to be purely departmental in character.[89] Any
possibility of a Ministry of Labour was therefore
ruled out. Likewise, the acquisition of new
responsibilities requiring legislative sanction,

whether relating to industrial conciliation or unemployment, was impracticable.[90]
    Administratively, the Home Office had no intention of allowing the Board of Trade to pre-empt fresh powers over labour questions. Indeed, the permanent officials were adamant that if all labour administration *was* to be concentrated within one department, the Home Office was 'the only Office of State to which it ought to belong.'[91] Similarly, as is demonstrated in Chapter 7, the Treasury was bitterly opposed to the Bureau's enlargement and determined to contain any new department. Moreover, even within the Board of Trade, there were personal factors working against the implementation of more than a minimal programme. Thomas Burt, appointed specifically to further the administrative interests of Labour, was essentially anti-collectivist, upholding still the trade unionist philosophy of the 1860s and 1870s, an ardent believer in self-help and orthodox classical economics, and an opponent of the Labour Party and New Unionism.[92] As the foremost exponent of the Lib-Lab tradition, he was 'more than half a conservative on all matters affecting the interest of capitalists'.[93] In many respects, Mundella shared Burt's social and economic philosophy, with his overriding commitment to the issues of traditional radicalism and industrial consensus. His perception of administrative reform was essentially paternalistic; a means of advancing specific measures deemed beneficial to the working classes, rather than a means of securing for Labour fuller participation in the policy-making process and a general shift in the social objectives of bureaucracy. Indeed, he explicitly rejected the progressive schemes of the social radicals for a Ministry of Labour with extensive powers of intervention in the labour market as 'class legislation' that would prove socially divisive and economically damaging.[94]
    Accordingly, when on 20 January 1893 the formation of a Labour Department at the Board of Trade was finally sanctioned by the Treasury, its terms of reference were confined to the collection and dissemination of labour statistics and no provision was made to transfer labour responsibilities from other departments. Nonetheless, the Labour Department represented a significant expansion in the machinery of civil intelligence. A permanent establishment of labour statisticians

The Origins of the Labour Department

and investigators, headed by a Labour Commissioner, was created in Whitehall and supported
by a team of fee-paid local correspondents
throughout the country. Provision was made for
the regular publication of a *Labour Gazette* to
complement the commercial intelligence provided by
the *Board of Trade Journal*. Moreover, the Labour
Department was accorded a separate identity within
a newly created Commercial, Labour and Statistical
Branch of the Board of Trade. Late-Victorian
government was now more fully equipped to identify
and measure the 'Labour Problem'. As Mundella
reflected:

> My Labour Department is a big thing - larger
> and more important than the Government itself
> apprehends. It will do great work in the
> future.[95]

The Origins of the Labour Department

NOTES

1. *Official Statistics Committee*, *Mins. of Ev.*, PP 1881
(39) XXX, pp.117-38.
2. H.S. Foxwell, 'Irregularity of Employment and
Fluctuations of Prices' in J. Oliphant (ed.), *The Claims of
Labour* (Edinburgh, 1886), p. 262.
3. O.R. McGregor, 'Social Research and Social Policy in
the Nineteenth Century', *British Journal of Sociology*, VIII
(1957), pp. 146-57. The *Journal of the Royal Statistical
Society* had, along with the *Proceedings of the National
Association for the Promotion of Social Science*, done most to
compensate for governmental deficiencies by providing 'a
quantitative commentary on the trends of social change and
the social incidence and running costs of expansive
industrialism' (H.L. Beales, *The Making of Social Policy*
(Oxford, 1946), p. 17).
4. *JRSS*, LVI (1893), p. 65. George Howell: (1833-1910)
Labour leader and writer, joined Chartists in 1847, prominent
in 'nine hours' struggle, 1859; joined the 'Junta' which
directed trade union affairs, 1860; Secretary to
Parliamentary Committee of Trades Union Congress, 1871-5;
prominent in securing Trade Union Acts of 1871 and 1876;
Liberal M.P. for Bethnal Green 1885-95.
5. C. Bradlaugh, 'Labour Statistics: their utility to
employers and employed', *Our Corner* (ed. Annie Besant), VII
(1886), p. 130.
6. *The Beehive*, 12 Feb. 1876.
7. PP 1881 (39) XXX, p. 5.
8. Ibid., p. 16. See also, below Ch. 8.
9. F.J. Mouat, 'The History of the Statistical Society
of London', *JRSS*, Jubilee Volume (1885), p. 49.
10. Ibid., pp. 10-11.
11. J.W. Nixon, *A History of the International
Statistical Institute* (The Hague, 1960), pp. 150-1.
12. *JRSS*, Jubilee Volume (1885), p. 146.
13. A.J. Mundella, T. Burt, R. Giffen, J. Burnett.
14. C. Bradlaugh in *Our Corner*, VII (1886), p. 129. The
Positivist, Frederick Harrison, later considered this aspect
of the Conference to have been its main contribution to the
movement for reform (Mundella Papers, fo. 4, Harrison to Miss
Mundella, 4 Dec. 1893).
15. *Industrial Remuneration Conference Report* (1885),
pp. 7-8; see also, E.H. Phelps Brown and M.H. Browne,
'Carroll D. Wright and the Development of British Labour
Statistics', *Economica*, 30 (1963), pp. 279-80.
16. R. Prouty, *The Transformation of the Board of Trade
1830-5: A Study of Administrative Reorganisation in the
heyday of laissez-faire* (1957).
17. P.R.O., MT9/261/M21040/1885, memo. on 'The nature and

object of the duties performed by the Marine Department of the Board of Trade', 1885.

18. H. Parris, *Government and the Railways in Nineteenth Century Britain* (1965), pp. 48, 125, 138, 225.

19. For a detailed breakdown of the distribution of administrative functions relating to Labour, see especially *R.C. on Labour, Appendices*, PP 1894 (C.7421) XXXV, pp. 575-94.

20. H. Llewellyn Smith, *The Board of Trade* (1928), p. 180.

21. R.M. MacLeod, *Treasury Control and Social Administration: A Study of Establishment Growth at the Local Government Board 1871-1905* (1928), pp. 60-1.

22. E. Troup, *The Home Office* (1925), pp. 50-1, 156, 213.

23. Prouty, *Transformation*, p. 8. The subsequent administrative efficiency of the Board compared with the 'superficial work' of other departments which continued to live a 'hand to mouth' statistical existence, was notable. (B. Mallet, *Sir Louis Mallet: A record of public service and political ideals* (1905), p. 44). In 1882, the Statistical Department was incorporated into a newly re-established Commercial Department.

24. P.R.O., BT12/27, memo. by R. Giffen on 'The Statistical functions of English Departments of State', 18 July 1889.

25. Ibid.

26. A.J. Mundella: (1825-97) Apprenticed hosier, 1836; Manufacturer 1848; Formed permanent conciliation board, Nottingham glove and hosiery trade, 1866; M.P. 1868-97; President of the Board of Trade, 1886 and 1892-4.

27. See *R.C. on the Depression of Trade and Industry, Mins. of Ev.*, PP 1886 (C.4621) XXI, QQ. 158-61.

28. *Hansard*, 3rd series, 302, col. 1771, 2 March 1886.

29. W.H.G. Armytage, *A.J. Mundella 1825-1897: The Liberal Background to the Labour Movement* (1951), p. 239.

30. *Hansard*, 3rd series, 302, col. 1788, 2 March 1886.

31. R.S.S. Council Minute Book, 12 Feb. 1885, 16 April 1885.

32. *Hansard*, 3rd series, 302, col. 1790, 2 March 1886.

33. PP 1886 (48) LXXI, pp. 2-3.

34. C. Bradlaugh, 'What a Labour Statistics Bureau Should Be', *Our Corner*, VII (1886), pp. 321-4.

35. The following critique is based upon D.F. Schloss, 'The Reorganisation of the Labour Department', *JRSS*, LVI (1893), pp. 44-69; C. Bradlaugh, 'A Starved Government Department', *The New Review*, III (1890), pp. 438-46; *Hansard*, 3rd series, 328, cols. 441-4.

36. P.R.O., T1/8369B/18036, minute by Sir Reginald Welby, 3 March 1887.

37. P.R.O., BT14/IND 20472, Treasury to R. Giffen, 28 April and 11 June 1886.

38. P.R.O., T1/8243B/11800, minute by Welby, 14 April 1886.

39. P.R.O., T9/27, Treasury to Board of Trade, 23 Jan. 1891.

40. P.G. Parkhurst, *Ships of Peace* (New Malden, 1962), pp. 102-4; Mundella Papers, fo. 3, R. Giffen to A.J. Mundella, 7 May 1886.

41. PP 1888 (433) CVII, p. 2.

42. *R.C. on Civil Establishments*, *Mins. of Ev.*, PP 1888 (C.5545) XXVII, QQ. 18088-91, 19168-70, 20021.

43. Schloss, 'The Reorganisation of our Labour Department', p. 45.

44. PP 1888 (433) CVII, p. 3.

45. Schloss, 'The Reorganisation of our Labour Department', p. 59; For details of the appropriation of American State Bureaus, see PP 1894 (C.7421) XXXV, p. 228.

46. A.B. Cooke and J. Vincent, *The Governing Passion: Cabinet Government and Party Politics in Britain 1885-86* (Brighton, 1974), pp. 257-8.

47. P. Smith, *Disraelian Conservatism and Social Reform* (1967), pp. 93, 130, 141-2, 166, 320; A. Sykes, *Tariff Reform in British Politics 1903-13* (Oxford, 1979), pp. 24-6.

48. *Dictionary of National Biography*, *2nd Supplement*, Vol. 1 (1912), pp. 495-6.

49. Ibid., Vol. III, pp. 48-50.

50. *Dictionary of National Biography*, *1912-21* (Oxford, 1927), p. 71; Lady Frances Balfour, *A Memoir of Lord Balfour of Burleigh* (1925), p. 58.

51. P. Smith, *Disraelian Conservatism*, p. 323.

52. Ibid., p. 324.

53. C. Bradlaugh, 'A Starved Government Department', p. 441; *Hansard*, 3rd series, 328, cols. 443-4.

54. Smith, *Disraelian Conservatism*, p. 323.

55. *Annual Reports of the T.U.C.* (1886-1892); Hicks Beach Papers, PC/PP/60, memo. by J. Burnett, 30 April 1892.

56. See, e.g., *Hansard*, 3rd series, 302, col. 1783.

57. See, e.g., *Annual Report of the A.S.E.* (1886), p. 11; *Labour Leader*, 7 May 1892. The issue of Labour's attitude towards government investigations and statistics is treated at length in Chapter 9.

58. *Hansard*, 3rd series, 302, col. 1772.

59. Foxwell in Oliphant, *The Claims of Labour*, p. 264. Significantly, this volume of essays was sponsored by the trustees of the Industrial Remuneration Conference.

60. *Workman's Times*, 7 May 1892; *Daily Chronicle*, 14 Jan. 1893.

61. Smith, *Disraelian Conservatism*, pp. 53-7; 231-2.

62. Ibid.

63. Armytage, *A.J. Mundella*, p.251.

64. See, e.g., 'The Progress of the Working Classes in the Last Half Century', *JRSS*, 46 (1883), pp. 593-622;

The Origins of the Labour Department

'Further Notes on the Progress of the Working Classes', *JRSS*, 49 (1886), pp. 28-91; J.G. Hutchinson, 'Progress and Wages: A Workman's View', *Nineteenth Century* 26 (1884), pp. 630-2.

65. *Hansard*, 3rd series, 337, col. 724, 25 June 1889.

66. L.A. Clark, 'The Liberal Party and Collectivism 1886-1906', unpublished M. Litt thesis, Cambridge University, 1957, pp. 33-7. The front was centred on 'the five' (Haldane, Asquith, Grey, Acland, Buxton), the leaders of the New Unionism, and L.C.C. Progressivism.

67. *Workman's Times*, 7 May 1892.

68. Hicks Beach Papers, PC/PP/60, memo. by J. Burnett on 'A Proposed Ministry of Labour', 30 April 1892.

69. Smith, *Disraelian Conservatism*, p. 324.

70. PP 1892 (44) II.

71. P.R.O., HO45/10122/B12457/4, E.J. Stapleton to C.E. Troup, 1 June 1892.

72. Hicks Beach Papers, PC/PP/60, memo. by R. Giffen on 'A Ministry of Labour', 30 April 1892.

73. Acland Diary, 21 and 22 July 1892.

74. W.E. Gladstone Papers, B.M. Add. MS 44258, fo. 274-7, Mundella to Gladstone, 9 June 1892.

75. Acland Diary, 21 and 22 July 1892; Passfield Papers, II4d, A.H.D. Acland to B. Webb, 19 Feb. 1909.

76. Acland Diary, 21 July 1892.

77. Ibid., 5 and 13 Aug. 1892; Sir Algernon West, *Private Diaries* (1922), p. 45.

78. As quoted in D. Sommer, *Haldane of Cloan, His Life and Times, 1856-1928* (1960), p. 88. See also, Acland Diary, 13 Aug. 1892.

79. Ibid., 8, 10, 13 Aug. 1892.

80. Ibid., 16 Aug. 1892; Sir Algernon West, *Private Diaries*, p. 49.

81. W.E. Gladstone Papers, B.M. Add. MS 44515, fo. 221, Gladstone to Burt, 19 Aug. 1892. Thomas Burt: (1837-1922) Miner; General Secretary of Northumberland Miners' Association 1865-1913; M.P. 1874-1918; President of T.U.C. 1891; Parliamentary Secretary to Board of Trade, 1892-5.

82. *R.C. on Labour, Digest of Ev.*, PP 1894 (C.7421) XXXV, p. 363.

83. *R.C. on Labour, Mins of Ev.*, PP 1893-4 (C.7063) XXXIX Pt 1, Q. 6751. For a detailed analysis of comparative developments on the Continent, see E.R.L. Gould, 'European Bureaus of Labour Statistics', *Yale Review*, II (1893-4), pp. 386-403. For a study of the American influence in the formation of the Labour Department, see Brown and Browne, 'The Development of British Labour Statistics', pp. 277-86.

84. Beatrice Webb Diary, Vol. 14 (1), 15 Feb. 1890; *R.C. on Labour, Mins of Ev.*, PP 1893-94 (C.7063) XXXIX Pt 1, QQ. 3755, 3763-6, 4399-4402.

85. Beatrice Webb Diary, Vol. 14 (1), 19 Sept. 1892.

Herbert Gladstone Papers, B.M. Add. MS 45989, fo. 4, H.H. Asquith to H. Gladstone, 14 Oct. 1892.

86. Passfield Papers, S. Webb to B. Potter, 13 May 1892; *JRSS*, LVI (1893), pp. 44-69.

87. Ibid., p. 56.

88. Beatrice Webb Diary, Vol. 14 (2), 24 Dec. 1892.

89. *The Times*, 13 Jan. 1893; E. Porritt, 'English Labour in and out of Parliament in 1893', *Yale Review*, II (1893-4), p. 419.

90. *Liberal Magazine*, 1 (December 1893), pp. 90-1.

91. P.R.O., HO45/10122B/12457/1, C.E. Troup to G. Lushington, 3 May 1892.

92. T. Burt, 'Labour in Parliament', *Contemporary Review*, 55 (1889), pp. 679-90; 'Mr Chamberlain's Programme: The Labour Question', *Nineteenth Century*, 32 (1892), pp. 865-74.

93. H.V. Emy, *Liberals, Radicals and Social Politics 1892-1914*, (Cambridge, 1973), p. 23; J.M. Bellamy and J. Saville, *Dictionary of Labour Biography*, Vol. 1 (1972), pp. 61-2.

94. P.R.O., T1/8743A/10410, Mundella to Sir W. Harcourt, 21 Dec. 1892.

95. Armytage, *A.J. Mundella*, p.295.

Chapter 4

THE PRODUCTION STRUCTURE OF LABOUR STATISTICS

FUNDING

An outstanding feature of the late-Victorian and
Edwardian Board of Trade was the size of its
expenditure on social enquiry relative to other
departments of social administration, and the
dramatic growth in such appropriation. It is
impossible to assess precisely the Board's
financial outlay on labour statistics. Its
annual accounts lack sufficient disaggregation.
Many of its commercial enquiries such as the
Fiscal Blue Books and Census of Production
incorporated a significant amount of data relating
to the labour market. Furthermore, there was no
clear demarcation within the Commercial, Labour
and Statistical Branch between commercial and
labour statisticians. Finally, within the senior
establishment, there were a number of
administrators who were heavily involved in
statistical work and *vice versa*. Nonetheless, a
rough estimate of the Board's expenditure on
labour statistics can be obtained. (See Figure
4.1)
     Figure 4.1 clearly illustrates that the rise
in expenditure on social statistics was at an
uneven rate. Four main upswings can be
identified, associated with the creation of the
Bureau of Labour Statistics in 1886, the
establishment of the Labour Department in 1893,
the incorporation of a new class of labour
investigators and statisticians within the Board
in 1899, and the initiation after 1902 of a series
of massive enquiries relating to working-class
remuneration, employment and living standards.
This pattern is confirmed by an overview of the
manpower deployed for the accumulation, collation

The Production Structure of Labour Statistics

Figure 4.1: Expenditure on Labour Statistics 1880–1914[1]

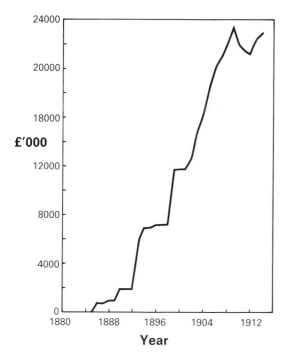

Table 4.1: Manpower Allocated to Labour Statistics[2]

	UPPER DIVISION			LOWER DIVISION		
	Assistant Secre- taries	Principal/ First Class Clerks	2nd Class Clerks	Staff Officers	2nd Division Clerks	Abstractors
1886				1	1	1
1893		1		5	4	2
1900	1	1	1	6	7	5
1914	1	2	1	10	23	6

and interpretation of labour statistics within the
Board of Trade over the same period. (See Table
4.1).

RECRUITMENT

The mode of recruitment of Board of Trade statisticians was also distinctive. With the notable
exception of F.H. MacLeod, labour statisticians
and investigators were appointed without
competitive examination from outside the Civil
Service.[3] Their average age at appointment was
roughly 35 and, typically, they possessed
extensive experience of social and economic
research and of the labour market.[4] As the
Board's enquiries became progressively more
complex and comprehensive after 1900, its establishment was further reinforced by the employment
on a part-time basis of leading experts in the
theory and application of statistical and
quantitative techniques.

This recruitment pattern was designed to
maintain the Labour Department as an effective
research and intelligence unit.[5] As statisticians
such as Llewellyn Smith, the first Labour
Commissioner, were promoted to more generalist
posts or diverted to industrial negotiation under
the 1896 Conciliation Act, or as new areas of
labour administration were contemplated, fresh
expertise was recruited. Thus, in response to
mounting concern at the economic and social
effects of industrial unrest, D.F. Schloss, an
expert on wage determination, was employed in the
1890s to investigate alternative forms of
industrial remuneration, such as profit-sharing.
Similarly, A. Wilson Fox, a specialist on the
rural labour market, was enlisted to assess the
viability of land reform and agricultural labour
colonies as methods of reducing unemployment and
contemporary fears of 'urban degeneration'. After
1900, the concern with national efficiency, tariff
reform, and a more scientific treatment of
poverty, shifted the focus of investigation to
working-class purchasing power and consumption
patterns and the cost structure of British
industry. The Board of Trade therefore undertook
a series of enquiries into working-class wage
rates, earnings and standards of living in the
United Kingdom as compared with those prevailing
in other advanced economies; including the

construction of an official Cost of Living Index.
For the task, it recruited the two leading wage
and price statisticians of the day, A.L. Bowley
and G.H. Wood, together with the theoretician
G. Udny Yule.

Meanwhile, as the demand for a national
unemployment policy moved to the centre of
political debate, W.H. Dawson, the leading
specialist on German social legislation, was
engaged to make exhaustive enquiries into the
German system of labour exchanges; to be joined in
1907 by W.H. Beveridge, a prominent member of the
Central (Unemployed) Body for London, and an
expert on the problems of under-employment and
unemployment and on the structure and viability of
foreign schemes of unemployment insurance. The
Board of Trade responded to impending minimum wage
legislation in similar fashion, recruiting as
statistical investigators G.T. Reid, a specialist
in the economics of sweated labour at the L.S.E.
and activist for the Anti-Sweating League, and
Ernest Aves, an expert on the casual labour market
and Home Office adviser on Australian and New
Zealand wage boards.

The Board of Trade was able to sustain such a
recruitment pattern despite increasing
representations from the Treasury, supported by
the Civil Service union, that such staff should be
appointed by open competition.[6] Most of the
Board's senior labour and commercial
administrators had themselves entered Whitehall as
social scientists and statisticians and were
insistent that such posts 'be retained for
exceptional men attracted by a definite prospect
of congenial work of sufficient scope, but not
attracted by so nebulous a thing as the Civil
Service as a whole'.[7] A common procedure was to
employ social statisticians on a part-time basis
out of the Comptroller-General's personal
allowance for 'clerical and other assistance'.
Only later were they incorporated fully within the
establishment, when the public demand for labour
or socio-economic information was at its most
intense and the Treasury more readily persuaded of
the need for their expertise.

PAY AND PROMOTION

As Table 4.1 clearly indicates, within the Board
of Trade, statistical work was not viewed as

purely 'mechanical' work within the competence of junior clerks. A significant proportion of its statisticians and investigators were appointed at the rank of staff officer or above, while the supervision of official labour statistics was firmly regarded as First Division work. As a result, the salaries of the Board's statistical personnel compared very favourably with equivalent officials in other departments such as the Home Office and Local Government Board.[8]

They also enjoyed highly favourable promotion prospects. A separate five-rung promotion structure (see Table 4.2) provided labour statisticians and investigators within the Board with ample scope for career development:

Table 4.2: Board of Trade Pay and Promotion Structure (1904)[9]

Principal for Statistics	£650-800
Senior Labour Investigator & Statistician	£400-500
Labour Investigator & Statistician	£300-400
Assistant for Special Enquiries	£150-200
Statistical Assistant	£100-150

Furthermore, those displaying broader administrative talents were elevated to key posts within the senior secretariat of the Board. For example, D.F. Schloss and A. Wilson Fox, appointed investigators in 1899, had become respectively Director of the Census of Production and Comptroller-General of the Commercial, Labour and Statistical Branch by 1907, while F.H. MacLeod rose from the rank of lower division clerk in 1889 to become Director of the newly established Department of Labour Statistics in 1912.

Another favourable feature of the administrative environment was that, during this period, the post of Comptroller-General - the vital link between the Board's statisticians and its permanent and political chiefs - was occupied by officials who clearly perceived the value of statistical data to policy-making. For example, Robert Giffen regarded the provision of statistical 'intelligence', as opposed to routine data, as vital for informed debate and for the effective formulation and evaluation of policy options. In his opinion, the Board was unique as a department in producing statistics purely for policy-making purposes, and the status accorded to statistical work within the Board not only enhanced the efficiency with which it performed its administrative functions but also rendered it the more capable of an 'enlightened' response to commercial and industrial developments.[10]

Similarly, Llewellyn Smith was convinced of the need for policy makers to 'take frequent sections and soundings' of 'the flow of social and economic phenomena' and to draw heavily upon quantitative investigation in decision-making. Defending in 1910, as Permanent Secretary, the prominent role of statisticians within contemporary welfare and fiscal debate, he voiced doubts as to whether the 'economic animal was a biped after all' in that abstract analysis and historical investigation had to be underpinned by 'concrete statistical measurement' at every stage of the policy-making process.[11] Such sentiments were reflected in the degree to which senior statisticians and investigators were consulted on a range of policy issues and their findings incorporated in ministerial briefings and policy memoranda.

Two additional factors reinforced this access to policy making. Firstly, the solution of the 'Labour Problem' was a comparatively new area of government expansion in which the traditions of administration were as yet unsettled and unconstrained by a vast body of statute law needing uniform treatment. Thus, although the channels of advice and file procedure did become increasingly more formalised within the Commercial, Labour and Statistical Branch of the Board of Trade, there was no cult of the generalist at the expense of the expert.[12] Secondly, because of the recruitment pattern and career development of the Board's labour officials in the 1890s, after 1900 many senior administrators such as Llewellyn Smith and Wilson Fox shared a range of pre-service experience with their statistical advisers and investigators, including involvement in the University Settlement Movement, in the Booth Enquiry, and in trade unionism and progressive politics, quite apart from active participation in the Royal Statistical and Economic Societies.[13] Both sets of officials also shared a common commitment to the more scientific treatment of social problems and the

elimination of the worst imperfections and
exploitative features of the labour market.

BACKGROUND AND MOTIVATION

In terms of motivation and operational philosophy,
Board of Trade statisticians can broadly be
grouped into two categories. Firstly, there were
several statisticians who viewed social enquiry
from an essentially conservative perspective. The
most prominent member of this group was Robert
Giffen, in charge of Board of Trade statistics
throughout the period 1876-97 as head of the
Statistical and Commercial Departments and
Comptroller-General of the Commercial, Labour and
Statistical Branch.

Born in 1837, the younger son of a small
Lanarkshire merchant, Giffen had been educated at
a mixed village school and begun his career at the
age of 13 as a solicitor's clerk in Glasgow.
However, by 1860, he had gravitated to journalism
as a profession and in 1862 had moved to London as
sub-editor of the *Globe*, the government organ of
Lord Palmerston's administration. After serving
for a time with John Morley on the *Fortnightly
Review*, Giffen had joined *The Economist* as
assistant-editor (1868-76) under Walter Bagehot.
From 1873 to 1876, he had also acted as City
editor of the *Daily News*, as a regular contributor
on finance and commerce to *The Times* and the
Spectator, and as a founder of the *Statist*. After
his appointment in 1876 as head of the Board of
Trade's Statistical Department, he had remained a
prolific writer and publicist on a wide range of
economic, financial, and statistical issues. In
addition, he had played an influential role in the
development of the Royal Statistical Society (as
Secretary and President 1876-84), the
International Statistical Institute, and the
Economic and Statistical Section of the British
Association. Meanwhile, in his official capacity,
Giffen had, quite apart from overseeing the
production of Britain's commercial data, made a
significant contribution to a variety of
government enquiries relating to trade, taxation,
currency, commercial law, official statistics and
economic depression.[14]

In his social and economic beliefs, Giffen
was a confirmed free-market Liberal individualist
and a vigorous opponent of State intervention in

industrial affairs. In particular, he resisted the tendency of government growth after 1880 to involve Whitehall in problems relating to the labour market. He considered that State arbitration and conciliation would distort the cost structure of British industry, that the provision of public works and other forms of job creation would divert funds from private enterprise, and that the more stringent regulation of working conditions might compromise the necessary prerogatives of industrial management.[15] Giffen seriously questioned the severity of the so-called 'Labour Problem', believing that the working classes were the major beneficiaries of economic growth, that pauperism was declining, and that, where it persisted, lack of thrift rather than exploitation was the major determinant.[16]

Thus, although a leading advocate in the 1890's of more extensive and systematic industrial data, Giffen perceived the role of official labour statistics as being primarily the containment of State intervention. In his view, they would further 'efficient and economical' government by centralising all labour intelligence at the Board of Trade.[17] Meanwhile, the fundamental community of interest between industrial management and workforce would be revealed and 'irrational' conflict eliminated, voluntary effort focussed more effectively upon the crisis points of urban deprivation, and collectivist measures rendered unnecessary. Giffen regarded labour statistics quite explicitly as a means of discrediting 'sensational politics and sociology' generated by the contemporary debate over the standard of living of the working classes and by 'collectivist agitators' such as Henry George.[18] In accordance with his minimalist philosophy of labour administration, he actively opposed the creation of a separate Labour Department in 1893 and its assumption of non-statistical duties such as conciliation work as an unwarranted invasion of the labour market.[19] Just as G.R. Porter had used his position as chief government statistician to advance the cause of free trade in the 1830s and 1840s, so Giffen exploited it in the 1880s and 1890s to stem the tide of collectivism.[20]

Moreover, several other influential statisticians within the Board of Trade subscribed to similar views, including A.E. Bateman (who succeeded Giffen as Comptroller-General)[21] and F.H. MacLeod, who had worked under Giffen for sixteen years before joining the Labour Department as Superintendent of Statistics, and who as Senior Investigator and Principal for Labour Statistics after 1899 played a pivotal role in the investigatory work of the department. In MacLeod's case, the conservatism of his economic and social philosophy was strongly reinforced by his pattern of career development. As a former lower division clerk, his overriding concern in supervising the collation of labour statistics was 'bureaucratic precedent and procedure' rather than 'social truth and utility'.[22] He was hostile towards the more innovative statisticians and economists within the Labour Department and resistant to new enquiries and statistical techniques.[23]

An additional conservative element amongst the investigators was provided by Labour Correspondents such as John Burnett. Born in Alnwick, Northumberland in 1842 and educated at the local charity school, Burnett had spent his early teens as an errand boy before being apprenticed in a Tyneside engineering works. He had compensated for his lack of formal education by attending evening classes in Newcastle, emerging by the early 1860s as one of the leaders of the skilled labour groups on Tyneside. Thereafter, he had played a prominent role in the campaigns for electoral reform and for shorter working hours, providing the leadership for the Nine Hours League and for the celebrated North-East engineering strike of 1871. After a period of employment on the *Newcastle Chronicle*, Burnett had been elected in 1875 as General Secretary of the Amalgamated Society of Engineers. For the next ten years, he had directed the Union's defence against increasingly aggressive management strategies designed to lower wage costs and to raise output within a deteriorating market environment. As a member of the Parliamentary Committee of the T.U.C., he had also led the trade union lobby for the repeal of the Criminal Law Amendment Act. However, by the mid-1880s, his leadership of the A.S.E., with its stress on stable bureaucratic control, industrial conciliation and a commitment to Gladstonian Liberalism, had come under mounting attack from rank and file militants, and when in 1886 Mundella had offered him the post of Labour Correspondent at the Board of Trade, Burnett had relinquished his union responsibilities in favour of a career in the Civil Service.[24]

Several other Labour Correspondents such as C.J. Drummond and J.J. Dent, and many of the Board's fee-paid Local Correspondents, had emerged from similar backgrounds, and likewise viewed social enquiry as labour aristocrats who, faced with the emergence of a new and more militant trade unionism, had gravitated from labour politics to the security and prestige of public office.[25] Although advocating a range of social reforms as a solution to the 'Labour Problem', they also were hostile to Socialist ideology and deprecated the divisiveness of New Unionism. Their advocacy of welfare rights and measures was not identified with any support for an independent working-class political programme and they viewed the mechanism of social amelioration as primarily the growth of 'wisely directed trade-unionism', with State intervention fulfilling only a residual role. In addition, they shared with Burnett a respect for hierarchy and a propensity to interpret the broader aspirations of Labour in terms of the relatively structured and pragmatic motions of the T.U.C.[26]

Accordingly, this group of investigators regarded the prime function of labour statistics as being to 'educate' the Labour Movement, on the assumption that accurate data on employment, on the costs and benefits of strike action, and on the cost structure of British industry, would rehabilitate the consensus tactics of mid-Victorian craft unionism and serve to preserve industrial peace. They also anticipated that more reliable and comprehensive labour market intelligence would enable the Trade Union Movement to focus its energies on eliminating the more contentious aspects of the 'Labour Problem', without recourse to legislative measures which might endanger the cost efficiency of enterprise and the self-sufficiency and motivation of the labouring classes.[27]

The motivation and operational philosophy of the second group of statisticians and investigators can most accurately be described as 'progressive', and within this group a further distinction may usefully, though more arbitrarily, be drawn between 'social innovators' and 'technical innovators'. The most prominent 'social innovators' were Hubert Llewellyn Smith, Clara Collet, David Frederick Schloss and Arthur Wilson Fox.[28]

The Production Structure of Labour Statistics

Hubert Llewellyn Smith, the first Labour Commissioner, had been born in Bristol in 1864 of middle-class Quaker extraction.[29] After a grammar school education, he had entered Oxford in 1883 to read mathematics. The University had provided a milieu which was to prove of immense significance to the development of British social policy. For it was from the Oxford of the 1880s that emerged a new generation of public servants who, in the pursuit of constructive administration, were to combat the prevailing negative attitude to domestic policy within the Civil Service. The 'new Oxford Movement' had been characterised by an unprecedented outburst of concern over the condition of the working classes. The teachings of Jowett and T.H. Green, with their stress on obligation, the arrival of a more socially relevant, empirical school of economics, and the advent of the radical historiography of Arnold Toynbee, had provided the preconditions, while the immediate cause had been the appearance of a series of sensational exposés of urban squalor, of which *The Bitter Cry of Outcast London* had been the most prominent.

Llewellyn Smith had readily responded to the social and intellectual challenge of this environment. He had participated in several societies devoted to the debate and investigation of economic and social issues, his most vital attachment being to the 'Inner Ring', a discussion group presided over by Arthur Acland for those who shared his concern with the 'Labour Problem'. Llewellyn Smith had also participated in the University Settlement Movement, playing host to parties of working men from Bethnal Green. Academically, his record had been equally impressive. His formal studies had yielded a First Class degree in mathematics, while he had capitalised on his informal work in applied economics by winning the Cobden Prize in 1886 for an essay on 'The Economic Aspects of State Socialism'.

The years between university and office had been for Llewellyn Smith ones of hectic and protean activity. Immersed in the kaleidoscopic world of late-Victorian progressivism, he had built up an array of social, political and academic contacts. Integrated early on into the aristocratic, radical milieu of the Carlisles at Castle Howard, he had progressed to that 'mecca' of social reformers and of future Labour

Department personnel - the East End of London, where at Toynbee Hall and later at Beaumont Square, where he founded a sub-colony called the 'Swarm', he had participated further in the University Settlement Movement. Meanwhile, in the Booth inquiry, at the British Association, the Royal Statistical and Economic Societies, at the Denison Club, and in his travels as an Extension Lecturer, he had made contact with the elite of social scientists and the leading statisticians of the day - both academic and governmental. Additionally, his espousal of the cause of the 'New Unionism' and his participation in London politics had made him the confidant of the Labour leaders. Above all, his political and educational activities had soldered him to the radical wing of the Liberal Party, while at the same time introducing him to the elder statesmen of labour reform, especially A.J. Mundella.

Consistent with this background, Llewellyn Smith upheld an advanced radical view of the 'Labour Problem'. Deeply influenced by the works of Stanley Jevons, he condemned the Manchester School for its doctrinaire rigidity and cruel administrative complacency, welcomed the emergence of a more constructive, socially meaningful economics, and sympathised with the cause of Socialism.[30] Given the absence of any other options, he preferred to be 'wrong with Karl Marx than right with David Ricardo'.[31] However, although Llewellyn Smith accepted the economic evils that Socialism set out to remedy as 'a just and valid cause for action', he was fundamentally opposed to revolutionary measures of social reform. Rather than the overthrow of existing economic and social institutions and relationships, he advocated a 'limited Socialism' which focussed upon 'the breaking down of the barriers of class exclusiveness, the development of the spirit of class union and social sympathy' and 'the education and moralisation of society'.[32] Llewellyn Smith's brand of social and welfare philosophy was informed with the characteristic middle-class missionary perspective of late-Victorian social radicalism. In his view, social progress had to incorporate both the moral as well as the material advancement of Labour, and this could only be achieved by maintaining overall social harmony during a process of gradual change. He considered that the value of government intervention in the labour market should be judged on purely pragmatic grounds, according to specific social priorities, rather than doctrinaire theory, and that self-reliance and working-class associative effort must remain the linchpin of social reform if the moral calibre and economic effic'ency of the labour force were to be maintained.[33]

Clara Collet's social background and philosophy were strikingly similar to those of Llewellyn Smith. Her middle-class upbringing had originally destined her for a career in school-teaching, but in the mid-1880s, she had gravitated instead to the social milieu of Toynbee Hall and the Denison Club, where she had become an ardent social worker for the University Settlement Movement and the Charity Organisation Society. From 1885 to 1888, she had studied political economy under Foxwell at University College London. However, the most vital influence upon her views had been the lectures of Arnold Toynbee with their stress on social obligation as an essential adjunct to economic enquiry, which she had attended at Oxford in the early 1880s. Toynbee had remained her inspiration when, with Llewellyn Smith, she had founded the London Economic Club in 1890 for 'progressive economists' with the aim of promoting a systematic investigation of the 'Labour Problem'. Meanwhile, her growing reputation as a social investigator and statistician had led to her recruitment as a member of Charles Booth's London Enquiry, to her appointment as an Assistant Commissioner of the Royal Commission on Labour, and to her recognition as a leading expert on the industrial condition of women.[34]

Politically, Clara Collet was a Liberal progressive, favouring the growth of trade unionism as an antidote to social exploitation, and more vigorous and wide-ranging State regulation of the working hours and conditions of Labour. Nevertheless, she viewed the function of industrial combination as being primarily defensive, and her commitment to social reform incorporated strong elements of conventional middle-class paternalism. She rejected what she considered to be the 'naive and dangerous' panaceas advocated by Socialism, whose doctrine of 'divine discontent' would, she claimed, merely destroy an economic system upon which the means of working-class subsistence were necessarily dependent. Not only did she object on orthodox

C.O.S. principles to the indiscriminate provision
of social benefits proposed by some trade union
militants, but she was also concerned to protect
'sweated' labour and other problem groups within
the so-called 'residuum' against the more
autocratic measures propounded by left-wing
intellectuals such as the Fabians.[35]
    Her colleague, David Schloss, had been a
former Oxford scholar, a barrister, and prominent
Jewish social worker, with distinguished
connections in the world of politics and high
finance. He was a prolific writer on all aspects
of the 'Labour Problem' and a specialist on
industrial remuneration, 'sweating', co-operation
and profit-sharing. He also had contributed to
the Booth Enquiry and had been a founder-member of
the London Economic Club and Economic Society, and
had, like Llewellyn Smith, collaborated with John
Burns to promote trade unionism amongst the
unskilled labour force of East London in the late
1880s and early 1890s. He had also played an
influential part in the campaigns for metropolitan
housing reform, for anti-sweating legislation, and
for the reform of labour administration.[36]
    Schloss was a social radical in his political
views, a vigorous critic of Gladstonian Liberalism, and a member of the Fabian Society. A
measure of his radicalism can be seen in a letter
to Sidney Webb in July 1892 in which he had
proposed the formation of a 'Fourth Party' to
'prevent the official Liberals' getting 'off cheap
as to social legislation', centred upon progressive M.P.s such as Haldane, Acland and Buxton:

> who will push the social side; this Fourth
> Party to have a following outside the House,
> which following can be led by you [Sidney
> Webb] and by the Daily Chronicle. Fourth
> Party to include a few men with money -swells
> who dont get the plums they expect in the
> sharing of the spoils. Some organs will be
> wanted. Buy Star cheap, acquire the dull
> Speaker or kill it by starting a bright
> weekly - the Democrat perhaps. The National
> Liberal Club, to say nothing of the Fabians,
> against the old crusted Reform Club and
> Devonshire. The young blood will win in the
> end.[37]

    Yet, it should be noted that Schloss' 'Fourth
Party' was conceived essentially as a ginger group

within the existing framework of social politics rather than as an independent vehicle for working-class orientated views and measures. He was not a Socialist. While he accepted the need for a redistribution of national income in favour of Labour, he was equally concerned to preserve the existing social and economic structure. In the final analysis, like many other middle-class reformers, he viewed social reform more as an antidote to social unrest - as 'a means of enabling the naked proletariat to acquire those prudential instincts which possession of property can alone engender' - than as a means of augmenting working-class power.[38] Schloss dismissed Socialism as being merely 'the common selfishness of the numerical majority' and believed that the most hopeful road to social peace lay in the spread of 'responsible' unionism and the infiltration of its 'pragmatism' and 'scepticism of legislative panaceas' into every corner of the Labour Movement.[39]

In contrast to the urban - orientated Liberal radicalism of Schloss, Arthur Wilson Fox was motivated by a spirit of rural paternalism and Tory democracy. The eldest son of the Physician in Ordinary to Queen Victoria, he was a member of the Somersetshire branch of a distinguished Quaker family and very much a product of the landed gentry. After being educated at Marlborough and Cambridge, he had begun to practise at the Bar in 1886. However, his legal commitments had been soon overshadowed by an increasingly active role in Tory politics. Wilson Fox had played a prominent part in the extension of the Primrose League and campaigned extensively on behalf of a number of Conservative candidates in the 1892 General Election. Meanwhile, as a means of educating the Party and the electorate on the 'Land Issue', he had begun a detailed investigation of the agricultural labour problem which subsequently led to his appointment as Assistant Commissioner to the Royal Commissions on Labour and Agriculture and his recruitment to the Labour Department.[40]

Wilson Fox characterised that 'corps d'elite of younger, more democratic, and more militant conservatives' attracted to the Primrose League in its early years, whose aim was to galvanise the old party organisation into action to meet the social problems of an industrialising society.[41] As a Tory progressive, he addressed the 'Labour

The Production Structure of Labour Statistics

Problem' with a mix of social paternalism and economic iconoclasm. Indeed, on a range of industrial issues, Wilson Fox appeared more advanced than many of his Liberal colleagues. In particular, he rejected the rural idealism of Social Imperialists and of many middle-class social engineers in their efforts to contend with the threat of 'urban degeneration'.[42] He considered that, as solutions to the problems of urban deprivation and unrest, schemes such as land colonies and State-aided emigration were both simplistic and cosmetic, and threatened to obscure long-term structural problems within the rural and metropolitan labour markets. In Wilson Fox's view, both national efficiency and social stability were contingent upon a reappraisal of the 'system of the reward and the management of labour', a higher level of public investment in technical education, and a radical shift in the incidence of taxation on land and site values; designed to stimulate industrial development in the inner-city areas, to release idle resources to the community, to reduce the overhead costs of agrarian enterprise, and to transfer the fiscal and moral obligations of social welfare from local propertied interests to the State.[43]

The statistical philosophy of the 'social innovators' had been largely moulded by their participation in the Booth Enquiry, and their primary concern was to provide a scientific exposé of the 'Labour Problem'; a careful, minute, systematic observation of working-class life as affected by environment, heredity, and habit. This, they argued, would provide an impartial data base for debate on labour issues, avoiding both 'investigatory sensationalism' such as the *Bitter Cry of Outcast London*, which they regarded as 'seriously deficient in the scientific sense', and superficial legislative proposals of a socialistic or autocratic kind that ignored the realities of the labour market and the complexities of social administration.[44] Furthermore, this group of statisticians shared the contemporary fear of the disintegration of society into the chaos of class war. As with their Settlement work and Extension lecturing, they viewed labour statistics as a means of cementing social relations and diverting working-class discontent into constructive channels. As Kadish concludes:

They felt certain that if the working man

were given the correct knowledge as to the reasons for his condition ... he would come to realise the fallacy of revolutionary socialism and adopt the right and best form of progress - gradual reform.[45]

The fact that 'the so-called' "enemy" was volunteering the information would in itself prove that class warfare was not an inevitable outcome of social and material differences'.

At the same time, the commitment of the 'social innovators' to social enquiry, as with that of Booth, was problem - orientated to a high degree. They viewed statistics as the essential basis of a 'constructive, relevant economics'[46] and clearly anticipated that official labour statistics would accelerate the process of legislative reform both by mobilising public opinion and by providing a more scientific means by which economic and social policy options might be identified, selected, and monitored. The Labour Department might not necessarily prescribe any legislative programme but it *would*, they hoped, provide a data-bank for legislators and reveal those areas of the labour market most in need of reform. It would, Schloss predicted, 'guide by the light of indisputable facts and figures the demands of the working classes' and demonstrate how far it might 'be possible and prudent for legislators to comply with these demands'.[47] In the tradition of the Booth Enquiry, the 'social innovators' within the Labour Department intended their investigations to establish a statistical framework within which a comprehensive and objective picture of the British labour market would emerge, upon which effective social diagnoses and reforms might be based.

The 'technical innovators', led by Arthur Bowley, George Wood and Udny Yule, were to play a crucial role in the series of enquiries into working-class income, consumption and costs of living undertaken by the Board of Trade after 1902. Whereas the statistical philosophy and techniques of the 'social innovators' can be strongly identified with the Booth Enquiry and the spirit of empirical investigation which informed the social politics of the early 1890s, the 'technical innovators' derived their inspiration from the rise of sociometrics and mathematical statistics at the turn of the century, associated in part with Social Darwinism and in part with the more pragmatic demands for quantitative information generated by the Tariff Reform debate.

It must be emphasised that their interest in social and industrial statistics was very far from being purely technical or theoretical. George Henry Wood was a 'radical with a strong impulse towards social reform' and a 'great sympathy with the aims of the Socialists'. He had been born in Bristol in 1874. A limited formal education and artisan upbringing had been followed by an engineering apprenticeship. Thereafter, by means of a rigorous programme of self-education in local debating societies and improvement classes, he had become by the late 1890s a professional activist on behalf of the Bimetallic League and the Fabian Society in Bristol and South Wales. Meanwhile, however, motivated by a desire to confront the 'Labour Problem' with statistical science, Wood had also begun to accumulate a vast data base for the analysis of working-class income and expenditure patterns, and to cultivate a wide range of contacts at the Royal Statistical Society and British Association. After 1898, collaborative research projects into working conditions and remuneration with social investigators such as B.L. Hutchins and Eleanor Rathbone, and a series of influential, pioneering studies of wage statistics with A.L. Bowley, had culminated, in 1903, with his appointment as statistical investigator to the Board of Trade.[48]

Ideologically, Wood may best be described as a Liberal progressive with strong Socialist tendencies. As a lecturer and journalist, he had articulated a radical concern to minimise the social costs of market forces, to reduce income inequality and to reform the housing stock and working environment of Britain's labour force. Even his advocacy of Bimetallism had focussed upon the positive linkages between currency reform and working-class living standards. He charged the economic system 'with having failed entirely to bring the workers of the country any appropriate reward to their deserts.' 'Surely', he wrote in 1896:

> a mode of society which breeds the vice and misery and degradation and destitution which are to be seen in any thickly populated districts has something wrong in its foundations. And this is so. That wrong is the commercial system built up on lines of

> 'free competition' and the sooner some
> modification preparatory to its entire
> abandonment is adopted the better it will be
> for us all.[49]

However, Wood's flirtations with Socialism were
more in the nature of intellectual exercises than
any genuine ideological commitment, and his
concern to develop a welfare programme that was
community rather than class-based ensured that he
remained within the Liberal fold of Edwardian
social politics.

A.L. Bowley had emerged from a very different
social and educational background to that of Wood.
Born in 1869, the son of the Vicar of SS. Philip
and Jacob in Bristol, Bowley had been educated at
Christs Hospital. Thereafter, he had taken a
first class degree in mathematics at Trinity
College, Cambridge, while, under the influence of
Alfred Marshall, developing a keen interest in
applied statistics. Consequently, although
school-teaching had provided his main income
during the 1890s, his real commitment had focussed
on economic and social research; a commitment
reinforced by his appointment in 1895 as part-time
lecturer in statistics at the newly established
London School of Economics and Political Science.
A series of research papers on labour and income
statistics and on the use of averaging and index
numbers in social investigation, presented at the
Royal Statistical and Economic Societies, the
British Association, and the International
Statistical Institute, had by 1902 established
Bowley's reputation as an applied statistician
within both the scientific community and
Whitehall.[50]

Bowley's social and economic views, although
less explicit than Wood's, were in this period
distinctly progressive. He was critical both of
the Bismarckian paternalism of Conservative social
policy and the indecisiveness of orthodox Liberals
towards welfare issues. His sympathies in the
early 1900s lay with the social radicals and their
efforts to alleviate chronic destitution, to
rationalise the labour market, and to alter the
level and incidence of social investment.[51]

Udny Yule's views are more problematic. He
was reticent about his social, political and
philosophical attitudes, so there is a poverty of
information on which to draw. He had come from 'a
declining elite of army officers, civil servants

and orientalists', had been educated at Winchester and University College, London, and had graduated in engineering in 1892. After a year's research in Germany on experimental physics, Yule had been recruited by the eugenist and mathematical statistician, Karl Pearson, as demonstrator in Pearson's newly founded Biometric Laboratory. Thereafter, during the 1890s and early 1900s, Yule pioneered a series of statistical techniques for data analysis. In particular, he transformed Pearson's coefficient of correlation into a general-purpose tool for interpreting social statistics, and provided formulas for multiple-regression analysis and for the measurement of association between sets of nominal data.[52]

Ideologically, Yule was 'detached' and 'sceptical' in his response to the social politics of the period. Implicit within his quantitative studies of social issues, such as pauper relief, vaccination and old age pensions, was a fundamentally conservative welfare philosophy, and despite his early association with Karl Pearson, he regarded Eugenics and Social Darwinism with 'indifference and hostility', viewing the application of social data within a traditional ameliorative framework rather than one encompassing measures of structural reform and social engineering.[53]

Although the 'technical innovators' often viewed their work as a means of analysing specific social problems and the impact of the existing principles and machinery of social administration, as statistical advisers and investigators for the Board of Trade their motivation was characterised by an overriding concern to refine the methodology of official labour statistics. They were concerned that the work of Quetelet and other European statisticians had not produced a more progressive attitude within Whitehall to statistical theory and methodology. As Yule reflected in 1898:

> the majority of Governmental statisticians are untrained in method; their interests lie with sociology or economics ... and theory necessitating some mathematical knowledge seems a thing wholly apart from this. As a result, experience (as with the old-fashioned engineer) has to replace the co-ordinated concepts of theory as best it can, thus compromising the scope and validity of the

data produced.[54]

Bowley was equally critical of the failure of official statisticians to generate 'significant' data of relevance to the needs of social scientists, and of their proclivity to perpetuate 'mechanical methods of investigation' that were incapable of testing the interdependence of social phenomena and of providing the type of quantitative data demanded by contemporary social and economic debate.[55] In his view, labour policy-makers were confronted in the Edwardian period with an unprecedented data problem: 'To measure the inaccessible, to describe the animal from the single bone, to make firm observations from a shifting base'.[56]

Such a problem, he argued, could only be resolved by the systematic application of mathematical techniques to the conduct of social investigations undertaken by the State. The value of existing labour statistics was, he maintained, seriously impaired by the neglect of summary measures such as the mean, the median, and the coefficient of variation. The evaluation of the causes and incidence of complex social and economic problems was constrained by the lack of systematic time series analysis and of the rigorous application of measures of association and correlation. Furthermore, many contentious welfare issues, such as the cost of living, required the analysis of a range of variables over time for which accurately weighted indexes were wanting.[57] Above all, Bowley contended that, faced with the massive deficiencies of existing social and industrial data (the lack, for example, of a census of consumption and distribution), it was imperative that official statisticians should confront the problem of imperfect data with the theory of probability and statistical sampling; thus providing not only a reliable insight into social problems and trends from a relatively small and economical data base, but also a precise measure of the significance to be attached to official intelligence.[58]

Yule and Bowley did not consider social statisticians within Whitehall to be wholly resistant to statistical theory and methodological innovation and they viewed the Board of Trade as a promising vantage point from which to permeate the production structure of government data with more advanced quantitative techniques.[59]

The Production Structure of Labour Statistics

NOTES

1. Sources: P.R.O., T1, Treasury Board Papers; T9, Treasury Out-Letters; BT13, Board of Trade Establishment Department, Correspondence and Papers; Department of Employment Library, Series 9070, Board of Trade Staff Lists; PP, *Annual Civil Service Estimates* and *Appropriation Accounts*.

2. Ibid.

3. For a full description of the origins and nature of civil service recruitment procedures, see *Majority Report of the Royal Commission on the Civil Service*, PP 1914 (Cd.7338) XVI, Chs. 1-2.

4. For a breakdown of their curricula vitae, see R. Davidson and R. Lowe, 'Bureaucracy and Innovation in British Welfare Policy 1870-1945' in W.J. Mommsen (ed.), *The Emergence of the Welfare State in Britain and Germany* (1981), pp. 265-7.

5. P.R.O., T1/10054B/21516, Board of Trade to Treasury, 13 June 1903.

6. P.R.O., T1/10241B/2068, minute by T.L. Heath, 9 Feb. 1905; T1/8857C/13679, F. Mowatt to G.L. Ryder, 26 Aug. 1894; *Civil Service Gazette*, 10 Nov. 1894, 13 July 1907.

7. *Royal Commission on the Civil Service*, PP 1912-13 (Cd.6535) XV, Q. 13,110.

8. The extent of pay differentials and their impact upon the calibre of statistical work elsewhere in Whitehall are discussed more fully in Chapter 8.

9. Sources: P.R.O., T1/9397B/11241;T1/10054B/21516.

10. P.R.O., BT12/27, memo. by R. Giffen on 'The Statistical Functions of English Departments of State', 18 July 1889.

11. *Report of the British Association for the Advancement of Science*(1910), p. 667.

12. See P.R.O., BT13/134, memo. on 'The Organisation of the Commercial, Labour and Statistical Department' by H. Fountain, 13 March 1909.

13. See Davidson and Lowe, 'Bureaucracy and Innovation in British Welfare Policy', p. 267.

14. *D.N.B.*, *2nd Supplement*, Vol. 2 (1912), pp. 103-5; *Economic Bulletin*, 3 (1910), pp. 140-2.

15. See, e.g., R. Giffen, 'Depression Corrected', *Edinburgh Review*, CLXXXII (1895), pp. 2-26.

16. See, e.g., R. Giffen, 'The Gross and Net Gain of Rising Wages', *Contemporary Review*, LVI (1889), pp. 832-43.

17. Hicks Beach Papers, PC/PP/60, memo. on 'A Minister of Labour' by R. Giffen, 30 April 1892.

18. Ibid., memo. on 'Board of Trade Labour Statistics and the Labour Commission' by R. Giffen, 16 April 1891.

19. *Royal Commission on Labour, Mins. of Ev.*, PP 1893-4 (C.7063) XXXIX Pt 1, Q. 7068; Obituary by A.E. Bateman, *JRSS*,

LXIII (1910), p. 532.

20. L. Brown, *The Board of Trade and the Free Trade Movement: 1830-42* (Oxford, 1958), Ch. 5; P. Abrams, *The Origins of British Sociology* (1968), pp. 21, 29.

21. See *JRSS*, 92 (1929), pp. 641-3; *The Times*, 8 Aug. 1929, Obituary by H. Llewellyn Smith.

22. Clara Collet Diary, 20 Aug. 1904.

23. See below, Ch. 10.

24. J.M. Bellamy and J. Saville (eds.), *Dictionary of Labour Biography*, Vol. 2 (1974), pp. 71-5.

25. C.J. Drummond: Former Conservative Secretary of London Society of Compositors. J.J. Dent: Apprenticed bricklayer. Prominent in London Radical politics of 1870s and 1880s. Leading figure in Co-operative Movement, W.E.A., and Working Mens' Clubs and Institute Union.

26. Beatrice Webb Diary, 18 Oct. 1887; J. Burnett, 'Trade Unions as a means of improving the conditions of labour' in J. Oliphant (ed.), *The Claims of Labour* (Edinburgh, 1886), pp. 18, 29, 33, 36.

27. Burnett, 'Trade Unions', pp. 8, 30, 39; E. Howe and H.E. Waite, *The London Society of Compositors* (1948), pp. 193-4.

28. H.L. Smith: 1893-7 Labour Commissioner; 1897-1903 Deputy C(omptroller) - G(eneral); 1903-7 C-G; 1907-19 Permanent Secretary of Board of Trade.

C.E. Collet: 1893-1903 Labour Correspondent; 1903-20 Senior Investigator for Women's Industries.

D.F. Schloss: 1893-9 Personal Staff C-G; 1899-1902 Investigator; 1902-7 Senior Investigator; 1907-8 Director, Census of Production.

A.W. Fox: 1895-7 Agricultural Labour Correspondent; 1897-1903 Assistant Labour Commissioner; 1903-7 Labour Commissioner and Deputy C-G; 1907-9 C-G.

29. Llewellyn Smith's early career is reviewed in detail in R. Davidson, 'Llewellyn Smith, the Labour Department and government growth 1886-1909' in G. Sutherland (ed.) *Studies in the growth of nineteenth-century government* (1972), pp. 239-45. See also, A. Kadish, *The Oxford Economists in the Late Nineteenth Century* (Oxford, 1982), pp. 18-30, 70-5.

30. Davidson, 'Llewellyn Smith', p. 240.

31. Kadish, *Oxford Economists*, p. 73.

32. Ibid., p.73.

33. Ibid., pp. 72, 94-5, 100, 119; Davidson, 'Llewellyn Smith', pp. 240-3.

34. Clara Collet Diary, 9 June 1878 to 28 Aug. 1891, *passim*; C.E. Collet, 'Obituary: Henry Higgs', *Economic Journal*, 50 (1940), pp. 559-61.

35. Clara Collet Diary, 10 Sept. 1876 to 28 Aug. 1891, 4 Oct. 1898-31 Dec. 1914, *passim*.

36. *Economic Journal*, 22 (1912), pp. 636-8; D.F. Schloss, 'The Jew as a Workman', *Nineteenth Century*, 29 (1891),

p. 107; 'The Sweating System', *Fortnightly Review*, 42 (1887), pp. 835-53; 'Healthy Homes for the Working Classes', *Fortnightly Review*, 43 (1888), pp. 526-37.

37. Passfield Papers, Schloss to Webb, 3 July 1892.

38. D.F. Schloss, 'Industrial Co-operation', *Contemporary Review*, 57 (1890), p. 568.

39. D.F. Schloss, 'The Road to Social Peace', *Fortnightly Review*, 49 (1891), pp. 255-7.

40. Wilson Fox Papers, 'In Memoriam'; A.E. Bateman, 'Arthur Wilson Fox', *JRSS*, 72 (1909), pp. 64-6.

41. J.H. Robb, *The Primrose League 1883-1906* (Columbia, 1942), pp. 9-10, 37.

42. See especially, Wilson Fox Papers, satirical poem by Fox on 'The Strength of the Race'.

43. See, e.g., PP 1906 (Cd.2978) LXXVI, pp. 26-7; Wilson Fox Papers, Rider Haggard to Fox, 25 July 1905.

44. See H. Llewellyn Smith, *Methods of Social Inquiry* (Oxford, 1890), p. 4; Clara Collet Diary, 10 Sept. 1876-20 Aug. 1891, *passim*; D.F. Schloss, 'The Road to Social Peace', *Fortnightly Review*, XLIX (1891), pp.255-6; Schloss, 'The Reorganisation of our Labour Department', *JRSS*, LVI(1893), p. 61.

45. Kadish, *Oxford Economists*, p. 100.

46. Clara Collet Diary, 16 Nov. 1890.

47. *JRSS*, LVI (1893), p. 61.

48. G.H. Wood Papers, unpublished biography, pp. 1-12, *JRSS*, 108 (1945), pp. 485-7.

49. Wood Papers, unpublished biography, p. 5.

50. R.G.D. Allen, 'Arthur Lyon Bowley' in *International Encyclopaedia of the Social Sciences*, Vol. 2 (1968), pp. 134-6.

51. Ibid., p. 134; Bowley Papers, 'Socialism and Social Reform', unpublished address by A.L. Bowley, c.1896.

52. D.A. MacKenzie, *Statistics in Britain 1865-1930: The Social Construction of Scientific Knowledge* (Edinburgh, 1981), pp. 180-1; M.G. Kendall, 'G. Udny Yule' in *International Encyclopaedia of the Social Sciences*, Vol. 16 (1968), pp. 589-91.

53. R.A. Kent, *A History of British Empirical Sociology* (1981), pp. 96-7; MacKenzie, *Statistics in Britain*, pp. 173-4, 181-2.

54. Yule Papers, Box 39, History of Statistics: Notebook.

55. A.L. Bowley, 'Address to the Economic Section of the British Association', *JRSS*, 69 (1906), pp. 540-8.

56. Ibid., p. 540.

57. Ibid., pp. 546-54.

58. A.L. Bowley, 'The Improvement of Official Statistics', *JRSS*, 71 (1908), pp. 469-77.

59. Pearson Papers, File 905, G.U. Yule to K. Pearson, 15 May 1900; Bowley, 'Address to the British Association', p. 542.

Part Three

THE   OUTPUT

Chapter 5

THE COMMODITY STRUCTURE OF LABOUR STATISTICS:
RATIONALE AND CONTENT

Figure 5.1 provides an overview of the commodity
structure of the Board of Trade's output of labour
statistics and of the major shifts in the
allocation of its investigative resources during
the period 1886-1914. Six main areas of enquiry
may be identified; industrial unrest, trade
unionism, labour remuneration, working-class
expenditure and costs of living, unemployment, and
foreign and colonial welfare provisions.

INDUSTRIAL UNREST

As Figure 5.1 reveals, in terms of funding,
information with respect to industrial relations
constituted a significant percentage (c.17%) of
the Labour Department's statistical output
throughout the period but was especially prominent
during the sub-periods 1889-94 and 1910-13, when
strikes and lockouts were most numerous and
protracted. The information was designed to
fulfil four main objectives. The overriding
concern was to explain the apparent breakdown of
labour relations which, it was feared, would not
only endanger social stability but also disrupt
production, intensify resistance to technical
innovation and weaken Britain's cost-
competitiveness in world markets.[1] By presenting
a clear picture of the nature and extent of
industrial disputes, it was intended to provide an
informed basis for contemporary debate on labour
unrest, to indicate its deviancy from accepted
norms of industrial relations and to facilitate
the operation of private and statutory collective
bargaining machinery.[2]
    Secondly, the Labour Department attempted to

Figure 5.1: Labour Statistics 1886-1914: Allocation of Budget[3]

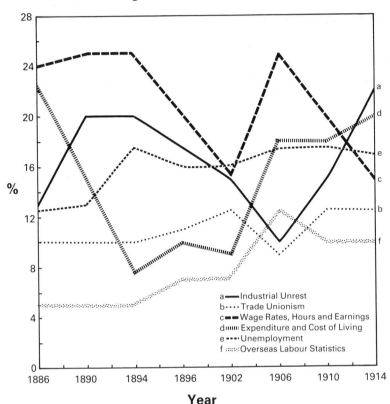

relate the incidence of unrest to the state of the
labour market, on the assumption that disputes
were primarily generated not by any fundamental
conflict of interest between Capital and Labour
but by their uncertainty as to the realities of
the wages and profits funds due to fluctuations in
the employment cycle.[4] Thirdly, the Department's
enquiries into strikes and lockouts were intended
to demonstrate the cost-ineffectiveness of
disputes in terms of earnings and profits, and,
increasingly, in terms of their repercussions upon
national efficiency.[5] Finally, they were designed
to identify and to publicise the scope of existing
conciliation and arbitration procedures within
British industry, the value of such consensus
strategies available to management and trade-union
leaders, including the facilities provided by the

Board of Trade under the 1896 Conciliation Act, and the relative merits and demerits of statutory provisions for the maintenance of industrial order.

The basis of government intelligence on industrial relations during the late-Victorian and Edwardian period - the Labour Department's *Annual Reports on Strikes and Lockouts* - clearly reflected these objectives. They provided: firstly, an increasingly detailed analysis of strikes and lockouts, including their causes, incidence, occupational and geographical distribution, their duration and magnitude, mode of settlement and outcome; secondly, data on the relationship between the number, extent and duration of labour disputes and fluctuations in the level of unemployment and business activity; thirdly, an estimate of the costs incurred by unions and employers during stoppages (including wages foregone, strike pay, fixed capital laid idle, outlays in stopping and re-opening works, and payment of fixed charges and salaries) and of the aggregate number of working days lost to industrial output; and fourthly, information on the preventive role of local and district trade boards in adjusting wage rates and working conditions in many staple sectors of the British economy.

In addition, during and immediately after periods of exceptional labour unrest, the Board of Trade undertook separate enquiries into specific aspects of industrial relations. In particular, as for example in its reports on profit-sharing, gain-sharing and co-partnership, it examined the viability of schemes designed to reinforce an identity of interest between employer and employed, and to enhance work incentives and productivity. It also focussed its enquiries (for example, those undertaken in the early 1890s by John Burnett for the Royal Commission on Labour and by George Askwith after 1909 on overseas legislation relating to dispute procedures) upon the likely costs and benefits of the State imposing compulsory conciliation and/or compulsory arbitration with legally binding awards as a means of reducing the economic and social effects of industrial strife. Meanwhile, the Labour Department carefully monitored proceedings under the Conciliation Act, providing extensive information on the origins, duration, size, trade distribution, and outcome of disputes in which the

Board of Trade became involved, on how and in what form (whether conciliation, arbitration, or mediation) government intervention under the Act was initiated, and on the success rate of such intervention.

TRADE UNIONISM

The level of expenditure on trade union data by the Labour Department was less volatile, remaining relatively static between 1886-94 and, thereafter, slowly rising on trend. Information on the extent and 'relevant' characteristics of trade unionism was perceived as performing three main functions: Firstly, to validate the stabilising and conciliatory roles of unionisation, and to 'erode the illusion' that its main objective was to foster strikes and that its leaders were pre-eminently 'social disturbers or industrial incendiaries inflaming the passions of their constituents'.[6] Secondly, the provision of detailed intelligence on trade union developments at both national and local level was considered vital to the success of the Board of Trade's conciliation and arbitration services.[7] Thirdly, the Labour Department was concerned to stress the role of unions as provident institutions in the social life of the community. In the 1880s and 1890s, such concern focussed upon their welfare potential as primary agencies of accident, sickness and unemployment insurance.[8] In the Edwardian period, the emphasis shifted to the inadequacy of trade union provisions, to their vulnerability to variations in business activity and the age structure of the labour force, and to their utility as a justification or model for State welfare initiatives.[9]

Accordingly, the Board of Trade annually reported upon the estimated level and distribution of unionisation within British industry, and on the survival rate of existing trade union organisations. These reports also incorporated a breakdown of the income and expenditure patterns of leading trades unions, with information on the ratio of strike to benefit expenditure, on the number and percentage of unionists in receipt of each type of benefit, on the level of contributions and benefits *per capita*, and on the working expenses, financial reserves and accumulated funds of selected unions together with details of their investment portfolios.

WAGE RATES, HOURS AND EARNINGS

Data on wage rates, hours and earnings figured prominently in the commodity structure of the Labour Department's statistical output throughout the period, especially in the years 1886-94 and 1904-10, and accounted for as much as 25 per cent of the Department's budget for enquiries. Their primary function was to determine the 'question of social distribution' central to a range of contemporary economic and welfare debates, and their provision reflected both a conservative and progressive rationale. From a conservative viewpoint, it was desirable to clarify both the long-term upward trend in labour remuneration and the legitimacy of short-term fluctuations in wage rates according to market forces.[10] Earnings and wage data were perceived as essential components in the education of the workforce as to the 'facts of life' of wage determination within a mature economy. More generally, it was anticipated that such data would reduce social discontent by demonstrating a secular rise in the real earnings of the British working classes and by deflating inflammatory claims as to the extent of low-income destitution and of the so-called 'submergeable population'.[11]

From a progressive standpoint, systematic information on working-class incomes was seen as vital as a basis from which welfare measures such as minimum wage legislation or poor law reform might be justified and their effects monitored.[12] As one leading radical statistician observed, enquiries into the wages and earnings of the labouring classes 'proceed tacitly on the assumption that as a matter of social expediency and social justice, the mass of the community should have a comfortable subsistence'.[13] The growing concern of New Liberalism after 1905 with the social and economic costs of income inequality and underconsumption and with the relationship between unemployment and destitution, generated additional demand for earnings data.[14]

Such information was also intended to address the equally contentious question of 'technical economic distribution'; to provide, in conjunction with comprehensive production data, the basis for analysing the wage costs of British industry, the relationship of wages to profits, the cost-effectiveness and productivity of the labour force, and the impact upon wage levels and differentials of technical innovation.[15] The Tariff Reform controversy constituted yet another strand of demand for information on wage rates and working-class earnings, as, implicit within the debate over fiscal reform was a range of assumptions with regard to British working-class incomes and purchasing power, the social depth and elasticity of domestic demand and the cost (pre-eminently labour cost) competitiveness of British industry.[16]

The Board of Trade's response to these demands was twofold. Firstly, it provided regular reports on the principal shifts in the recognised market rate of wages and working hours affecting the industrial workforce, and on the estimated cost of such shifts to the wages bill of the country. These reports provided details of the relative and absolute magnitude of wage increases and decreases, of their seasonality and method of determination, and of the number, occupation, and locality of workers involved. Increasingly, such data was provided in the form of time series to provide an overview of both trends and fluctuations in the market rate of labour remuneration. In addition, at irregular intervals, to facilitate the interpretation of wage-rate statistics and their use in computing working-class earnings, the Labour Department issued supplementary volumes on the methods of wage payments in force in various industries and the principal piece lists and standard time rates operating in British industry.

Secondly, during the late-Victorian and Edwardian period, the Board of Trade produced two massive wages and earnings censuses - for the years 1886 and 1906. They varied significantly in their coverage and degree of statistical sophistication, but together they provided extensive data on the average wage rates and earnings of the manual labour classes in the leading sectors of the British economy. The census reports incorporated detailed breakdowns of the level and distribution of annual and weekly rates of pay and earnings according to the age, sex, trade, locality, and occupational status of the workforce.

WORKING CLASS EXPENDITURE AND COST OF LIVING

Wages and earnings data were a vital adjunct to the fourth category of Labour Department enquiries; those relating to the cost and standard of living of the working classes. During the period 1886-1914, the level of resource allocation on cost of living enquiries was extremely variable. It accounted for over 20 per cent of the Board of Trade's appropriation for labour statistics in the late 1880s, but for less than 11 per cent throughout the period 1890-1902. Thereafter, however, it absorbed a rapidly growing proportion of the Department's investigative resources; in the range of 17 to 20 per cent between 1903 and 1914.

As with other areas of the Department's statistical output, the supply of expenditure and cost of living data was designed to address a range of contemporary economic and social issues and ideologies. Firstly, it was viewed by both right and left-wing collectivists as vital in exposing the insufficiency of wage earnings to maintain large sections of the workforce at a level consistent with social justice and economic efficiency, and the severe social costs consequent upon rigid adherence to orthodox market criteria in wage determination.[17] Such information would, it was anticipated, provide invaluable national and comparative regional data on the extent of destitution and urban degeneration, thus illuminating the poverty debate generated by the local studies of Booth and Rowntree, by the findings of the Physical Deterioration Committee, and by the polemics of the National Efficiency Movement and Social Darwinism.[18] Meanwhile, by revealing the realities of working-class income and expenditure patterns, cost of living enquiries would demonstrate the inability of even organised labour adequately to protect its purchasing power against irregular earnings due to accident, sickness, unemployment and old age, and the consequent need for statutory schemes of insurance, superannuation and income maintenance.[19]

Secondly, demand for cost of living data sprang from the quest of social radicals for some form of scientific and defensible basis for a shift away from the conventional market determinants of wage rates to the social criterion of a 'minimum living wage' related to local variations in rents and commodity prices.[20] Armed with cost of living information, it was anticipated that labour negotiators would abandon their traditional tendency to bargain within the bounds of established relativities and comparative market criteria.[21] This strand of demand was reinforced by concern within Whitehall itself, especially the Post Office, to determine the pay scales of public employees on the basis of systematic comparisons with the *real* wages obtaining in similar occupations in the private sector and of regional variations in the cost of living.[22]

Thirdly, the demand for data on working-class family budgets reflected an increasing focus within contemporary economic and welfare debate upon the participation of women within the labour market. A range of 'progressive' ideologies, including the National Efficiency Movement and Social Imperialism, were anxious to quantify the degree to which female employment merely reflected inadequate remuneration of the male workforce, with an attendant rise in infant mortality and degeneration of the moral and physical potential of the urban home environment.[23] Data on the relationship of female earnings to family subsistence was also of intense interest to professions such as schoolteaching and the Civil Service, anxious to establish suitable criteria for the remuneration of female employees (especially single women) whose share of the workforce had risen dramatically since 1870.[24]

Fourthly, as with its wage and earnings data, the Board of Trade's cost of living enquiries were very much a function of the Tariff Reform Debate and the most vital consumption and price indexes produced by the Labour Department were incorporated within the celebrated Fiscal Blue Books on British and foreign trade and industrial conditions.[25] The fiscal debate raised a variety of issues relating to the standard of living of British Labour, to the trend of real wages in the United Kingdom as compared with that of its major industrial competitors, to the resilience of working-class purchasing power, and to the relative costs and benefits for working-class consumption of cheap supplies of food and raw materials as opposed to more stable employment consequent upon a protected domestic and imperial market.[26]

Finally, after 1908, cost of living data were

increasingly viewed in government circles as a valuable 'index of industrial discontent'. Indeed, the cost of living enquiry undertaken in 1912 was a direct outcome of the protracted and violent labour unrest of 1911. It was specifically designed to elucidate the economic and social pressures underlying working-class militancy and to establish the relative significance of falling real wages as compared with rising social expectations.[27]

Accordingly, during the Edwardian period, the Board of Trade produced a mass of information on the average retail prices of the main components of working-class consumption (i.e. food, clothing, rent, fuel and light), both in the United Kingdom and other leading industrialised economies, including the United States and Germany. Such data provided the basis of a series of retail price indexes measuring chronological, regional and international variations in the urban cost of living. When integrated with the Department's extensive earnings data, its cost of living statistics generated additional estimates as to approximate levels and variations in real wages according to occupation and locality, and more importantly, some measure of the relative purchasing power of the British urban workforce as compared with its counterpart in other maturing economies. In an effort to obtain an accurate 'weighting' for its cost of living indexes, the Labour Department also undertook a series of investigations into the patterns of working-class expenditure in the United Kingdom and abroad. In the process, it produced a range of information on the economic and sociological determinants of working-class consumption patterns, and in particular, on their relationship to variations in income levels and family structure, and on the significance of female and child earnings in working-class family budgets.

UNEMPLOYMENT

As Figure 5.1 indicates, the level of resources allocated by the Board of Trade to the production of unemployment data and intelligence followed a broadly cyclical pattern fluctuating around a rising trend. The fluctuations, with upswings in 1892-4, 1903-5 and 1908-10, reflected both the varying intensity of governmental and public concern over the social and economic costs of unemployment and the level of trade and business activity,[28] while the trend was symptomatic of the increasing stress of economic and welfare debate after 1880 upon labour utilisation, and the shift of a range of political ideologies towards a commitment to more extensive State intervention in the labour market.[29]

Throughout the period 1886-1914, employment and unemployment data were used by the Board of Trade to modify and interpret a range of information on working-class earnings, consumption and industrial unrest.[30] However, their collection had also a number of discrete objectives. The enquiries undertaken between 1886 and 1900 were largely motivated by social fear of the unemployed and under-employed mobs of 'outcast London' produced by its crisis of social and industrial development in the last quarter of the nineteenth century and by the inability of existing Poor Law provisions to cope with the problem of urban destitution.[31] As Stedman Jones has demonstrated, this crisis engendered a fundamental re-orientation of middle-class attitudes towards the unemployed, reinforced by the radical empiricism of the 1890s and by Social Imperialist and Darwinist theories of 'urban degeneration'.[32] This, in turn, created an upswing in demand for unemployment data with which to categorise the unemployed and the causes of 'want of employment'. In particular, there existed an overriding concern to provide a scientific base upon which the so-called 'residuum' or 'industrial sediment' might be quantified and differentiated from the respectable working-class unemployed, thus enabling the 'rational' selection and systematic application of appropriate policy options, including measures of positive or negative eugenics designed to improve national efficiency and reduce the financial burden of Poor Law expenditure upon the ratepayer.[33]

A similar rationale underlay the Board of Trade's unemployment enquiries during the years 1900-5. The element of social fear remained with the recurrence of organised demonstrations during the downswing of the trade cycle 1901-4, backed by the Labour Movement and radical press.[34] These developments, coupled with the further erosion of confidence in the existing agencies of welfare crisis control created by the Select Committee on Physical Deterioriation, inspired a Conservative initiative to rationalise the local provision of relief and to create more permanent machinery to mitigate the impact of unemployment upon the income and efficiency of the respectable able-bodied workforce, culminating in the 1905 Unemployed Workmen Act.[35] Such an initiative required extensive data on the level and incidence of unemployment, on its relationship to pauperism and the trade cycle, and on the efficiency and clientele of existing schemes administered by local authorities.

Meanwhile, as Harris has documented, the unemployment data of the Board of Trade had become a veritable *vade mecum* for participants in the tariff reform debate. The protectionist argument begged a range of questions relating to the level of labour utilisation within the British economy as compared with that obtaining in protected industrial economies such as Germany and America; also to the displacement effect upon the British workforce of foreign competition, and to the relationship between unemployment and industrial productivity.[36] More generally, unemployment data was vital as a rough indicator of the structure and performance of the British economy when operating within a free trade policy and as a means of identifying variations in the sectoral impact and relevance of protectionist legislation.

Finally, between 1905 and 1914, the Board of Trade's output of employment and unemployment statistics was a direct response to the developing programme of New Liberalism to construct a national policy of unemployment provisions outwith the Poor Law.[37] Its motivation was, therefore, a need to monitor the merits and demerits of existing statutory and voluntary unemployment provisions, to furnish a series of feasibility studies on a range of policy options designed to co-ordinate the labour market and insulate working-class living standards against cyclical unemployment, and to monitor the effect of fresh legislation with a view to its application to additional areas of the workforce.

The Board of Trade's efforts to satisfy these varying strands of demand for unemployment data can best be viewed within a tripartite framework; the course, causes and cure of unemployment. Firstly, using union benefit records and employers' returns on the continuity of production, the *Labour Gazette* and *Annual Abstract of Labour Statistics* provided rough estimates of the level and trend of unemployment in the major industrial regions and sectors of the economy. Extensive data were produced on seasonal and cyclical fluctuations in employment in the main capital-intensive industries such as engineering and shipbuilding, supplemented after 1904 by an employment index extending back to the 1860s. For selected trades, a more detailed breakdown of the aggregate and *per capita* duration of unemployment was supplied. In addition, the Labour Department devoted increasing attention in its statistical output to the relative incidence of unemployment and able-bodied pauperism.

This information complemented the special enquiries of the Department into the causes of unemployment and under-employment undertaken in the mid-1890s. In the preface to its *Report on Agencies and Methods for Dealing with the Unemployed* and its statistical evidence to the Select Committee on Distress from Want of Employment, the Department provided a two-dimensional classification of different types of trade fluctuation and different types of unemployed workmen, which, with minor variations was used as the standard framework of analysis throughout the period. These enquiries also incorporated new insights into the relationship between economic fluctuations, industrial structure, and the disorganisation of the labour market, and into the interaction between moral or individual and environmental or aggregative factors in the determination of patterns of unemployment; insights which furnished the basis after 1903 of quarterly intelligence reports to the Cabinet on the state of the labour market, which integrated a growing range of financial and commercial indicators.

The Labour Department also afforded late-Victorian and Edwardian parliamentary and public debate with some means of appraising the policy options available for stabilising employment and reducing the social and economic costs of unemployment. It examined the performance of a range of existing welfare measures, including trade-union benefit, outdoor relief, private and municipal labour bureaux, labour colonies, and public works; monitoring especially their impact upon the labour market and work incentives and their moral and financial credibility. In addition, the Department attempted to provide a data bank for the appraisal of a similar variety of innovative proposals, including land reform, subsidised emigration, tariff reform, immigration controls and contra-cyclical public works, culminating in its celebrated briefings for the Poor Law Commission on the viability of a national system of labour exchanges and compulsory, contributory unemployment insurance.

FOREIGN AND COLONIAL WELFARE PROVISIONS

Late-nineteenth and early-twentieth century British welfare debate created an unprecedented demand for information on the content and outcome of overseas welfare ideas and measures,[38] with a consequent shift in the method of enquiry from largely random private investigations to more fully institutionalised and systematic official reports. This transition was reflected in the pattern of the Board of Trade's resource allocation. The collection of foreign welfare data absorbed only a modest percentage of the Board's budget for enquiries during the years 1886-1900 but its share rose sharply during the Edwardian period (see Figure 5.1). As with fluctuations in other areas of the Department's statistical activities, the explanation for this upswing is complex. However, three broad categories of motivation may be identified.

Firstly, in a very general sense, the demand for information on overseas welfare measures reflected a concern to establish the practicality of proposed policy innovations within British welfare debate, or alternatively, to legitimate existing patterns of social provision. Countries such as Germany and Australasia were effectively perceived as social laboratories whose welfare experiments might be monitored and subsequently adopted,[39] subject to stringent import controls as to their applicability to Britain's social and industrial structure, their accordance with prevailing economic and financial ideology and their compatibility with native, middle-class assumptions concerning the appropriate mechanism and objectives of the labour market.

Secondly, this search for information on the level and efficiency of public and private social investment abroad was invigorated after 1900 by the tariff reform debate. In particular, protectionists were concerned to demonstrate the linkages between tariff revenue and welfare expenditure and the ability of protectionist regimes to fund social reform without eroding profit margins or managerial incentives.[40] The increasing focus of official inquiry upon foreign welfare provisions, and in particular upon German social legislation, was also a logical corollary of the National Efficiency Movement. As Hay has demonstrated, the concern shared by the political elite of the efficiency school and the British business community at the competitive threat of German industry in overseas and domestic markets engendered a growing interest in the relationship between German social collectivism and the productivity of its workforce.[41]

Finally, an appraisal of overseas labour market legislation was viewed by the governmental elite as essential in devising new strategies of social control. Faced with the social strains of a maturing economy, British policy-makers were concerned to monitor overseas legislation (as in Canada and Australasia) designed to contain major industrial disputes and to maintain the continuity of essential services and output.[42] They were equally anxious to examine the use of welfare policy (as in Germany) to alleviate the long-run social pressures arising out of discontinuities in economic development and the revolutionary threat of social democracy; a welfare strategy which appeared to provide a positive response to Socialism while retaining industrial control both at the point of production and at the level of the national economy.[43]

The Board of Trade employed a range of outlets in disseminating information on overseas welfare developments. From 1893, it used the *Labour Gazette* to provide regular reports on the content and progress of foreign labour legislation. A somewhat more quantitative appraisal of such developments was provided after 1899 in a series of *Abstracts of Foreign Labour Statistics*. Initially, they concentrated upon wage levels, industrial unrest, levels of unionisation and hours of employment, but increasingly their focus shifted to conciliation and arbitration procedures and measures of social insurance. In addition, the Labour Department provided comparative statistical and descriptive analyses for a range of official investigations into the more serious imperfections of the British labour market, such as the Select Committees on Home Work, on Distress from Want of Employment and on Trade Disputes and Trade Combinations. Finally, as specific welfare issues moved to the forefront of public debate, the Board of Trade undertook independent enquiries into the relevance and efficiency of foreign welfare policies. Its reports on overseas provisions for invalidity and old age (1899), on foreign agencies and methods for dealing with the unemployed (1904), on the Canadian Industrial Disputes Act, and on Dominion and foreign laws relating to stoppages in public utilities (1912), well illustrate this aspect of the Board's intelligence work.

NOTES

1. R. Davidson, 'The Board of Trade and Industrial Relatioɩɩs 1896-1914', *Historical Journal*, 21 (1978), pp. 571, 584.

2. A.J. Mundella, 'Labour Statistics and Industrial Peace', *Ielp*, 3 (April 1891), p. 49; D.F. Schloss, 'The Reorganisation of our Labour Department', *JRSS*, LVI (1893), pp. 51-2.

3. Sources as for Ch. 4, Figure 4.1.

4. See, e.g., *6th Report on Strikes and Lockouts*, PP 1894 (C.7566) LXXXI Pt 1, pp. 10-11.

5. *3rd Report on Strikes and Lockouts*, PP 1890-1 (C.6476) LXXXVIII, p. 8; *5th Report on Strikes and Lockouts*, PP 1894 (C.7403) LXXXI Pt 1, p. 34.

6. See especially, *2nd Report on Trade Unions*, PP 1888 (C.5505) CVII, p. 5; *5th Report on Trade Unions*, PP 1893-94 (C.6990) CII, p. 4.

7. R. Davidson, 'Social Conflict and Social Administration: the Conciliation Act in British Industrial Relations', in T.C. Smout (ed.), *The Search for Wealth and Stability* (1979), pp. 183-4.

8. *8th Report on Trade Unions*, PP 1896 (C.8232) XCIII, pp. xv-xvi; *10th Report on Trade Unions*, PP 1898 (C.9013) CIII, p. xxvi.

9. See, e.g., *16th Report on Trade Unions*, PP 1909 (Cd.4651) LXXXIX, pp. xxvii-xlii.

10. See, e.g., *1st and 5th Reports on Changes in Wages and Hours of Labour*, PP 1894 (C.7567) LXXXI Pt II, p. ix; 1898 (C.8975) LXXXVIII, p. xi.

11. *Memorandum on the Progress made in carrying out the Arrangements for Collecting and Publishing Statistics relating to Labour*, by R. Giffen, PP 1888 (433) CVII, p. 4; P.R.O., Lab 2/1555/L1099/1903, memo. by H. Llewellyn Smith, 18 July 1903. Llewellyn Smith regarded a wage census as 'the best (though bad at best) method of applying some statistical test to the wild assertions made as to the "submergeable" population'.

12. A.L. Bowley, 'Address to the Economic Science and Statistics Section of the British Association', *JRSS*, 69 (1906), pp. 554-5.

13. 'Extracts from an essay on wage statistics and the next Census of the United States' by Professor R. Mayo Smith, PP 1888 (433) 107, p. 9.

14. M. Freeden, *The New Liberalism: An Ideology of Social Reform* (Oxford, 1978), pp. 128-32; P. Ford, *Social Theory and Social Practice* (Shannon, 1968), pp. 105-7.

15. A.W. Flux, 'Gleanings from the Census of Production Report', *JRSS* 76 (1913), pp. 561-89; P.R.O., BT11/2/C6378/1906, proceedings of a conference between Lloyd George and M.P.s interested in manufactures, 25 Oct. 1906.

16. For an explicit statement of this role of labour statistics, see P.R.O, T1/10241B/2068, minute by G. Barstow, 7 Feb. 1905.

17. See, e.g., Henry Higgs, 'Workmen's Budgets', *JRSS*, 56 (1893), pp. 264-5; *Report of the British Association for the Advancement of Science*, (1899), pp. 817-8.

18. P.R.O., LAB2/1555/L1099/1903, minute by H. Llewellyn Smith, 18 July 1903.

19. G.H. Wood Papers, DC/30, unpublished lecture on 'Labour statistics and the prevention of destitution' n.d.

20. H.V. Emy, *Liberals, Radicals and Social Politics 1892-1914* (Cambridge, 1973), pp. 29-30; Freeden, *New Liberalism*, pp. 163-4; *Report of the B.A.A.S.* (1898), p. 823.

21. P.R.O., LAB2/29/C7067/1910, minute by G.R. Askwith, 14 Aug. 1910.

22. *S.C. on Post Office Servants, Mins. of Ev.*, PP 1906 (380) XII Pt 1, p. 510.

23. C. Dyehouse, 'Working Class Mothers and Infant Mortality in England 1895-1914', *Journal of Social History*, 12 (1978-79), pp. 248-67; A. Davin, 'Imperialism and Motherhood', *History Workshop*, 5 (1978), pp. 9-65.

24. *R.C. on the Civil Service, Mins. of Ev.*, PP 1914 (Cd.7340) XVI, pp. 403-5.

25. PP 1903 (Cd.1761) LXVII; 1905 (Cd.2337) LXXXIV; 1909 (Cd.4594) CII.

26. A. Sykes, *Tariff Reform in British Politics* (Oxford, 1979), pp. 56-7, 135,139; P.R.O., 30/60/44, G.W. Balfour Papers, Llewellyn Smith to Sir F. Hopwood, 12 Sept. 1904, memo. on 'The social effects of fiscal proposals'.

27. *S.C. on Post Office Servants, Appendices to Mins. of Ev.*, PP 1913 (268) XIII, p. 2; *R.C. on the Civil Service, Mins. of Ev.*, PP 1914 (Cd.7340) XVI, pp. 403-4.

28. S. Pettit, 'Contemporary Perceptions of the Trade Cycle in the Context of Social Policy 1886-1914', unpublished M.A. thesis, Edinburgh University (1982), Ch. 2.

29. J. Harris, *Unemployment and Politics: A Study in English Social Policy 1886-1914* (Oxford, 1972).

30. See, e.g., *5th Report on Strikes and Lockouts*, PP 1894 (C.7403) LXXXI Pt 1, p. 7.

31. Harris, *Unemployment and Politics*, Chs. 1-2.

32. G. Stedman Jones, *Outcast London: A Study in the Relationship between Classes in Victorian Society* (Oxford, 1971), Chs. 16-17.

33. D.A. MacKenzie, *Statistics in Britain 1865-1930* (Edinburgh, 1981), p. 40.

34. K.D. Brown, *Labour and Unemployment 1900-1914* (Newton Abbot, 1971), Chs. 1-2; P.R.O., LAB2/1478/L211/1903, memo. by J.J. Dent, 4 Feb. 1903.

35. R. Soloway, 'Counting the Degenerates; The Statistics of Race Deterioration in Edwardian England', *Journal of*

Contemporary History, 17 (1982), pp. 137-64; Harris, *Unemployment and Politics*, Ch. 4.

36. Harris, *Unemployment and Politics*, pp. 213-7, 221-2; Sykes, *Tariff Reform*, Chs. 2-3.

37. Harris, *Unemployment and Politics*, Chs. 5-6.

38. .T. Higgins, *States of Welfare, Comparative Analysis in Sociaι Policy* (1981), Ch. 3.

39. J.R. Hay, *The Origins of the Liberal Welfare Reforms 1906-1914* (1975), pp. 15-16.

40. Sykes, *Tariff Reform*, pp. 42-3, 56.

41. J.R. Hay, 'Employers and Social Policy in Britain: the evolution of welfare legislation, 1905-14', *Social History*, 2 (1977), pp. 443-4; G.R. Searle, *The Quest for National Efficiency* (Oxford, 1971), pp. 29-32.

42. See, e.g., P.R.O., CAB37/107/98, 9 Aug. 1911; Lord Askwith, *Industrial Problems and Disputes* (1920), Ch. XXIV.

43. J.R. Hay, 'The British Business Community, Social Insurance and the German Example' in W.J. Mommsen (ed.), *The Emergence of the Welfare State in Britain and Germany* (1981), pp. 107-32.

Chapter 6

THE COMMODITY STRUCTURE OF LABOUR STATISTICS: THE
SHORTFALL

While, in comparison with other departments of
social and industrial administration, the
commodity structure of the Board of Trade's labour
statistical output was highly impressive in its
range, it also exhibited severe and significant
limitations in all its main areas of enquiry. Not
only did their terms of reference ignore vital
aspects and areas (both geographical and social)
of the labour market, there also existed a marked
shortfall between the Board's investigative aims
and its achievements.

INDUSTRIAL UNREST

Such deficiencies were especially evident in its
efforts to identify and to measure the
determinants of industrial unrest. Its categories
of analysis tended to reflect the traditional
priorities of mid-Victorian consensus unionism
rather than the broader socio-economic motivation
and confrontation ideology of late-nineteenth and
early-twentieth-century labour militancy. Hence,
while issues of hours and wage rates and working
conditions (narrowly defined) received extensive
coverage, those relating to long-term trends in
real wages, occupational status, labour intensity,
and the impact of technical and managerial
innovation upon the social relationships of
production, were relatively ignored. This
tendency was strongly reinforced by the fact that
the Board's data over-represented unrest within
the more conservative and bureaucratic sectors of
trade unionism. Unofficial stoppages were not
systematically monitored and small disputes, which

often reflected rank and file unrest, were
arbitrarily excluded from the Board's detailed
returns, without regard to their potential
significance.[1]   Its attempts to relate the
incidence of industrial unrest to fluctuations in
the labour market were equally deficient.   There
was a noticeable failure to produce a reliable
index of unrest and to correlate it with available
information on levels of employment and economic
activity, even after the Department had
constructed an employment index.[2] Similarly, no
reliable measure was provided of the linkages
between the incidence of strikes and lockouts and
the chronology and amplitude of the business
cycle.
    The Labour Department's efforts to
demonstrate the cost-effectiveness of industrial
stoppages as compared with conciliation and
arbitration procedures were also superficial.   In
its coverage and reliability, the data base for
its calculations actually regressed after 1900.
Significant social and economic costs, such as
dissaving by strikers and unemployment and loss of
output in related industries, were discounted.[3] No
precise measure of the effect of strikes on
British output, still less on productivity and
cost-competitiveness, was attempted.   Meanwhile,
such estimates as the Department provided on the
annual costs and benefits of conciliation and
arbitration to trade unions were both highly
speculative and tangential to the central issues
of their net effects over the duration of the
trade cycle, their impact upon labour costs
relative to that of free collective bargaining,
and their long-term repercussions for the share of
wages in national income.

TRADE UNIONISM

Official data on unionisation displayed a similar
range of defects and a similar disinclination, as
the leading American labour statistician, Carroll
D. Wright, observed, to measure the structural
determinants and effects of labour market
phenomena as well as their more formal
characteristics.[4] As Figure 5.1 indicates,
compared with other areas of the Board's
statistical output, the share of investigative
resources devoted to such data after 1895 remained
markedly constant.   This was reflected in an

equally noticeable lack of progression in the statistical techniques applied to trade union material, which remained virtually static until the First World War.

The Department could provide only a 'guesstimate' of the level of unionisation within the British workforce as a whole.[5] Occupation or industry-specific unionisation rates were rarely obtained. As a result, no measure was provided of the relationship between labour solidarity and a range of variables, such as the degree of industrial concentration, the capital and labour intensity of production, and the skill and sexual characteristics of the workforce. The absence of adequate time series analysis not only prevented an assessment of shifts in the relative significance of such variables over the period, but also precluded the evaluation of the effect of cyclical fluctuations and of long-term trends in economic performance upon the structure and tactics of British organised labour.

In view of the rationale behind the Labour Department's annual trade union reports, their lack of systematic data on the impact of unionisation is even more notable. No attempt was made to correlate sectoral and temporal variations in unionisation with either direct or indirect indicators of the level and cost-competitiveness of industrial output. Furthermore, the disparity in wage levels and working conditions between unionised and non-unionised groups within the labour force was never systematically examined, nor were their relative income, expenditure and employment patterns.

Even the more routine data on trade-union membership and budgets were vulnerable to criticism. Until the early 1890s, the Board's information related to less than 50 per cent of total union membership. Thereafter, its coverage improved, recording by 1900 68 per cent of the membership and over 80 per cent of the income and accumulated funds of the Trade Union Movement.[6] Yet, detailed statistical analysis was limited to only 100 so-called 'leading unions', selected, according to one official statistician, in a 'highly promiscuous fashion'.[7] Although, in addition to vague criteria of 'membership and solidity', the unions were chosen with regard 'for some representation of each branch of industry',[8]

the fact that among other anomalies, the largest
and arguably most militant union - the South Wales
Miners' Federation - was omitted, cast serious
doubts as to the representativeness of the Board
of Trade's data and its reliability in monitoring
shifts in the composition and industrial policy of
the Union Movement.[9]

WAGE RATES, HOURS AND EARNINGS

There was a similar shortfall between the range of
objectives   (both   conservative   and   progressive)
which motivated the Board's investigations into
working   hours   and   remuneration,   and   the   data
produced.   Four dimensions of weakness may be
broadly   identified;   sectoral,   temporal,
social/distributional, and lateral.   The Board's
earliest investigations covered only 25 per cent
of the workforce with less than a 15 per cent
completion rate for the schedules submitted during
the   1886   census.[10]   Moreover,   this   limited
coverage was focussed upon a few staple sectors of
the economy, while wage data for 'new industries'
and for the retailing and distributive trades were
markedly   absent.   No   recourse   to   systematic
sampling was adopted.   The Board merely observed,
with a hint of desperation, that the average rates
of   remuneration   for   the   staple   industries
represented 'so large a mass of the population'
that they could reliably 'be taken as indicating
the general average for the labour force as a
whole'.[11]   No   statistical   proof   for   such   an
assertion was furnished.
    Subsequent supplementary investigations were
equally partial.   Wage data for domestic service,
which   still   represented   the   second   largest
category of employment, were based merely on a
scatter of returns collected by members of the
Royal Statistical Society and the Metropolitan
Association   for   Befriending   Young   Servants,[12]
while agricultural wage statistics were primarily
dependent on the observations of a small group of
local   farmers,   tradesmen,   and   Poor   Law
administrators.[13]   Admittedly,   the   1906   wage
census vastly extended the coverage of official
data.   Nevertheless, the fact that as late as 1912
the Labour Department's wage index represented
only   five   industries,   excluding   among   other
leading sectors, iron, steel and shipbuilding,
testified to the lack of confidence of the Board

in the reliability of its wages and earnings data.[14]

Such data were also unequal to the task of measuring wage variations over time, and their social and economic implications. In the absence of systematic and regular wage censuses, it was impossible for the Board to monitor shifts in wage differentials and in the pay distribution of the workforce. In addition, no reliable estimate could be made of the impact of variations in piece-rates upon wage levels and earnings.[15] Meanwhile, failure to allow for fluctuations in the level of unemployment seriously compromised the value of the Board's statistics as a measure both of shifts in actual wage earnings, and in labour costs of production. At best, only a general indication of their direction could be deduced.[16]

The official wage indexes developed after 1902 suffered from a range of deficiencies which seriously eroded their credibility as a means of time series analysis. They were openly admitted to rest on a 'narrow and unconvincing basis', and excluded a variety of leading industries and occupations.[17] The use of one base year instead of the average of a number of years over the trade cycle severely reduced the effectiveness of such indexes for the purpose of measuring wage trends, especially as the Board selected the year 1900 which was widely regarded by statisticians and economists as peculiarly unrepresentative.[18] Many of the Labour Department's wage series were inadequately 'weighted'. For example, the wage index for the construction industry was based on only three occupations and remained static throughout the period 1900-12 despite over seventy recorded changes in wage rates.[19] Meanwhile, the wage index for the engineering sector excluded data from several of its leading industrial centres as well as from trades such as boilermakers, smiths and machinemen, and was based on a 'highly questionable amalgam' of average piece, hourly and weekly wage rates.[20] The index of coal wages made no allowance for variations in the ratio of surface to face workers nor for the short-term volatility of rates within the industry. Based as it was on wage rates prevailing in specific months, it could entirely misrepresent the extent *and* direction of the mean annual variation.[21] The Board's wage series for piecework trades were even more distorted as they

merely reflected published piece-rates and were
not appropriately weighted for shifts in labour
and capital intensity, in productivity, and in the
age and sex structure of the workforce.[22]
      The 'distributional' objectives of the
Department's wage and earnings enquiries were
similarly frustrated. Its wage censuses provided
no reliable measure of the distribution of actual
earnings or nominal purchasing power within the
working classes and between various sectors of the
labour market, still less of the share of wages in
the national income. As a post-war labour
statistician reflected:

> pre-war data provided no precise statistics
> with which to confront the issues of low-
> income destitution and the 'progress' of the
> working classes; no datum line from which
> changes could be reliably measured and the
> need for the development of social policy
> determined.[23]

The Board's wage and earnings data related almost
entirely to organised labour, virtually ignoring
the casual labour force and the more exploitative
areas of the labour market. Its information on
the wages of out-workers and home workers was
minimal and largely derived from a few non-random
samples taken by Toynbee Hall, the Amalgamated
Tailors Union and C.O.S. relief societies.[24]
Despite the increasing focus of welfare debate
upon the social and economic condition of women,
there was a marked absence of data on levels of
female remuneration. Official national and
regional wage indexes were primarily based upon
the more skilled sections of the workforce and
were not representative of semi-skilled and
unskilled groups. They did not, therefore,
provide any basis for estimating the level of
poverty within Britain and could furnish little
enlightenment to contemporary debates over the
extent of 'urban degeneration', over the need for
Poor Law reform and minimum wage legislation, and
over the severity and repercussions of
underconsumption.[25]
      The Board's statistics on working-class
remuneration were also characterised by a serious
lack of what Charles Booth termed 'lateral
extension'.[26] They did not, for example, relate
shifts in the level of employment to variations in
the level of earnings, and therefore evaded the

central issues of the impact of the trade cycle on working-class incomes, and conversely the effect of wage movements on the level of business activity. They did not correlate temporal, occupational, and regional variations in wage rates either with welfare variables such as the incidence of destitution and poor housing, or with economic variables such as the level of industrial profits and technical innovation.

Absence of data on the relationship of wage costs to costs of production was especially marked. The enquiry of 1890 was more a 'gesture' than a 'serious statistical investigation' and was based on information gleaned from the published accounts of a few public companies.[27] Until the censuses of earnings and production of 1906-7, social and tariff reform politics remained uninformed as to the relationship of labour costs to the value of output within the British economy. Even then, only very crude aggregative estimates of labour productivity could be obtained from official statistics.[28] Finally, it should be noted that the welfare and economic implications of the Board of Trade's data on hours of employment were never properly explored. They were used primarily as a necessary variable by which to interpret wage data and to calculate earnings. There was little or no attempt to identify the impact of variations in the length of the working week upon levels of output or upon industrial safety.[29]

WORKING CLASS EXPENDITURE AND COST OF LIVING

The efforts of the Labour Department to provide a reliable estimate of trends in the real wages and standard of living of the British working classes were inevitably hampered by deficiencies in its earnings data and indexes. Such efforts were also severely handicapped by inadequacies in its price data. Ideally, in order to monitor movements in the cost of living, the Department needed to construct a series of indexes which were based on retail prices, which included all commodities in the basket of goods commonly purchased by as wide a spectrum as possible of the working classes, which were accurately weighted according to ascertained patterns of working-class expenditure, which differentiated between different regions or between town and country, and which related to a

period sufficiently long to provide a basis for
long-run assessment. Most of the Board of Trade's
indexes may be faulted on all or most of these
desiderata.

Firstly, its price indexes were predominantly
based on wholesale and not retail price data and
excluded a variety of small but significant items
of working-class consumption.[30] Its food prices
were entirely obtained within the London area and
primarily reflected prices ruling in large
distributive concerns. Its clothing series was
grossly inadequate, based as it was on a crude
estimate of shifts in the price of raw material
inputs. Meanwhile, the Board's index of working-
class rents was based on estimates for only five
years. For 1890, 1895 and 1900, reliance was
placed on house valuation returns which
undoubtedly under-stated the rate of rent
increases. Rent data for 1905 and 1912 were more
complete but still incorporated a metropolitan
bias and obscured the wide range and volatility of
rental payments. They were over-reliant on the
'impressionistic' judgements of overworked
investigators as to 'predominant rents' and failed
to provide sufficient information as to their
frequency distribution.[31] Statisticians such as
Bowley and Sauerbeck were also critical of the
base years of 1871 and 1900 adopted by the Board
in its price indexes, on the grounds that they
gave a distorted picture of prevailing trends.[32]

The 'weighting' of such indexes, and
especially the rent and fuel sub-indexes, was
seriously compromised by the lack of official
statistics on working-class expenditure. The
Board of Trade's enquiry of 1889 had less than a 5
per cent completion rate for its schedules and
generated insufficient data upon which to base
'any meaningful conclusions as to working class
consumption patterns',[33] still less by which to
weight existing price indexes. Moreover, the
Board failed to produce any additional consumption
data throughout the 1890s, despite the growing
international awareness of the work of Le Play and
the utility of family budget data to social
scientists and policy-makers, and despite the
refinement of the statistical techniques
involved.[34] As Henry Higgs protested to the
British Association for the Advancement of Science
in 1899, British labour administrators were almost
entirely dependent on the work of foreign
observers, such as Lavollee's study of *Les Classes*

Ouvrier en Europe (1896).[35]
Even the Board of Trade's budget data for
1903 were highly derivative, being primarily
reliant on the previous studies of Booth,
Rowntree, the Economic Club and the American
Commissioner for Labour.[36] Only a non-random
sample of 400 budgets was investigated, largely
from the London labour aristocracy, (a function of
the Board's reliance on co-operative and thrift
societies), and excluding significant items of
working-class expenditure such as fuel and light.
The celebrated family budget enquiry of 1904,
which was to remain the data base for welfare
debate and social policy for another 35 years, was
also severely limited, retaining the social,
regional and occupational bias of previous
investigations.[37] Although its 2,000 budgets had
a more even geographical spread, it was heavily
orientated towards the London area. Unskilled and
casual labour groups as well as workers in the
clerical and distributive occupations, and female
employees in general, were under-represented.[38]
Moreover, as there was no further budget survey
before the First World War, there could be no
revision of the official Cost of Living Index to
allow for subsequent shifts in the pattern of
Edwardian working-class consumption.[39]
The weaknesses of the Board's wage, price and
consumption data meant that it failed to fulfil
its declared aim of constructing a reliable real
wage index from which movements in the standard of
living of the labouring classes might be deduced.
Nor did its information define the linkages
between the level of real wages and a range of
economic and social variables such as the
technical and organisational structure of
industry, the level and stability of employment,
and the pattern of skill differentials,
occupational mobility, industrial militancy, and
family structure. In addition, the scope of the
Board's cost of living enquiries bore little
relationship to the data requirements of
contemporary welfare and fiscal debate. They
provided no reliable basis for determining the
causes and extent of 'primary' and 'secondary'
poverty within Britain, and for establishing the
representativeness of the findings of local
surveys such as those of Booth and Rowntree.[40]
They were even less suited to calculating the
relationship between destitution and the more
prominent environmental and industrial symptoms

associated with 'urban degeneration' (e.g. poor housing, high infant mortality and low productivity) or to furnishing 'some degree of objective data' with which the increasingly contentious issue of minimum wage legislation might be addressed.[41]

Meanwhile, Board of Trade statisticians were acutely aware of the inability of its labour statistics to predict and to monitor the net impact of fiscal reforms upon working-class incomes and purchasing power.[42] They were resistant both to the inclusion of such data in the Fiscal Blue Books and to Cabinet pressure to produce precise estimates of the social costs and benefits of free trade and protection on the basis of the Board's standard of living data. Its labour statistics could provide no reliable basis for international comparisons.[43] As the Treasury had predicted, it proved impossible to obtain reliable and comprehensive information as to working-class earnings, consumption patterns and costs of living abroad.[44] The Board's overseas inquiries were severely limited in scope and technique, and despite the secondment of investigatory teams, were largely reliant on the 'impressions' of local industrialists, labour leaders and consular officials.[45] The process of data accumulation was thoroughly unscientific, a non-random sample of only 28 towns being selected as representative of American income and expenditure patterns on grounds of their 'intrinsic importance', with scant regard to the likely statistical significance of such findings.[46]

UNEMPLOYMENT

Recent studies by Buxton, Mackay and Garside have clearly demonstrated the limitations of pre-war official data in measuring the volume, incidence and duration of unemployment.[47] Such data provided, at best, a rough indication of the direction and extent of fluctuations in employment. They did not furnish an exact statistical measure or even close estimate of the total amount of unemployment among the labour force.[48] Still less could they evaluate the magnitude of under-employment and hidden unemployment within the late-Victorian and Edwardian economy. Employment statistics supplied by industrialists were highly selective and lacked any measure of the percentage of the total labour force represented or of the relationship of the numbers employed to those seeking employment.[49] Likewise, information derived from union benefit records could only provide a guide to fluctuations in unemployment and not an accurate indication of its volume. Its failure accurately to reflect the industrial distribution of the workforce seriously impaired its value as a basis for the construction of a reliable employment index.[50] Furthermore, as Garside has indicated, even the data produced by the establishment of a national system of labour exchanges and unemployment insurance proved inadequate as a measure of the real level of unused labour resources in the economy.[51]

Official statistics were similarly ill-equipped for monitoring the industrial, occupational, regional, temporal and social incidence of unemployment. Reliable information on the industrial and occupational distribution of unemployment was unavailable before 1912. The data that were available were very limited and selective and virtually useless for the purposes of time series analysis.[52] Manpower and benefit returns from employers and trade unions did not incorporate a systematic breakdown by trade or industry nor any measure of the representativeness of the workforce covered in the returns. Some industries such as engineering and shipbuilding were markedly over-represented. Other more stable areas of employment such as agriculture, transport and domestic service, or sectors such as mining and textiles which tended to counter downswings in economic activity by recourse to short-time, were either under-represented or entirely excluded. The occupational coverage of official employment and unemployment statistics was subject to similar anomalies.

Meanwhile, the pattern of variations in regional unemployment also remained largely uncharted; official intelligence as to local unemployment conditions being dependent upon mainly verbal, non-statistical, subjective assessments by employers, Board of Trade correspondents, and Poor Law officials.[53] The Board did provide more comprehensive data with regard to cyclical and seasonal fluctuations in the level of labour utilisation, but here again, there were serious weaknesses in the official statistics. The partial and unsystematic

industrial weighting of the Board's employment
index and the inappropriateness of its base years
severely limited its ability to monitor accurately
the duration and amplitude of cyclical
variations.[54] Furthermore, except for dock
labour, official statistics were insufficient to
quantify seasonal fluctuations in employment with
any degree of precision.[55] In consequence, there
was no provision of a seasonally-adjusted series
which might have provided a clearer picture of the
underlying trend in unemployment.

Most surprising perhaps, in view of the
rationale behind late-Victorian and Edwardian
unemployment enquiries, was their lack of precise
information concerning its social incidence and
its degree of concentration among specific groups
within the labour market. Reliable information on
trends in unemployment related only to a small
proportion of the workforce - to a minority of
skilled, male trade unionists whose unions
administered out-of-work benefit schemes and whose
conditions of employment were far from
representative. In addition to significant
numbers of trade unionists and non-unionised
skilled workers, such data therefore ignored the
female workforce and the mass of low-skilled and
manual labour - the very 'residuum' upon which so
much of contemporary welfare and efficiency debate
focussed.[56] The Board of Trade's efforts to
monitor unemployment within the lower strata of
the workforce by reference to the returns of Poor
Law officials and distress committees proved
abortive.[57] Pauperism was only related to but not
synonymous *with* unemployment. Moreover, the
returns reflected a range of social and
administrative variables other than the level of
unemployment and could in no way be statistically
related to the class or status specificity of
other employment data.[58]

Official statistics were also uninformative
with respect to the duration of unemployment. The
information derived from isolated case studies of
particular trades and from the pre-history of
claimants before distress committees and labour
exchanges was wholly inadequate for the needs of
proper duration analysis.[59] In the absence of
flow statistics, it was impossible to identify the
level of turn-over within the unemployed, the
proportion of long and short-term unemployment at
any given time, and the relationship of duration
to other variables such as age, sex, skill, and

the general level of unemployment.

The inadequacies of official statistics on the extent, incidence and duration of late-Victorian and Edwardian unemployment inevitably frustrated the efforts of government statisticians to identify and to measure its causes. For example, lack of data on the social incidence of unemployment rendered abortive any attempt to identify the existence of an 'unemployed class' or to differentiate between the so-called 'residuum' and 'respectable unemployed'.[60] In the absence of occupational and skill-specific information, it was impossible to evaluate the significance of technological change as a causal factor. Absence of duration data impaired any precise appreciation of the role of frictional unemployment, while the importance of structural factors was similarly obscured by the lack of systematic regional and industrial information. Likewise, the dearth of information on the industrial history of the unemployed prevented any rigorous examination of the relationship between unemployment and personal attributes such as education, health, 'character' and motivation, which could have provided some statistical basis for contemporary debate over the respective roles of moral and environmental influences in generating want of employment. It was also impossible to measure the differential impact of supply and demand factors upon the level of labour utilisation. Only rough estimates could be given as to the displacement effects of female, rural and immigrant labour.[61] Indeed, in the absence of comprehensive data on the mechanics of the labour market, the whole concept of 'urban degeneration' remained immune to statistical verification. Furthermore, the lack of reliable time series seriously inhibited official analysis of seasonal and cyclical fluctuations in employment and their sensitivity to the various strands of demand.

On the basis of available data, it was equally futile to attempt to measure the impact of unemployment, despite the fact that its effects on a range of social and economic variables, such as the level of working-class earnings, purchasing power, health, crime, civil and industrial unrest, pauperism, output and productivity, were the focus of welfare debate.

Inevitably, these shortfalls in official statistics of the causes, extent and repercussions of unemployment impeded labour administrators in their attempts to establish the relevance and feasibility of various policy options. For example, detailed information on the regional and sectoral incidence of unemployment would have been required to establish the likely impact of land reform and protectionist legislation. Without comprehensive data on the social and ethnic mix of the unemployed, it was impossible to estimate the cost-effectiveness of labour colonies or immigration controls. Similarly, the relative merits of relief schemes and labour exchanges could have been established only by reference to systematic information on the causes and duration of unemployment and on the mobility, skill and status characteristics of the unemployed, while, as Bowley pointed out in 1906, the limited coverage and lack of predictive potential of British unemployment data not only prevented a proper actuarial assessment of insurance proposals but also seriously undermined the credibility of contra-cyclical strategies such as the forward-budgeting of local authority capital expenditure.[62]

FOREIGN AND COLONIAL WELFARE PROVISIONS

The value of overseas welfare provisions as positive or negative models for British policy-makers was similarly impeded. As with commercial intelligence, the welfare intelligence of Britain's industrial competitors was markedly superior. The Board of Trade's *Abstracts of Foreign Labour Statistics* were highly selective and derivative. They contained little indication of the reliability of their data base and failed to collate information suited to worthwhile comparative analysis of international labour conditions. Indeed, until 1904, the processing of a mass of foreign and colonial labour intelligence was entrusted to a translator and second division clerk. Two statistical investigators were subsequently employed by the Comptroller-General, but it was only after 1907 that the Treasury sanctioned the permanent appointment of an expert statistician and linguist to supervise the collection and analysis of international labour statistics.[63] Inevitably, the utility of such information to social scientists and policy-makers in monitoring overseas labour market trends and the suitability of overseas industrial and welfare

provisions for domestic consumption, was seriously
eroded.

Board of Trade investigations provided little
indication of the cost-effectiveness of foreign
and colonial labour legislation. The impact of
social investment upon workforce productivity and
discipline was rarely estimated, while the
earnings and cost of living data collected by the
Board were widely regarded as 'wholly inadequate'
to support 'defensible propositions' concerning
the 'relationship between specific social
provisions and international disparities in
working-class conditions'.[64] Statistical
information tended to be confined, as with the
Board's feasibility studies of European schemes of
labour bureaus and unemployment insurance, to the
actuarial soundness of overseas legislation, and
emerged in response to specific public enquiries
such as the Poor Law Commission rather than as
part of the normal production schedule of the
Department.

Nor did the Board's enquiries into foreign
and colonial social provisions provide a
comparative analysis of the range of social,
political and economic variables which might
determine the speed and content of welfare
transfer; such as the degree of industrialisation,
urbanisation and social stratification, the
solidarity and relative strengths of Capital and
Labour, the influence of other pressure and
interest groups and of localism and voluntarism,
the pattern of income distribution, the demographic, financial and legal structure, and
cultural responses to social 'deviancy' and
bureaucracy.

NOTES

1. *21st Report on Strikes and Lockouts*, PP 1909 (Cd.4680) XLIX, p. 9.
2. *5th Report on Strikes and Lockouts*, PP 1894 (C.7566) LXXXI Pt 1, pp. 10-11; *Report on British and Foreign Trade and Industry*, PP 1905 (Cd.2337) LXXXIV, pp. 79-81.
3. See, *7th Report on Strikes and Lockouts*, PP 1895 (C.7901) XCII, pp. 56-7.
4. C.D. Wright, 'English Labor Statistics', *Publications of the American Statistical Association*, 2 (1890-1), pp. 68-9.
5. *9th Report on Trade Unions*, PP 1897 (C.8644) XCIX, p. xvi.
6. *8th Report on Trade Unions*, PP 1896 (C.8232) XCIII, p. xiv.
7. G.H. Wood Papers, OA/26, Notes on 'Blue Books of the Month', 1909.
8. *11th Report on Trade Unions*, PP 1899 (C.9443) XCII, p. xiv.
9. G.H. Wood Papers, OA/26, Notes on 'Official Trade Union Statistics', *c*. 1909.
10. P.R.O., LAB41/161/L1070/1908, memo. on 'The Progress of the Census of Wages' by F.H. MacLeod, 6 March 1908.
11. See, *Report on Rates of Wages in the Principal Textile Trades*, PP 1889 (C.5807) LXX, p. xxv.
12. *Accounts of Expenditure of Wage-earning Women and Girls*, PP 1911 (Cd.5963) LXXXIX, p. 4.
13. *Report on the Wages and Earnings of Agricultural Labourers*, PP 1905 (Cd.2376) XCVII, pp. 7-8.
14. P.R.O., LAB41/213, G.H. Wood to F.H. MacLeod, 1 April 1912.
15. Wood Papers, CB/95, Wood to MacLeod, 3 July 1906.
16. P.R.O., LAB41/151, minute by MacLeod on 'Wages Enquiry', 6 Dec. 1906; LAB41/213, Wood to MacLeod, 5 Sept. 1905; A.L. Bowley, 'The Improvement of Official Statistics', *JRSS*, 71 (1908), pp. 472-3.
17. P.R.O., LAB41/213, minute by MacLeod on 'Wages Index', 14 May 1912.
18. P.R.O., LAB41/213, memo. by A.L. Bowley on 'Wages Index', 4 Dec. 1905.
19. Ibid., Wood to MacLeod, 15 April 1912.
20. P.R.O., LAB41/213, memo. by Wood, 25 Jan. 1906.
21. Ibid., memo. by Bowley, 4 Dec. 1905.
22. Wood Papers, CB/95, Wood to MacLeod, 3 July 1906.
23. Royal Statistical Society Archives, Box 3, File 19, A.L. Bowley to Minister of Labour, 21 Jan. 1936. See also *Statist*, 58 (1906), pp. 915-16.
24. *Report on Sweating in the East End of London*, PP 1887 (331) LXXXIX, p. 11.
25. See especially, Bowley's critique, *JRSS*, 69 (1906),

p.   555-8.   According to Bowley, Edwardian policy-makers had 'nothing to go on but guesses as to the real extent of poverty'.

26. *S.C. on Distress from Want of Employment, Mins. of Ev.*, PP 1895 (365) IX, Q. 10520.

27. *Report on the Relation of Wages in Certain Industries to the Cost of Production*, PP 1890-1 (C.6535) LXXVIII, p. 5.

28. A.W. Flux, 'The Census of Production', *JRSS*, 87 (1924), pp. 355-6.

29. *Report of the British Association for the Advancement of Science* (1915), p. 347, Interim report of the Committee on the Question of Fatigue from the Economic Standpoint.

30. For a general critique, see T.R. Gourvish, 'The Standard of Living 1890-1914' in A. O'Day (ed.), *The Edwardian Age: Conflict and Stability 1900-1914* (1979), pp. 16-18.

31. Yule Papers, R.S.S. Archives, Box 15, MacLeod to Yule, 11 Sept. 1907.

32. Wood Papers, 1A/80, draft letter to *The Times*, 6 Jan. 1910.

33. *Returns of Expenditure by Working Men*, PP 1889 (C.5861) LXXXIV, p. 4.

34. See, e.g., H. Higgs, 'Workmens' Budgets', *JRSS*, 56 (1893), pp. 255-7; *Bulletin of the International Statistical Institute*, 5 (1890), pp. 45-89; *Publications of the American Statistical Association*, 2 (1890-1), pp. 70-1.

35. *Report of the B.A.A.S.* (1899), pp. 818-19.

36. *Report on British and Foreign Trade and Industrial Conditions*, PP 1903 (Cd.1761) LXVII, pp. 209-10.

37. *2nd Report on British and Foreign Trade and Industrial Conditions*, PP 1905 (Cd.2337) LXXXIV, pp. 3-4.

38. Despite the fact that women constituted around 30% of the total occupied population in 1911, throughout the period 1886-1914, the Board of Trade undertook only one minute enquiry into the expenditure of female employees, based on schedules for 30 women and girls. See, PP 1911 (Cd.5963) LXXXIX, p. 4.

39. P.R.O., LAB17/2, memo. by H. Wolfe on 'Family Budget Enquiry', 9 Dec. 1926.

40. P.R.O., LAB2/1555, memo. by A. Wilson Fox on 'The extent of destitution', 16 July 1903; *Statist*, 52 (1903), pp. 681-2.

41. A.L. Bowley in *JRSS*, 69 (1906), pp. 553-4.

42. P.R.O., LAB2/1598/L263/1904, C.P. Sanger to H. Llewellyn Smith, 3 Feb. 1904.

43. P.R.O., LAB2/1598/L263/1904, memo. on 'The Comparative Progress in the Economic Condition of the Working Classes in the United Kingdom, the United States, France and Germany since the period 1840-45', by W. Layton and C.P. Sanger, 1904.

44. P.R.O., T1/10241B/2068, minute by G. Barstow, 7 Feb.

1905.

45. P.R.O., LAB2/1598/L549/1907, memo. by F.H. MacLeod on 'Foreign Towns Inquiry', 27 April 1907; *Statist*, 65 (1910), p. 998.

46. *Report on the Cost of Living of the Working Classes in American Towns*, PP 1911 (Cd.5814) LXXXVIII, p. x.

47. N.K. Buxton and D.I. MacKay, *British Employment Statistics* (1977); W.R. Garside, *The Measurement of Unemployment: Methods and Sources in Great Britain* (1981).

48. Garside, *The Measurement of Unemployment*, p. 244; P.R.O., LAB2/1478/L270/1906, memo. on 'A recent estimate of the number of unemployed' by H. Llewellyn Smith, 8 Jan. 1895; PP 1905 (Cd.2337) LXXXIV, p. 81.

49. Buxton and MacKay, *Employment Statistics*, pp. 52-3; Garside, *The Measurement of Unemployment*, pp. 24-7.

50. J. Harris, *Unemployment and Politics*, (Oxford, 1972), p. 371; Garside, *The Measurement of Unemployment*, p. 17; PP 1905 (Cd.2337) LXXXIV, p. 79.

51. Garside, *The Measurement of Unemployment*, p. 28.

52. Ibid., pp. 17, 227.

53. Ibid., p. 26.

54. See, *Report on British and Foreign Trade and Industry*, PP 1905 (Cd.2337) LXXXIV, pp. 79-85, memo. on 'Fluctuations in Employment'.

55. Garside, *The Measurement of Unemployment*, pp. 207-8.

56. See, P.R.O., LAB2/1478/L270/1906, memo. by H. Llewellyn Smith, 8 Jan. 1895; *The Economist*, 51 (1893), p. 601.

57. P.R.O., CAB37/38, 'The Unemployed' by H. Llewellyn Smith, 23 Jan. 1895, pp. 3-4.

58. Garside, *The Measurement of Unemployment*, pp. 167-8; M.A. Crowther, *The Workhouse System 1834-1929* (1981), pp. 252-8.

59. Garside, *The Measurement of Unemployment*, p. 183.

60. P.R.O., LAB2/1555/L1099/1903, memo. by H. Llewellyn Smith, 18 July 1903; Charles Dilke, 'Presidential Address', *JRSS*, 70 (1907), p. 575.

61. See, e.g., *Report on the Employment of Women and Girls*, PP 1894 (C.7564) LXXXI Pt 2, p. 71; *S.C. on Distress from Want of Employment*, *Mins. of Ev.*, PP 1895 (365) IX, p. 79; *R.C. on Alien Immigration*, *Mins. of Ev.*, PP 1903 (Cd.1742) IX, pp. 829-34.

62. *JRSS*, 69 (1906), pp. 556-7.

63. P.R.O., T1/10612/5461, Board of Trade to Treasury, 2 Feb. 1907.

64. See, e.g., Charles Dilke in *JRSS*, 70 (1907), pp. 567-9; P.R.O., LAB2/1717/C8502/1909, memo. by A.A. Wotzel on 'The Foreign Intelligence Branch of the Labour Department', 19 Oct. 1909.

Part Four

THE   CONSTRAINTS

Chapter 7

TREASURY CONTROL AND LABOUR STATISTICS

A number of explanations may be advanced for this
shortfall between the Board of Trade's
investigative aims and its statistical
achievements in measuring the 'Labour Problem'.
It was a function of a range of logistical,
technical and ideological factors, many of which
were, in practice, closely interdependent.
Despite the fact that the Board of Trade's
intelligence work was better staffed and funded
than that of other departments of social
administration, one of the more persistent and
erosive constraints upon British labour statistics
was undoubtedly Treasury control. Throughout the
period 1886-1914, the Treasury maintained a
consistent opposition to the expansion of official
statistics both as an issue of financial policy
and one of routine appropriation. Its attitude
had been clearly articulated in its minute of 1882
that:

> the collecting and digesting of public
> statistics is a duty that should be carefully
> watched and guarded in order that it may not
> degenerate into extravagance. There is a
> dangerous tendency to magnify work and extend
> functions beyond the limits required at once
> by economy and expediency.[1]

Despite the economic and social crises of the
period and the growing demand for an effective
system of civil intelligence, the Treasury
sustained this minimalist philosophy. It
explicitly rejected 'the doctrine that the general
taxpayer should fund the dissemination of more
comprehensive labour and commercial statistics on
the grounds that it would produce an increasing

volume of trade and employment to the benefit of the community'.[2] In the Treasury's view, the provision of 'routine administrative' rather than 'promotional' data was entirely consistent with efficient government, and it was symptomatic that on the eve of the First World War, the Treasury itself still lacked any 'organisational arrangements for collecting information' on a range of vital issues relevant to the financial position of the nation, including the level of domestic liquidity and the movement of foreign exchanges and overseas capital.[3]

In effect, the Treasury imposed a 'Catch-22' situation upon late-Victorian and Edwardian social administrators. It expected Whitehall to demonstrate the cost-effectiveness of its measures but resisted the deployment of resources by means of which both short and long-term policy options and objectives might be evaluated and the social and economic repercussions of decision-making monitored. Predictably, its resistance focussed on 'speculative enquiries' (i.e. investigations which might generate fresh areas of government expenditure), and on the appointment of professional statisticians who might foster such 'departures' while discrediting the orthodox Treasury view of official statistics as 'mechanical work' within the competence of the Lower Division secretariat. As Charles Dilke observed in 1907, in terms of their claims upon public expenditure, expert statisticians were essentially regarded by the Treasury 'in the light of sturdy beggars'.[4]

In the case of labour statistics, the normal bureaucratic constraints of Treasury control were further reinforced by more personal, ideological prejudices. The political and social ideology of most Treasury officials was conservative,[5] and they were innately hostile towards the extension of labour statistics, viewing it as a populist strategy of social radicalism and the thin end of the socialistic expenditure wedge. The Labour Department was therefore perceived as a permanent conspiracy to extravagance and its efforts to fund the measurement of the 'Labour Problem' systematically frustrated.

An indication of the aggregate effects of Treasury control upon such funding can be obtained by comparing the Board of Trade's provisional estimates for statistical staff and investigations with the respective appropriations for the period

1886-1914.[6] As Figure 7.1 reveals, the shortfall,
both in absolute and percentage terms, is
significant throughout, with a long-run upward
trend. However, there are marked fluctuations
around the trend which reveal the influence in the
short run of shifts in the political environment,
and underlying the aggregative picture, a number
of broadly chronological phases of Treasury
constraint upon labour statistics can be detected.

Figure 7.1:   **Provisional Financial Estimates and
Appropriations for Labour Statistics 1886-1914
(Percentage Shortfall)**

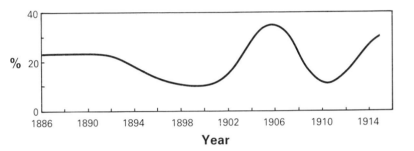

1893-1900:

As we have seen in Chapter 3, the history of the
Labour Statistics Bureau at the Board of Trade
from 1886 to 1892 had been dominated by the
triumph of economy, and the Treasury proved
equally obstructive towards the Bureau's
enlargement in 1893. While reluctantly forced to
accept the establishment of a separate department
as 'a political matter out of which our chiefs
wish to make political capital', the primary
objective of Welby's successor, Sir Francis
Mowatt, was to prevent 'its growth and expansion'
by appointing a conservative statistician (Robert
Giffen) as its Director at the outset and
collaborating with him 'in fixing some limits
beyond which' he would not 'allow its activity to
extend'; on the grounds, as Mowatt evocatively
expressed it, that: 'No kicking straps or leading
reins which it will take quietly enough now will
really confine its action when it begins to feel
its legs'.[7]

The narrowing of the shortfall between provisional estimates and appropriation for statistical expenditure between 1893 and 1900 reflects the success with which the Treasury achieved these aims rather than a failure in Treasury control. As Mowatt had predicted, Giffen was primarily concerned with commercial issues and lacked commitment to the Labour Department. Demands by the Board of Trade upon the Exchequer for additional funding of labour statistics in the latter half of the 1890s were therefore relatively modest. Nonetheless, Treasury control seriously delayed the formation of a staff of 'skilled investigators and statisticians' as recommended by the Royal Commission on Labour.[8] As a result, the Board was forced to rely heavily on fee-paid local correspondents recruited from the Trade Union Movement, and upon information provided by community leaders, such as landowners and Poor Law Guardians, a reliance which seriously compromised the confidence of both Capital and Labour in the objectivity of the Board's industrial statistics.[9] Furthermore, a number of the more critical lacunae in the statistical investigations of the Board, such as the failure to develop its analysis of the links between industrial unrest and structural variations in the labour market, were in part due to pressure from the Treasury to avoid what it regarded as 'illegitimate and speculative exercises'.[10]

1900-1907:

However, the most serious impact of Treasury control upon labour statistics occurred during the Edwardian period when the Board was confronted with an unprecedented demand for industrial intelligence. The Treasury fought determinedly to restrict the scope of the Board's statistical output. For example, it refused to sanction a fresh census of wages in 1901 and 1903 in view of the 'state of the national finances' consequent upon the Boer War, and its 'scepticism' as to its 'practical utility'.[11] It seriously eroded the value of the 1906 census by restricting the coverage of the enquiry to twelve representative weeks and confining the industrial base proposed for an official wage index.[12] Similar economies reduced the coverage of the Board's cost of living enquiries in Britain and inhibited the collection

of reliable and comprehensive data on working-
class rents and consumption patterns.[13] It was
equally obstructive towards the Board of Trade's
proposals in 1905 for a series of major
investigations into the earnings and cost of
living of workforces in other industrialised
economies. The Treasury deployed a range of
arguments with varying degrees of conviction and
consistency; that such investigations were
incompatible with the general 'financial
exigencies of the time'; that they would lack
relevance to contemporary economic and social
issues unless comprehensive data was obtained on
the level and pattern of employment and the
purchasing power of wages overseas, which would
prove impractical and prohibitively expensive; and
that 'the subject was so vast that it would be
practically impossible to draw any general
deduction from the figures received' which would
'inevitably tend to become a mere accumulation of
statistical lumber'.[14] Only after the issue had
been fought in Cabinet did the Board of Trade
obtain formal sanction for the enquiries. Even
then, a series of minor economies imposed by the
Treasury threatened to abort the project and
succeeded, by modifying its timing and scope, in
markedly reducing its value to contemporary fiscal
and welfare debate.[15]
    The value of the Board's investigative work
and its ability to perform as an 'intelligence
department' was also impaired by the Treasury's
reluctance to sanction the recruitment of
additional statisticians into the higher grades of
the Board's secretariat. Repeatedly, after 1900,
crucial enquiries such as the Fiscal Blue Books
were compromised by the lack of senior
statisticians to co-ordinate and interpret data
and to generate new series on economic and social
trends. Writing to Mowatt in June 1903, Llewellyn
Smith succinctly summed up the seriousness of the
situation:

        The Board of Trade have for a long time
        viewed with growing apprehension the danger
        that is continually being incurred through
        the necessity of hastily "getting up"
        questions of the most vital importance to
        meet sudden calls for information - questions
        that ought to be systematically watched
        instead of being allowed to sleep until an
        emergency arises. We live from hand to mouth

engrossed in the compilation and publication
of masses of statistics but without the
leisure to study the meaning of our own
figures.
    If the department is to fulfil a genuine
and effective "intelligence" role, it is
necessary to ensure that a certain number of
well-trained officers shall be employed in
analysing and interpreting the facts and
figures instead of merely compiling and
editing them.[16]

    Llewellyn Smith therefore proposed that
instead of relying upon the *ad hoc* appointment of
temporary investigators, there should be
established within the Board a proper career
structure for investigators so that a continuity
of expertise might be obtained, headed by a small,
permanent cadre of professional statisticians
recruited from leading social scientists and
empiricists; and that the ratio of senior statisticians to abstractors should be radically
altered. Despite the fact that the Board of Trade
pressed the issue in Cabinet, the gains were
limited. The Treasury was hostile to Llewellyn
Smith's proposals, arguing that the Labour
Department was 'the spoiled child of the service'
and that it was merely 'taking advantage' of
'public interest in the topics with which it dealt
in order to make exorbitant demands upon the
exchequer'.[17] A new career structure for
abstractors and investigators *was* established, but
the Treasury continued to resist the recruitment
of statisticians from outside Whitehall on three
counts; that it would serve as formal recognition
that the production of official statistics
required professional expertise, that it would
provide a pretext for political jobbery, and that
it might in the case of some investigators,
reinforce 'the invidious precedent' established by
the Labour Department in 1893 of conceding
professional status within the Civil Service both
to women and former tradesmen.[18]
    Consequently, as Llewellyn Smith bemoaned to
Lloyd George in 1907, Board of Trade enquiries
continued to suffer from a lack of 'statistical
expertise at the top' (for the 1906 wage census,
the final estimates provided for only three
trained statisticians as compared with fifty
checkers, compilers and abstractors), and from an
over-reliance upon inexperienced investigators

equipped at best with a limited grounding in economics and detailed instructions designed to ensure some unspecified degree of comparability between their findings.[19]

1907-1914:

Between 1907 and 1910, there was a marked convergence between the estimates submitted by the Board of Trade for statistical and investigative work and its financial vote. This convergence was not due, as with the period 1893-1900, to any moderation of the statistical objectives of the Board, but most probably to the advent of a more progressive political environment receptive to welfare-related expenditure, and to the arrival of Lloyd George at the Board of Trade with an urge to capitalise upon the more popular aspects of the Department's functions and to expand both its labour and commercial intelligence as an adjunct to a major programme of social and industrial legislation.[20] His successor, Winston Churchill, also accorded the Board's intelligence work a high priority consistent with the respect for the persuasive power of statistical information that he had imbibed from the Webbs, and with his ambition to establish a 'Civil Committee of Imperial Defence against poverty and unemployment' armed with a comprehensive overview of the labour market.[21]

However, between 1910 and 1914 there was, as Figure 4.1 indicates, a downturn in the rate of growth of statistical expenditure by the Board of Trade. In part, this reflected the increasing focus of departmental concern with the funding of a range of welfare legislation, including the introduction of minimum wage boards and unemployment insurance.[22] It was also, as Figure 7.1 reveals, a function of Treasury control. The Treasury was hyper-sensitive to the fact that the stimulus of additional intelligence about the labour market produced as a spin-off from the Liberal welfare reforms, and the growing pressure from social radicals within government circles for more scientific investigation of the causes and incidence of destitution, might initiate a further innovative and expensive phase of social investigations. It was determined that, in evaluating any such 'expansive tendencies', considerations of cost would 'not be sacrificed on the altar of some specious arguments as to utility'.[23]

In the event, the main victim of Treasury control after 1910 was the Board of Trade's efforts to develop a reliable and comprehensive series of indexes relating to working-class earnings, consumption patterns, and costs of living, based upon the mass of British and overseas labour statistics accumulated by the Board and by private investigators over the previous decade.[24]

Meanwhile, the Board's ability to monitor industrial and economic developments continued to suffer from a want of sufficient personnel of suitable calibre. The Comptroller-General reported in 1909 that the Labour Department still lacked 'trained experts capable of taking the results of an investigation, extracting the salient features, and presenting a reasoned summary or report upon the whole'.[25] As a result, the Board's senior officials could not readily be up-dated on the range of issues relating to the labour market with which the Department was increasingly involved, and were inadequately briefed for policy-making purposes. As the Permanent Secretary, Llewellyn Smith, concluded in 1913 in a review of the Board's organisational weaknesses:

> The Board is working with too small a margin for unexpected contingencies. I have for the past few years been living so to speak on my capital, so far as my stock of knowledge of the true economic situation and its changes is concerned. At present, I live intellectually from hand to mouth, having only time to organise inquiries and little or none to study their results and apply their lessons.[26]

In view of recent work which has sought to explain and justify the rationale behind late-Victorian and Edwardian Treasury control,[27] the history of labour statistics at the Board of Trade between 1886 and 1914 presents a salutary warning to the welfare historian. However much negotiations between a department and the Treasury may have resembled merely a very formal and elaborate game, the rules of which were well known to both contestants, and in which the Treasury would in most instances eventually yield, the fact remains that Treasury control played a significant role in frustrating the efforts of the Board both to measure the 'Labour Problem' and to interpret the policy implications of its findings.

Treasury Control and Labour Statistics

NOTES

1. P.R.O., HO45/11787/B32589/2, Treasury minute, 21
April 1882.
2. P.R.O., T1/11170/25785, memo. by G. Barstow, 5
Nov. 190'.
3. P.R.O., T1/11791/13516, Treasury minute, 24 March
1915.
4. *JRSS*, LXX (1907), p. 557.
5. H. Roseveare, *The Treasury* (1969), Chs. 6-7;
R.M. MacLeod, *Treasury Control and Social Administration*
(1968), *passim*.
6. Sources as for Chapter 4, Figure 4.1.
7. P.R.O., T1/8743A/10410, memo. by Mowatt, 30 Dec.
1892.
8. See, e.g., P.R.O., T1/8857C/13679.
9. P.R.O., T1/9891A/18946; Ch. 9 below.
10. See, e.g., P.R.O., T1/9109B/18813.
11. P.R.O., T1/9636A/1448; LAB2/1555/L1099/1903.
12. P.R.O., LAB41/151.
13. P.R.O., T1/18410/10518A.
14. P.R.O., T1/10241B/2068; T1/10524A/19025.
15. P.R.O., T1/10562/22706; LAB41/213, G.H. Wood to F.H.
MacLeod, 25 May 1909.
16. P.R.O., T1/10054B/21516, Llewellyn Smith to Mowatt,
13 June 1903. For the inability of the Board of Trade to
cope with the statistical demands of the Tariff Reform
controversy, see also Walter Layton Papers, unpublished
autobiography, pp. 13a, 15.
17. P.R.O., T1/10241B/2068, minute by T.L. Heath, 9 Feb.
1905.
18. P.R.O., T9/31/pp. 583-4; T1/10054B/21516; T1/
10659A/13618.
19. Lloyd George Papers, B/1/1/10, Llewellyn Smith to
Lloyd George, 24 Dec. 1907; *S.C. on Post Office Servants
(Wages and Conditions of Employment)*, *Mins. of Ev.*, PP 1906
(308) XII Pt 1, Q.7237; 1913 (268) XII, Q.27274.
20. *Hansard*, 4th Series, 177, Col. 164, 27 June 1907.
Lloyd George: 'The Statistical Department of the Board of
Trade was the Intelligence Department of the commerce and
industry of the country ... and should be as efficient as the
Intelligence Department in War'; P.R.O., T1/10562/22706,
minute by Sir George Murray, 31 Dec. 1906.
21. P.R.O., BT13/134, Churchill to Llewellyn Smith, 8
April 1909; Passfield Papers, Beatrice Webb Diary, 24 March
1908.
22. P.R.O., LAB41/213, G.H. Wood to F.H. MacLeod, 11 June
1909.
23. P.R.O., T1/11700/26594, minute by R.G. Hawtrey, 3
March 1909; T9/41, Treasury to Board of Trade, 22 Feb. 1912.
24. P.R.O., LAB41/213, G.H. Wood to F.H. MacLeod, 11

178

April 1912.

25. P.R.O., BT13/134, memo. on 'The Organisation of the Commercial, Labour, and Statistical Department' by G.J. Stanley, 30 March 1909.

26. P.R.O., T1/11646/13667, Llewellyn Smith to Sydney Buxton, 24 March 1913. Equally symptomatic of the Treasury's lack of appreciation of the data needs of welfare administration was its refusal to sanction the appointment of a permanent actuarial adviser to the Board to assess the viability of existing and projected schemes of insurance. See P.R.O., BT13/E37900; T1/11481/22621.

27. See, e.g., M. Wright, 'Treasury Control 1854-1914' in G. Sutherland (ed.),*Studies in the growth of nineteenth century government* (1972), pp. 195-226.

Chapter 8

THE FAILURE OF ANCILLARY PRODUCERS

The second major obstacle with which the Board of
Trade was forced to contend was the compartmental-
isation of official social and industrial
statistics. As a result, its statistical output
was heavily dependent upon data inputs from a
range of other government departments; in
particular, the Home Office, the Local Government
Board, the Registrar General's Office, and the
Registry of Friendly Societies; data which in many
instances such departments were either unable or
unwilling to supply. This reliance not only
reduced the range and reliability of the Board's
labour market intelligence, but constituted a
positive disincentive to those of its more
innovative statisticians who wished to identify
and to measure the linkages between a range of
contemporary social and economic problems.

THE HOME OFFICE

The Home Office proved singularly unresponsive
towards the objectives of the Board of Trade. In
theory, its potential for producing labour
statistics rivalled, if not surpassed, that of the
Labour Department itself. Its administration of
the Factory and Workshop Acts and of industrial
legislation relating to employment conditions,
truck, home work and workmen's compensation, gave
the Home Office access to extensive data on the
employment, remuneration and health of the labour
force in the leading sectors of the British
economy. Its factory, mines and workshop
inspectorates had an unrivalled knowledge of local
labour markets - of conditions at the point of
production, of procedures and levels of pay, of

the more exploitative and dangerous trades and processes, of the impact of technical innovation on wage differentials and unemployment, and of the social and economic determinants of labour unrest.

Yet, there was a signal failure to collate the mass of available information arising from their field work and from the implementation of a growing range of industrial regulations.[1] Prior to 1896, Home Office returns of the numbers employed in British industry were highly irregular and, in the case of non-textile employment, 'so unreliable as to be statistically valueless'.[2] Thereafter, under pressure from the Board of Trade, an annual return of employment was issued but, in clear disregard for the advice of Llewellyn Smith and Robert Giffen, it excluded all workshop employees and was collated according to an 'idiosyncratic amalgam of industrial and occupational classifications' (by the nature of the raw material worked on, the process to which it was subjected, and the purpose for which the finished article was made), thus seriously reducing its value to the Board of Trade for the purposes of integration and comparability with its own data.[3] The Home Office proved similarly obstructive during the 1890s in withholding from the Board detailed information on wages, unemployment and unrest in key industries such as coalmining and cotton textiles, at a time when the Board was endeavouring to extend the industrial basis and thus the credibility of its labour statistics.[4] Meanwhile, as the Board's fiscal enquiries into the comparative efficiency and standard of living of British labour revealed, the Home Office failed to capitalise upon its knowledge of working conditions so as to furnish a statistical basis for the measurement of their relationship to industrial fatigue and productivity. As late as 1907, its statistics on home work and the female labour market were openly admitted to be in 'a very primitive state' and of 'no real value'[5]; the introduction of minimum wage legislation relying instead upon the data and expertise of the Labour Department. Likewise, despite representations from Llewellyn Smith, Home Office returns relating to the medical inspection of juvenile employees were not exploited so as to provide a worthwhile index of the degree of fitness or unfitness of the factory population.[6]

Several explanations can be advanced for this lack of Home Office commitment to labour statistics. Firstly, it reflected the overriding concern of the Home Office secretariat to preserve the existing hegemony of the Office over industrial administration. Since 1880, the Home Office establishment had been transformed by the appointment, by open competition, of a new generation of First Division clerks led by Edward Troup. Whereas the 'old guard' within the secretariat had adopted a negative attitude to government growth and had willingly devolved a range of functions upon other authorities such as the Local Government Board and the newly established Scottish Office (1885) and Board of Agriculture (1889), by 1890, the younger officials were determined to consolidate and to expand the responsibilities of the Home Office.[7] They were especially sensitive to criticisms in the labour and radical press of its administration of industrial statistics and of the Factory and Workshop Acts, and to the proposal that the labour functions of the Home Office should either be incorporated within a new ministry or transferred to the Labour Bureau of the Board of Trade.[8] In their view, an improvement in the efficiency and status of the 'industrial work' of the Home Office was the more logical and defensible solution. The establishment of a Labour Department at the Board of Trade in 1893 was therefore regarded by Home Office officials as a fundamental intrusion into their bureaucratic domain, and much of their subsequent antipathy towards the statistical objectives of the Labour Department, such as their abortive effort in 1894 to 'confine the scope of the *Labour Gazette* to those small sections of Labour over which the Board of Trade exercised administrative control',[9] reflected this territorial imperative.

However, the deliberately obstructive attitude of the Home Office towards the efforts of the Labour Department to accumulate and disseminate meaningful social data was not simply the product of inter-departmental rivalry. It was also a function of its economic philosophy.[10] Although its secretariat rejected the social insensitivity of orthodox political economy and accepted the challenge of Jevons and Marshall to its assumptions, their economic views were essentially conservative. They considered it imperative that the government should avoid fiscal and welfare measures such as progressive taxation, relief schemes, or minimum wage legislation, which might trench upon the profits fund, erode managerial incentives, and reduce the level of capital accumulation. Middle-class savings had to be accorded priority over unproductive working-class expenditure. It was equally vital that, whenever possible, labour costs should be freely exposed to market forces.

The Labour Department was viewed as a fundamental threat to such values. Troup was convinced that Llewellyn Smith had collaborated with the Fabians in their celebrated attack on Liberal social policy - 'To your tents O Israel' -in the *Fortnightly Review*, and feared that the Labour Department would initiate a range of welfare measures designed to modify income distribution, regulate the labour market and inhibit free collective bargaining.[11] In time, the Home Office came to hold a less sinister view of the Labour Department's objectives. Nonetheless, it continued to interpret adverse publicity towards Home Office statistics in ideological terms, and as late as 1910, Troup was disposed to dismiss a T.U.C. resolution stressing the relative merits of Board of Trade industrial data as nothing more than 'the blindness of affection which naturally belongs to a god-papa'.[12]

The contribution of the Home Office to official labour statistics during the late-Victorian and Edwardian period was further inhibited by the administrative philosophy of its permanent officials. It can be argued that the impact of open competition upon Home Office administration after 1870 was in many respects 'regressive'. The appointment of university-educated generalists meant that by the 1890s, the majority of the senior establishment had little specialist knowledge of the needs of industry and the realities of the labour market. Such officials were career rather than problem-orientated and viewed social administration primarily as a source of income and professional status. They constituted a bureaucatic elite which identified with the social, educational and professional views of peer groups in other areas of Whitehall rather than with specific areas of social reform.[13]

Consistent with this perspective was a minimalist attitude towards the role and utility of statistics. While they acknowledged that, without statistics, administration might degenerate 'into a blind mechanical process with no intelligent guide for its action',[14] they did not perceive the Home Office as having an 'investigative role' over and above the provision of routine administrative data sufficient to ensure the efficient enforcement of a code of industrial regulations. Indeed, the secretariat positively resisted the view that the Home Office should fulfil a broader intelligence function with respect to social and economic developments, as an adjunct to its regulatory duties.[15] Significantly, Home office officials favoured the establishment of a Factory Statistics Branch in 1895 as a means of relieving the inspectorate from 'over-pressure of work' rather than of capitalising upon their intelligence potential.[16] In 1894, its Factory Statistics Committee, while admitting the 'self-evident value' of regular anthropometric studies of representative samples of factory children, declined to recommend their implementation on the grounds that the matter lay 'beyond the ordinary range of the work of the department'.[17] Likewise, in 1910, Home Office officials were unreceptive to Churchill's proposals to establish a team of labour advisers modelled on the labour correspondents of the Board of Trade, as a means of improving Home Office industrial intelligence; although, on this occasion, the unwelcome prospect of admitting former trade unionists into the professional establishment and its overtones of populist gimmickry also weighed heavily with the secretariat.[18] Equally characteristic was the absence of Home Office representatives at the International Statistical Institute and its apathy towards the efforts of the International Labour Office to develop both the statistical techniques and data base for comparative analyses of the health and efficiency of industrial workforces.[19]

This negativism was clearly reflected in the low level of resources allocated to statistical work by the Home Office. Aggregate Home Office expenditure on statistical staff and investigations during the period 1886-1914 was on average 57 per cent below that of the Board of Trade and its rate of growth markedly lower.[20] Even the Treasury was impressed by the economy of the Home Office in view of the vast expansion of data-processing consequent upon industrial legislation such as the Workmen's Compensation and Factory and Workshop Amendment Acts.[21]

Furthermore, despite a comprehensive reappraisal of its statistical duties between 1892

The Failure of Ancillary Producers

and 1895, the Home Office continued to adhere to
the rule, established in the 1870s as part of the
general rationalisation of Civil Service
functions, that statistical work was 'mechanical'
and within the competence of the junior establishment. Senior officials such as Troup maintained
that, subject to technical advice from the
inspectorates, such work was ideally suited to the
Second Division; that it required intelligence and
background knowledge but 'not any demanding
technical expertise or high standard of training
in statistical methods' and that the primary
requirement was an 'administrative competence' to
oversee the 'routine aggregation of returns'.[22]
Thus, whereas the statistical work of the Board of
Trade was devolved upon professional statisticians
and supervised by officers of First Division rank,
the key statistical posts in the Home Office (i.e.
the heads of the Statistical Department, the
Factory Statistics Branch and Mineral Statistics
Branch) were all recruited from lower clerical
grades.[23] Despite mounting criticism from Press,
Parliament, and scientific organisations such as
the British Association and the Royal Statistical
Society, the Home Office resolutely refused to
appoint a trained statistician before the First
World War, believing that the policy gains from
statistical work were maximised at a relatively
low level of analysis.[24] A schedule of its
statistical staff in 1913 (Table 8.1) clearly
reveals their lack of status and the heavy
reliance on junior clerks and boy copyists.[25]

Table 8.1: Home Office Statistical Establishment
(1913)

Status	Statistical Dept.	Factory Statistics Branch	Mineral Statistics Branch
Staff Officers	1	1	-
2nd Div. Clerks	2	3	1
Ass. Clerks	6	5	2
Copyists	-	-	2
Boy Clerks	3	10	-

Moreover, such expertise as was acquired amongst

185

the lower clerical ranks within the various statistical branches was dissipated by the high turnover of staff due to the failure of the Home Office to establish, in accordance with the Board of Trade, a distinct promotion structure for statistical officers.[26]

Their pay reflected their low status within the Office. Between 1876 and 1914, the scale of remuneration within the Statistical Department actually declined.[27] The salary scale of its Superintendent remained virtually unchanged over the same period and was, along with those of the clerks in charge of factory and mineral statistics, virtually half the scale attached to equivalent posts within the Board of Trade.[28] As late as 1909, the statistical officer responsible for briefing the under-secretaries on parliamentary questions was a junior clerk on a remuneration of £98 per annum, and many such officials were forced to supplement their income by undertaking additional employment after office hours.[29] Given the fact that, even after the reforms of the 1890s, industrial statistics continued to be accorded lowest priority within the statistical work of the Home Office,[30] it is perhaps understandable that the Board of Trade found their value as an input to the measurement of the 'Labour Problem' sadly wanting.

THE LOCAL GOVERNMENT BOARD

As with the Home Office, the Local Government Board possessed enormous potential for generating data relevant to the labour market. Its administration of pauperism, vagrancy, housing, health, environmental pollution and distress from want of employment, gave it, in theory, a unique overview of the structural determinants of working-class living standards and physical efficiency; with access via its Poor Law Inspectorate, guardians and other local authorities to a mass of local information relating to the level and incidence of destitution, to unemployment, under-employment, labour mobility, industrial sanitation, housing stock, and to costs of living.

However, again, as with the Home Office, this potential remained largely unrealised. The Local Government Board 'had no technique of objective tests in its work of supervision, and no precise measurement of the results of particular policies'.[31] In 1892, reflecting upon the impetus of a paper by Charles Booth, Sidney Webb remarked: 'He will have done what I have tried for years to do, viz. get the Local Government Board to improve its statistics. If I were at that office I would have revolutionized its statistical department by this time'.[32] No reform followed, however, and it continued to be overburdened by 'introspective' data unrelated to the social issues of contemporary debate and merely designed to keep a routine check upon the Inspectorate.[33] Predictably, the committee appointed in 1897 to report on the staffing of the Department was particularly critical of its statistical deficiencies.[34] Thereafter, as the problems of destitution, unemployment and physical deterioration moved to the centre of political debate, this inadequacy represented a serious embarrassment to both the Conservative and Liberal administrations. In 1905, Charles Hobhouse wrote of its lack of statistical direction to Walter Runciman on his appointment as Parliamentary Secretary: 'I know how much waking up that Department requires - and if you can galvanise its officials - not into activity - but into common sense - you will have cleared an Augean Stable.'[35] Yet, as Runciman left for the Treasury in 1907, his Chief Inspector was still lamenting 'the deplorable state of the *Gazette* and the statistics'.[36]

The degree to which this statistical ineptitude handicapped the Board of Trade in its efforts to obtain comprehensive labour statistics is best illustrated with reference to unemployment and housing. The Labour Department tried in vain to obtain from the Local Government Board information bearing upon the origins and extent of unemployment.[37] Despite strong and sustained inter-departmental pressure, it was not until 1912 that the format of Poor Law returns was drastically revised in order to provide a breakdown of the level, duration and causes of destitution.[38] As a result, official pauper statistics could neither be used to supplement the Board of Trade's intelligence as to the state of the labour market nor to measure the critical relationship between unemployment and pauperism. Similarly, the efforts of the Board of Trade to analyse the casual labour market and the problem of under-employment was seriously inhibited by the

failure of official vagrancy statistics to monitor
the real level and incidence of 'casual pauperism'
within the community.[39]   The refusal of the Local
Government Board to synchronise its returns with
the monthly intelligence reports of the Board of
Trade's labour correspondents further reduced
their value.[40]

The Local Government Board was equally
unreceptive to the special investigations into the
causes, course and possible remedies of unemployment undertaken by the Board of Trade after 1893;
data from only 45 per cent of local authorities
being made available to the Labour Department for
the purposes of its evidence to the Select
Committee on Distress from Want of Employment.[41]
Thereafter, in spite of growing public and parliamentary criticism of the Local Government Board's
failure to quantify the social wastage which it
was supposed in part to administer, its permanent
officials continued to adopt a negative strategy
towards unemployment statistics, explicitly
dissociating their activities from the concept of
'labour' as such, in a desperate attempt to avoid
responsibility for such returns.[42]   In particular,
they declined to furnish the Board of Trade with
systematic information on local municipal and
voluntary schemes to alleviate exceptional
distress due to cyclical unemployment, and hence
to make an effective contribution to feasibility
studies of unemployment policy options.
Meanwhile, such statistics as the Local Government
Board *did* produce on unemployment and the state of
the labour market were 'universally regarded as
useless' and considered as a dilution of the real
situation 'to alienate sympathy from the
unemployed and avert executive action'.[43]   The
Local Government Board encouraged its Poor Law
Inspectorate and guardians merely to provide
'general impressions' rather than any 'illusory
and costly measure' of trends in regional and
local employment.[44]   As a result, so-called
'intelligence' furnished to the Board of Trade was
less a measure of labour utilisation than of the
prejudices with which such authorities perceived
the unemployment issue; as merely a creation of
scrounging, Socialist propaganda and indiscriminate charity, or in the characteristic terminology
of Local Government Board memoranda, 'wastrels',
'agitators' and 'a deluge of soup'.[45]

The Labour Department was similarly
handicapped by the absence of reliable data on

housing stock and rents. As recent studies by
Stedman Jones and Sutcliffe have revealed, the
price and availability of working-class housing
were central to the late-Victorian and Edwardian
urban crisis and to contemporary debate as to
urban degeneration and national efficiency, being
prime determinants of the standard of living of
the labour force.[46] They were therefore of vital
significance to the Board of Trade's enquiries
into working-class consumption patterns and costs
of living. However, Labour Department
investigators soon discovered that they could
place 'no reliance whatsoever' upon the 'scrappy
and limited information' at the disposal of the
Local Government Board.[47] Instead, in order to
establish an index of 'predominant rents' of
'typical' working-class housing, they were forced
to produce their own housing data virtually from
scratch, and given the constraints of having 'to
inaugurate in a very short space of time an
entirely novel enquiry', the quality of
statistical accuracy and refinement was inevitably
impaired.[48] Significantly, it was the rent
component of the Board of Trade's cost of living
index which attracted most criticism from the
Labour Movement and from the statistical profession, and evidence would suggest that its
weakness seriously eroded the overall credibility
of the Board's cost of living enquiries.[49]
     Several explanations can be advanced for the
lack of commitment of the Local Government Board
to social statistics in general and labour
statistics in particular. First and foremost, it
stemmed from the social and economic philosophy of
its permanent officials. Their outlook was over-
whelmingly conservative. 'With the possible
exception of the medical department the whole
administration was shot through with a reactionary
strain.'[50] The permanent secretaries, Owen,
Provis and Monro, were committed adherents of the
principles of the 1834 Poor Law Amendment Act, and
were unreceptive to the more 'progressive' and
environmentalist perceptions of destitution
invading government circles after the Chamberlain
Circular of 1886. Almost to a man, the Poor Law
Inspectorate shared the disposition of their
chiefs.[51] From this ideological standpoint, the
Board shared the Home Office's view that the
Labour Department was a front for the Socialist
wing of the Labour Movement and that its investigations were therefore designed to undermine the

orthodox principles of Poor Law administration.[52]

Underlying the apparent apathy of the Local Government Board towards the unemployment enquiries undertaken by the Labour Department after 1893 was a very real fear that such investigations would shift the emphasis of official enquiry from the distress consequent upon 'want of employment' to its structural determinants, and thus rupture the carefully delimited parameters of existing welfare debate. In identifying such causes and devaluing the significance of personal and moral factors, the Board feared that the Board of Trade would merely fuel left-wing demands for the State regulation of the labour market and for the fundamental reappraisal of the scope and rationale of the Poor Law.[53] The fact that, after 1900, Labour Department statistics were increasingly used by Labour spokesmen to indict the Local Government Board for its negative response to social deprivation, and that the Right to Work Campaign increasingly identified the Labour Department as the proper authority to co-ordinate public investment schemes designed to stabilise the level of employment,[54] only served to reinforce the reluctance of the Local Government Board to collaborate in the provision of official labour statistics.

The negative attitude of the Local Government Board to social statistics also stemmed from the administrative philosophy of its permanent officials. Apart from the Assistant Secretary of the Poor Law Division, the senior establishment of the Local Government Board was appointed by open competition. Officials were not expected to have any practical experience of workhouse administration, housing, unemployment, medical care or of any of the range of environmental problems for which the Board was responsible. Even the Poor Law Inspectorate possessed little previous expertise. They were appointed as 'laymen' for their 'tact' and 'savoir faire' and their general capacity to guide and influence local authorities.[55] This recruitment pattern engendered a conservative response to social and industrial problems. As 'professional' bureaucrats, the permanent officials of the Local Government Board conceived of their role as the performance of prescribed duties rather than the creation of new ones, with the emphasis on the efficient application of rules or a 'code' according to precedent.[56]

This disinclination to innovate was strongly reflected in their attitude to statistical work. The Board's senior officials viewed statistics as a routine adjunct of administration and not as a means of informing broader contemporary debate over poverty and efficiency. Indeed, they explicitly denied that the Local Government Board *had* an 'intelligence' role to play within the process of labour policy-making, that its functions had any relevance to those of the Labour Department, and conversely, that labour statistics, other than those relating to 'thrift and providence', might facilitate the work of the Board.[57] Any attempt by individual officers to undertake 'original investigation' into contentious issues relating to social policy was firmly suppressed.[58]

Thus, compared with the shift in public attitudes towards poverty and a range of related social problems during the period, the statistical returns of the Local Government Board remained markedly unchanged. Their overriding function was to identify the level of deserving as opposed to undeserving pauperism and thereby to monitor the enforcement of the principles of the 1834 Poor Law Amendment Act.[59] The Board's pauper and vagrancy statistics were therefore designed to ensure the conformity of Poor Law Unions with such principles rather than to illuminate the structural determinants of destitution and the relationship of pauperism to the dynamics of the labour market. Even the more detailed, *ad hoc* investigations after 1900 into the causes and incidence of pauperism and vagrancy, and the industrial and family profiles of recipients of relief, were primarily motivated by a concern to preserve the principle of less eligibility.[60] Social statistics produced by the Local Government Board were also designed to monitor the cost of Poor Law administration so as to minimise its burden upon the rates and to eradicate local, and specifically 'poplarist' anomalies in the provision of relief.[61] This narrow rationale behind Poor Law data was most tangibly expressed when, in 1897, as part of the general rationalisation of the Board's structure, the Statistical Branch was incorporated within the Local Taxation and Audit Division.[62]

In so far as one can disaggregate the Board's accounts, it is evident that the low functional status accorded to empirical investigation was

reflected in the level of resources allocated to
it. In evidence to the Departmental Committee of
1897 on the Local Government Board's establishment, the Principal of the Statistical Department
forcefully described his budget as a 'public
disgrace' and openly admitted his consequent
inability to fulfil 'any effective intelligence
function' either for decision-making within the
Board or for use in broader public and
parliamentary debate.63 The fact that as late as
1911 his salary scale was as low as £400 - £500
(i.e. 40 per cent below that of the comparable
post in the Labour Department) further reduced the
morale of his department.64

Moreover, the division of labour within the
Statistical Department meant that Higher Division
clerks focussed their efforts upon returns
relating to local taxation, agricultural rating,
and local authority loans. The bulk of the
collation and interpretation of pauper and
vagrancy statistics was devolved upon second and
third class clerks.65 It was not regarded in any
way as specialist work requiring professional
training. Indeed, prior to the First World War
'no-one [had] been recruited' to the Department
with 'a trained knowledge of the value of
statistics and their preparation'. Even its head
had started his Civil Service career as a junior
clerk in 1850 and had been forced to acquire such
limited expertise as the routine objectives of the
Board demanded 'in the course of his work'.66

In assessing the statistical inertia of the
Local Government Board, allowance has certainly to
be made for the enervating effects of Treasury
control.67 Equally, the dependence of the Board
for information upon local authorities has to be
stressed. Local officials were 'notoriously lax'
with respect to statistical returns, and apathetic
towards the production and use of social data.68
Sanitary authorities frequently ignored their
legal obligation to monitor industrial sanitation,
including outwork and home work conditions, and
were impervious to the possible application of
Census data in identifying housing and health
problems.69 Meanwhile, Poor Law guardians doggedly
resisted pressure from Whitehall to provide
additional information on poverty, unemployment
and local labour market conditions. They
maintained either that its value was
incommensurate with the additional labour and cost
involved or that 'information in the public

interest' should be funded by the Exchequer and not constitute an additional burden upon the rates.[70] Such data as were produced by local authorities were frequently unreliable for the purposes of aggregate or regional analysis and valueless for cross-tabulation with other social indicators. Many local officials were, as the Local Government Board freely admitted, 'illiterate, ignorant men'.[71] Only the more lavishly-funded unions maintained systematic pauper records, and the evidence suggests that, for want of motivation or resources, the bulk of pauper and vagrancy returns were at best guesstimates and often distorted so as to disguise evasions of the Poor Law.[72]

Nonetheless, the fact remains that on many occasions the Local Government Board merely used Treasury control or the deficiencies of local authority records as an excuse for its own failings. The Treasury files reveal no commitment on the part of the Board to elevate the status and funding of statistical work, nor to shift the cost of local enquiries onto the Exchequer. Moreover, despite a succession of public exposés (from the Report of the Official Statistics Committee of 1881 to the Minority Report of the Poor Law Commission of 1909) of its inability to monitor the social problems within its remit, the Board was unprepared to *compel* local authorities to comply with the statistical needs of central government.[73]

THE GENERAL REGISTER OFFICE

The limited range of industrial data presented in the Census constituted yet another impediment to the statistical work of the Board of Trade. As Alfred Marshall observed to the Treasury Committee on the Census in 1890, the fact that Census data was poorly suited to the needs of social scientists and administrators seriously impaired their ability to confront the 'Labour Problem'. 'We want', he submitted, 'the Government to supply us with straw - We cannot make bricks without it'.[74] Similar sentiments were subsequently expressed by the Labour Department in several of its major policy-briefing memoranda.[75]

The Department criticised the Census on five main counts: firstly, its failure to provide a reliable breakdown of the numbers employed in each industry, occupation and mode of production (for example, to differentiate between surface and face workers in the extractive industries, between workers employed in the various stages of iron and textile production, or in factory production as opposed to workshop employment or home work); secondly, its failure to monitor the employment, status and skill characteristics of the workforce; thirdly, its inability to provide a measure of the proportion of the workforce unemployed or irregularly employed; fourthly, its lack of reliable information on the extent and incidence of female participation in the labour market; and finally, its failure to ascertain the industries and occupations upon which 'non-workers' - in 1901, 53 per cent of those enumerated - were dependent for their income and subsistence.[76]

In the absence of any detailed study of the General Register Office, the reasons for such omissions can only be tentatively advanced. In part, they originated in doubts as to the feasibility of the Board of Trade's statistical objectives. Attempts to obtain accurate information on employment status, as in 1891, had proved abortive, as had previous efforts of the Registrar-General to secure a census of the unemployed.[77] Moreover, the experience of German and Swiss Census authorities appeared to indicate that detailed occupational schedules could not successfully be incorporated within the normal process of census enumeration.[78]

British Census authorities also lacked the staff and resources with which to address broader social and economic issues and the welfare implications of vital statistics. The Treasury refused to sanction an upper division establishment within the General Register Office. As a result, the staff were demoralised and lacked intellectual and statistical calibre.[79] Moreover, the Census officials were incapable of processing the type of schedules advocated by the Board of Trade. The Superintendent of Statistics at the General Register Office freely admitted that most enumerators were ignorant, untrained, and poorly paid, and that, for want of education or commitment, many Registrars and Superintendent-Registrars failed to exercise any effective quality control upon the Census.[80] Meanwhile, the Census Office itself was staffed by a temporary establishment of inferior clerks hastily recruited by the Treasury.[81] As Bowley complained to the

Royal Statistical Society in 1908, given the poor
quality of the personnel involved at all levels in
the Census machinery, 'the great part of the
utility of the data' for social and economic
administrators was inevitably wasted.[82]

However, resistance by the Registrar-
General's Office to the statistical proposals of
the Board of Trade and its defeatist response to
the data problems of the Labour Department also
appears to have had a more basic ideological
dimension. Correspondence between social
scientists, statisticians and leading social
administrators during the period contain a scatter
of references to the reactionary bent of the
Office, both in terms of its social and
operational philosophy,[83] and the contribution of
its senior officials to parliamentary enquiries,
such as the Royal Commission on Labour, and to
inter-departmental discussions on the Census,
confirms this viewpoint.

Until the appointment of Bernard Mallet and
T.H.C. Stevenson as Registrar-General and Superintendent of Statistics in 1909, the General
Register Office adopted a minimalist view of its
functions; as being those of enumeration and *not*
investigation. Its overriding concern was to
refine the accuracy of a narrow range of vital
statistics rather than to bring such data to bear
upon the more contentious issues in late-Victorian
and Edwardian social politics.[84] Even *The Times*
was critical of its 'sceptical turn of mind'
towards the value of census data for identifying
shifts in social structure and in the condition of
the working classes.[85]

In particular, the General Register Office
resisted the efforts of the Labour Department to
incorporate within the Census more systematic
schedules ·relating to the distribution and make-up
of the workforce. In the view of Sir B.P.
Henniker, Registrar-General from 1880 to 1900,
such schedules reflected merely the 'statistical
fad' of a minority of radicals and social
scientists, and would alienate public opinion from
the Census.[86] In general, until 1909, British
Census authorities remained apathetic towards
international advances in the application of
census intelligence to social administration, not
only in Germany and America, but also in Canada,
Australasia, and even India, and were unreceptive
to innovations in the techniques of tabulation and
in statistical theory which could have enabled the

more flexible use of vital statistics for the
purposes of social and economic policy-making.[87]
     While the precise reasons for this conserva-
tism still remain somewhat unclear, its effects
upon the labour statistics produced by the Board
of Trade are manifest. The absence of basic
information with regard to the size and distribution of the workforce inhibited systematic
analysis of a range of issues relating to the
labour market, such as the level of unionisation
and unemployment.[88] The ability of the Labour
Department to monitor shifts in the skill
characteristics of labour was drastically reduced
by the lack of consistent and precise occupational
data in the Census, as was its opportunity to
relate demographic factors, such as family size
and composition, to earnings, to workforce
mobility, and to the age and sex specificity of
employment.[89] Its ability to identify dangerous
or socially unacceptable trades and modes of
production for the purposes of preventative
legislation was similarly impaired.
     Furthermore, the lack of comparability
between Census and Board of Trade data seriously
eroded the value of the latter. In particular, as
the Census classifications did not conform with
the occupational breakdown in the Board's wages
and earnings investigations, its statisticians
could not safely extrapolate from departmental
data to provide reliable estimates on key issues
of contemporary welfare and economic debate, such
as the aggregate income of the working classes or
the extent of destitution.[90] There was no
scientific means of calculating whether the
Board's labour statistics constituted a representative sample, and this inability of the
Department to utilise the Census to establish the
statistical significance of its enquiries and
indexes was an important contributory factor in
retarding its adoption of the mathematical
techniques of sampling.[91]

THE REGISTRY OF FRIENDLY SOCIETIES

Yet another department with potential for
producing labour statistics was the Registry of
Friendly Societies. In the period 1886 to 1914,
the Friendly and Provident Society Movement still
constituted the largest area of working-class
associative effort. Numerically, it was still

more significant than the Trade Union Movement, possessing a membership of 4.8 million in 1897.[92] As by statute it was required to submit regular returns to the Chief Registrar of Friendly Societies on its membership and financial position, the Registry had access to a mine of information on the savings and expenditure patterns of the working classes. It could literally monitor the extent and incidence of thrift and self-help. In theory, it possessed a mass of invaluable data relating to the nature extent and viability of private welfare schemes (including the provision of accident, sickness and death benefits and medical facilities), to the impact of State welfare legislation upon such schemes, and to variations in the sickness and mortality experience of their membership.[93]

In practice, however, much to the dismay of the Labour Department of the Board of Trade, the information collected by the Registry proved to be 'virtually useless'. The bulk of the societies were either unreliable or inept, or positively evasive in submitting returns.[94] Moreover, primarily due to Treasury control, the Registry was incapable of monitoring their quality, still less of properly collating and interpreting the data within them.[95] Due to a chronic shortage of statistical staff, less than 50 per cent of the annual returns were even 'cursorily examined'.[96] As a result, as the Chief Registrar, Stuart Robertson, freely admitted in 1912, information compiled in the Registry was essentially 'an accumulation of unrefined and useless figures', widely and justifiably criticised by social commentators.[97]

As with the General Register Office, the statistical philosophy of the Registry of Friendly Societies was, for most of the period, extremely introspective; the broader implications of its statistics for industrial policy being obscured by an overriding concern to strengthen the actuarial review of Friendly Society finances. When, in 1912, Stuart Robertson sought to introduce a broader conception of the Registry's statistical role, the Treasury dismissed his efforts to produce data of 'more general social and economic relevance' as reflecting 'a statistical purism' and 'departmental imperialism' wholly inappropriate for what they considered to be 'rightly a backwater of the Civil Service'.[98]

This shortfall between potential and

performance in the provision of statistics relevant to the labour market also characterised a range of other departments. For example, in attempting to obtain information relating to unemployment policy options, the Board of Trade found the Board of Customs singularly unreliable for information on immigration flows.[99] Similarly, the data necessary to test the feasibility of various colonisation and emigration schemes were unforthcoming from the Colonial Office. The apathy of the Office towards colonial labour statistics was most clearly exemplified in the stunted development of the Emigrants Information Office administered by the Dominions Branch.[100] Meanwhile, in the provision of information on wages in the public sector and, in particular, on their adherence to the Fair Wages Resolutions, the War Office and the Admiralty proved very obstructive. As a matter of policy, they were opposed to providing such information.[101] Finally, comparative analysis by the Labour Department of labour market conditions and welfare legislation in Britain and overseas was seriously impaired by its inability to rely on the Foreign Office for data. Labour intelligence furnished by the diplomatic and consular services was regularly distorted by social prejudice and rarely constituted more than 'descriptive impressions'. Attempts to rely on them for hard labour statistics, as in the wages and cost of living enquiries, proved utterly abortive.[102]

A CENTRAL STATISTICAL OFFICE

In an effort to reduce its dependence for industrial data upon other departments of State, the Board of Trade urged upon successive governments the proposal that all social and economic 'intelligence', as distinct from purely administrative statistics, should be collated and interpreted by one Central Statistical Office attached to the Board. Before the Official Statistics Committee of 1879-81, Robert Giffen had striven to expose the lack of co-ordination and utility in British government information consequent upon its decentralised production structure.[103] The Committee had conceded that the major blame for statistical chaos lay 'in the sacrifice of the requirements of the public and of Parliament to those of the departments', and had accepted the need for 'strong centralisation and control', but its recommendations for structural reform had been tentative and ineffectual. While acknowledging that the Board's statistical branch could unquestionably 'claim to have made great and steady progress towards supplying the want of a Central Statistical Department', the Committee had not been prepared to sanction its further development.[104]

Nonetheless, throughout the 1880s and 1890s, Board of Trade officials continued to lobby for the formal recognition of what they considered to be the Board's *de facto* role as a Central Statistical Department. As the 'Labour Problem' moved to the forefront of public debate, they were increasingly concerned to secure an effective system of industrial intelligence based upon the rationalisation of the statistical apparatus of late-Victorian government.[105] Unfortunately, the Board's concern was not shared elsewhere in Whitehall, and the issue of a Central Statistical Office lacked sufficient political capital to carry weight within the corridors of power.

Nevertheless, faced after 1900 by the unprecedented demand for economic and social data occasioned by Edwardian fiscal and welfare debate, Board of Trade labour administrators determined to renew and to intensify their campaign. Between 1906 and 1914 they collaborated with a range of social scientists and reformers in advocating a Central Statistical Office at the Board of Trade, or for an alternative scheme, originally conceived by Giffen, of a standing commission headed by the chief statistical officer of the Board, by means of which the quality, comparability, and relevance of information generated by Whitehall might be constantly reviewed and improved.

In 1906, labour officials briefed Bowley for his influential address to the British Association for the Advancement of Science, in which he advocated a 'central thinking department of statistics'. Echoing their frustrations, he observed that:

> There is already collected by the various Government departments, partly in their routine work, partly for the dissemination of information, an immense amount of valuable facts; but whenever a scientific inquirer endeavours to describe accurately some social or industrial development, or wishes to bring

> to the test of statistics the effect of some
> proposed reform ... some essential
> information is found lacking, for the reason
> that it has been no one's business to collect
> it.[106]

In the same year, the Board collaborated with
Charles Dilke to introduce the question of a
Central Statistical Department before the Select
Committee on Income Tax. Dilke's exchange of
views with witnesses such as Bowley, Chiozza
Money, and T.A. Coghlan, statistical adviser to
the Australian Government, was designed to
underline the 'confusion amounting to chaos'
within British economic statistics, and the
consequent impairment of the policy-making
process.[107]

Dilke's presidential address to the Royal
Statistical Society in 1907, highlighting the need
for a genuine intelligence department with which
to confront economic and social problems and to
undertake the forward-planning of governmental
investigative work, was similarly inspired by the
views and aspirations of the Board of Trade.[108] In
briefing Dilke, A.E. Bateman, former Comptroller-
General, revealed the enduring obstacles to
reform:

> The Statistical Department of the Board
> should be strengthened, but there would be
> departmental jealousies and difficulties ...
> I think that a Central Commission such as
> exists in most European countries would help
> towards the solution. The Treasury would
> oppose as they did the scheme of 30 years ago
> of strengthening the Board of Trade.[109]

Thereafter, the Board endeavoured to sustain its
campaign in evidence before the annual sessions of
the Select Committee on Publications, but although
the Committee was sympathetic towards the concept
of a 'State school of statistics' linked to the
Board of Trade, it did not regard the establishment of a Central Statistical Office as within its
terms of reference, and continued resistance from
the Treasury and from other departments of social
administration to the proposal ensured that
nothing tangible was achieved prior to the First
World War.[110]

The Failure of Ancillary Producers

NOTES

1. J. Pellew, *The Home Office 1848-1914: From Clerks to Bureaucrats* (1982), p. 155.
2. P.R.O., BT13/23/E11499, minute by Llewellyn Smith, 28 June 1896.
3. P.R.O., LAB2/1481/L117/1896; *Report of Departmental Committee on Factory Statistics*, PP 1895 (C.7608) XIX, p. 10.
4. P.R.O., LAB2/1597/C2031/1894, minute by Llewellyn Smith, 2 May 1894.
5. *S.C. on Home Work, Mins. of Ev.*, PP 1907 (290) VI, QQ. 120, 124.
6. *Report of Factory Statistics Committee*, PP 1895 (C.7608) XIX, p. 5.
7. Pellew, *Home Office*, Ch. 3.
8. P.R.O., HO45/10122/B12457, E. Troup to G. Lushington, 3 May 1892.
9. P.R.O., LAB2/1597/C2031/1894.
10. See R. Davidson, 'The Ideology of Labour Administration 1886-1914', *Society for the Study of Labour History Bulletin*, 40 (1980), pp. 29-35.
11. P.R.O., HO45/B10296A/9837, Troup to Pemberton, 26 July 1894.
12. P.R.O., HO45/20284/R620/6; HO45/9901/B19183.
13. Pellew, *Home Office*, pp. 183, 190-1, 201-3.
14. *Report of Factory Statistics Committee*, PP 1895 (C.7608) XIX, p. 19.
15. Pellew, *Home Office*, p. 108.
16. P.R.O., HO45/9877/B15358, H. Gladstone to H.H. Asquith, 24 Nov. 1893.
17. PP 1895 (C.7608) XIX, p. 18.
18. P.R.O., T1/11356/22568.
19. *Bulletin of the International Statistical Institute*, (1886-1914); P.R.O., T1/11319/16216.
20. Home Office data from P.R.O., T1, Treasury Board Papers; T13, Treasury out-letters to Home Office; HO45, Home Office registered papers; PP, *Annual Civil Service Estimates and Appropriation Accounts*.
21. P.R.O., T1/8993A/18127.
22. *Report of R.C. on the Civil Service, Mins. of Ev.*, PP 1912-13 (Cd.6535) XV, QQ. 4918-9, 5023; P.R.O., HO45/17788/B32589/82.
23. For a detailed breakdown of the career development of the statistical officers of the Department, see P.R.O., HO45/17788/B32589/82.
24. P.R.O., HO45/17788/B32589/71, minute by Sir Edward Troup, 2 March 1913. For criticisms, see HO45/9901/B19183; HO45/20284/R620/6; *Daily News*, 3 Aug. 1899; *JRSS*, 70 (1907), pp. 570-2; *Report of the B.A.A.S.* (1903), pp. 315-7.
25. P.R.O., HO45/17788/B32589/73, 'Comparative Statement of Certain Portions of the Home Office Staff in 1878 and

The Failure of Ancillary Producers

1916' by W.J. Farrant (Clerk for Statistical Returns), 17 April 1917.
26. P.R.O., HO45/17787/B32589/71, memo. by W.J. Farrant, 13 March 1913.
27. P.R.O., HO45/17788/B32589/73, memo. by Farrant, 17 April 1917.
28. P.R.O., HO45/17787/B32589/64, Home Office to Treasury, 23 Aug. 1911.
29. P.R.O., HO45/17787/B32589/46, memo. by W.P. Byrne and G.H. Tripp, 16 Dec. 1909.
30. P.R.O., HO45/17787/B32589/20, minute by G.H. Tripp, 2 Oct. 1906.
31. K.B. Smellie, *A History of Local Government* (1946), p. 101.
32. Passfield Papers, S. Webb to B. Potter, 4 Jan. 1892.
33. R.M. MacLeod, *Treasury Control and Social Administration* (1968), p. 31.
34. Ibid., p. 35.
35. Runciman Papers, C. Hobhouse to W. Runciman, 21 Dec. 1905.
36. Ibid., J.S. Davy to W. Runciman, 30 Jan. 1907.
37. See, e.g., P.R.O., MH10/57, minute by Sir Hugh Owen, 29 March 1893.
38. P.R.O., MH10/76, Circular from L.G. Bd., 26 June 1912.
39. P.R.O., MH10/70, Circular on the criticisms by the Royal Commission on the Poor Law of Poor Law Returns.
40. P.R.O., CAB37/38, memo. on 'A Recent Estimate of the Number of the Unemployed' by H. Llewellyn Smith, 23 Jan. 1895; *S.C. on Distress from Want of Employment, Mins. of Ev.*, PP 1895 (365) IX, Q. 4677; P.R.O., LAB2/1597/L253/1905.
41. P.R.O., MH10/59, L.G. Bd. Circulars, 19 Feb. 1895, 20 March 1895.
42. P.R.O., T1/10224/12488/1903.
43. R. Giffen, *Statistics - Written about the Years 1898-1900* (ed. H. Higgs, 1913), p. 7; *Hansard*, 4th Series, 152, cols. 877-8, 26 Feb. 1906.
44. See, e.g., P.R.O., MH10/75, Circular, 6 Jan. 1911.
45. See P.R.O., LAB2/1478, memo. by J.J. Dent collating reports of Metropolitan Poor Law Authorities, 4 Feb. 1903.
46. G. Stedman Jones, *Outcast London*, (Oxford, 1971), Pt 2; A. Sutcliffe, *Towards the Planned City* (Oxford, 1981), Ch. 3.
47. P.R.O., RG19/48B, Proceedings of the Inter-departmental Committee on the 1911 Census, p. 51, 9 Feb. 1910.
48. Yule Papers, R.S.S. Archives, Box 15, F.H. MacLeod to Yule, 11 Sept. 1907.
49. P.R.O., LAB2/1555/CLS1617/1908, Post Office to B. of T., 11 Aug. 1908; *JRSS* 68 (1905), p. 178; 71 (1908), pp. 208, 211.

202

50. K.D. Brown, 'John Burns at the Local Government Board: a Reassessment', *Journal of Social Policy*, 6 (1977), p. 158.

51. M.E. Craig, 'Bureaucracy and Negativism: The Local Government Board 1886-1909', M.A. Dissertation, Edinburgh University (1975), Ch. 4.

52. Rosebery Papers, Ry 70, J. Bryce to Rosebery, 5 Feb. 1895.

53. Ibid., Ry 68, Shaw Lefevre to Rosebery, 30 Dec. 1894; Balfour Papers, File 121, Almeric Fitzroy to A.J. Balfour, 21 July 1905.

54. P.R.O., LAB2/1478/L211/1903, memo. on 'National Unemployed Committee', 15 Dec. 1902.

55. *R.C. on the Civil Service*, *Mins. of Ev.*, PP 1912-13 (Cd.6210) XV, pp. 179-90.

56. Brown, 'The Local Government Board', pp. 158-63; MacLeod, *Treasury Control*, *passim*.

57. P.R.O., MH19/203, minute by Sir Hugh Owen, 20 Dec. 1888; T1/10224/12488, L.G. Bd. to Treasury, 2 March 1903.

58. See, e.g., P.R.O., T1/8298A/6204.

59. P.R.O., MH10/59, L.G. Bd. Circular, 11 Feb. 1895; MH10/69, L.G. Bd. Circular, 3 June 1905.

60. P.R.O., MH10/72, L.G. Bd. Circular, 17 Sept. 1908.

61. P.R.O., MH78/1B, 'Statistical Department - Statement of Work' by F. Stevens, 7 Jan. 1897. More generally, see P.A. Ryan, '"Poplarism" 1894-1930', in P. Thane (ed.), *The Origins of British Social Policy* (1978), p. 67.

62. *Report of Departmental Committee on the sufficiency of the clerical staff and Secretariat of the Local Government Board*, PP 1898 (C.8731) XL, p. 5.

63. P.R.O., MH78/1B, Local Government Board Committee, unpublished mins. of ev., QQ. 2715, 2731-2733.

64. P.R.O., MH78/43.

65. P.R.O., MH78/1A, papers on work and personnel of the L.G. Bd; MH78/1B, Local Government Board Committee, unpublished mins. of ev., QQ. 2745, 2759.

66. *Select Committee on Publications*, *Mins. of Ev.*, PP 1916 (112) III, Q. 368.

67. See MacLeod, *Treasury Control*, *passim*.

68. See, e.g., P.R.O., MH15/91/112645/52 (1907); MH15/91/7318/105 (1904).

69. See P.R.O., MH78/46, memo. by Sir W.H. Power, Principal Medical Officer, L.G. Bd., 19 Jan. 1904.

70. See P.R.O., T1/11110/21480.

71. P.R.O., T1/14987/15492, 'Statistical Department - General Statement as to the Work', p. 62.

72. M.A. Crowther, *The Workhouse System 1834-1929* (1982), pp. 117-18.

73. P.R.O., MH10/70, L.G. Bd. Circular, 18 Sept. 1906.

74. *Treasury Committee on the Census*, *Mins. of Ev.*, PP 1890 (C.6071) LVIII, QQ. 1462, 1528.

75. See, e.g., P.R.O., BT13/23/E11499, memo. on 'The Recommendations of the Labour Commission', 8 Jan. 1895.

76. P.R.O., RG19/10, B(oard) of T(rade) memo. on Census schedules, 19 Oct. 1900; RG19/9, B.T. to R(egistrar) G(eneral), 7 May 1901.

77. O.P.C.S., *Guide to Census Reports: Great Britain 1801-1966* (1977), p. 51; *S.C. on Distress from Want of Employment, Mins. of Ev.*, PP 1895 (365) IX, p. 81.

78. *Treasury Committee on the Census, Mins. of Ev.*, PP 1890 (C.6071) LVIII, Q. 120.

79. P.R.O., RG20/73, T(reasury) to R.G., 30 July 1895; RG29/3. R.G. to T., 30 Aug. 1905.

80. *Treasury Committee on the Census, Mins. of Ev.*, PP 1890 (C.6071) LVIII, QQ. 10, 29, 34, 39, 57, 66.

81. Ibid., p. 11.

82. *JRSS*, 71 (1908), p. 477.

83. See, e.g., Bowley Papers, R.S.S. Archives, Bernard Shaw to Bowley, 19 Jan. 1901; Dilke Papers, B.M. Add. MS 43922, B. Mallet to Dilke, 14 June 1910.

84. See especially, *R.C. on Labour, Mins. of Ev.*, PP 1893-4 (C.7063) XXXIX Pt 1, pp. 118-19; P.R.O., RG29/19, correspondence between R.G. and B.T. over 1901 Census; RG19/45, memo. by A. Bellingham, 3 July 1908.

85. *The Times*, 22 Sept. 1887.

86. P.R.O., RG29/19, B.P. Henniker to Shaw Lefevre, 11 July 1894.

87. Tuckwell Papers, File 31, memo. by R.S.S. Census Committee, 1910; P.R.O., RG19/48B, Interdepartmental Committee on 1911 Census, p. 122; RG19/45, memo. by A. Bellingham, 3 July 1908.

88. P.R.O., BT13/23/E11499, memo. on 'The Recommendations of the Labour Commission', 8 Jan. 1895; *9th Report on Trade Unions*, PP 1897 (C.8644) XCIX, p. xvi; *Report on British and Foreign Trade and Industry*, PP 1905 (Cd.2337) LXXXIV, p. 79.

89. P.R.O., RG19/9, misc. correspondence between B.T. and R.G. over 1901 Census; RG19/48B, proceedings of Inter-departmental Committee on the 1911 Census, pp. 25, 103-21.

90. Ibid., p. 119; LAB2/1555/L1099/1903, memo. on 'The Extent of Destitution', by C.E. Collet, 14 July 1903; *Bulletin of the International Statistical Institute* (1906), pp. 292-3, 'Recensements industriels et statistique du Chomage'.

91. See A.L. Bowley's observations in *JRSS*, 69 (1906), pp. 550-66; Ibid., 71 (1908), pp. 475-6.

92. P.H.J.H. Gosden, *The Friendly Societies in England 1815-75* (Manchester, 1961), p. 7.

93. P.R.O., T1/11284/6986, memo. on the functions of the Registry by the Chief Registrar, J. Stuart Sim, 31 Oct. 1910; memo. by W.H. Tozer, (Statistical Clerk), 21 Nov. 1910.

94. P.R.O., T1/8519A/16314, Provisional Report of Departmental enquiry into the Establishment of the Registry (1890),

p. xxxvi.

95. P.R.O., T1/11706/27505, memo. by Stuart Robertson, 19 July 1913; T1/8519A/16314, Departmental Enquiry into the Establishment, Mins. of Ev. p. 6; T1/10249A/4026, correspondence between T. and R.F.S. over salary and status of W.H. Tozer.

96. P.R.O., T1/11705/27505, memo. by G. Stuart Robertson, 15 Nov. 1912.

97. Ibid., Stuart Robertson to Bradbury, 18 Nov. 1913.

98. P.R.O., T1/11705/27505, minute by Wilkins, 7 July 1911; memo. by J. Bradbury, 21 Nov 1913; Bentham Cox to Bradbury, 1 Nov. 1913.

99. P.R.O., BT12/34, R.T. Prowse to R. Giffen, 11 April 1893.

100. J.A. Cross, 'The Dominions Department of the Colonial Office: Origins and Early Years, 1905-1914', London PhD thesis (1965), Ch. 5.

101. See, e.g., P.R.O., LAB2/1479/L2343/1893, G. Lawson to H. Llewellyn Smith, 28 Nov. 1893.

102. See, e.g., P.R.O., LAB2/1480/L1078/1897, memo. by Llewellyn Smith, 25 Nov. 1897.

103. *Report of Official Statistics Committee*, PP 1881 (39) XXX, pp. 56-8.

104. Ibid., pp. xiv-xxxii.

105. See, e.g., P.R.O., BT13/23/E11499, memo. on 'The Recommendations of the Labour Commission', 8 Jan. 1895.

106. *JRSS*, 69 (1906), p. 541.

107. PP 1906 (365) IX, QQ. 490-9, 1156, 1613-15; Dilke Papers, B.M. Add. MS 43919, Dilke to Llewellyn Smith, 15 May 1906.

108. *JRSS*, 70 (1907), pp. 553-76; Clara Collet Diary, 30 June 1907.

109. Dilke Papers, B.M. Add. MS 43919, Bateman to Dilke, 2 June 1907.

110. *Proceedings of the Select Committee on Publications*, PP 1909 (285) VIII, pp. iv, 29-37; PP 1916 (112) III, pp. 15-16; Dilke Papers, B.M. Add. MS 43920, Sir George Murray to Dilke, 16 May 1908.

Chapter 9

INDUSTRIAL RESISTANCE

A third major obstacle confronting the Board of Trade in its efforts to measure the 'Labour Problem' can most aptly be described as industrial resistance. That the task of securing the co-operation of employers and workers in the provision of labour statistics proved a laborious and frustrating one is clearly indicated by the fact that about 85 per cent of the *Labour Gazette's* circulation was free, as an inducement to its contributors.[1] It has of course to be remembered that the opportunity cost to trade union officials and management of voluntarily completing detailed schedules on a range of labour issues was high. They could not be expected readily to appreciate the social benefits to be gained from improved official statistics, the more so as the schedules issued by the Labour Department generally reflected systematised bureaucratic expectations that ill-accorded with the often irregular and incomplete records compiled by union organisations and employers. The statistical philosophy of social scientists and administrators often produced empirical demands that bore little relationship to the comparatively modest and pragmatic information flows required by manufacturers and the workforce at the point of production.

Industrial resistance was not, however, merely a function of logistics. It also reflected fairly deep-rooted ideological distrust on the part of both Capital and Labour towards the enquiries undertaken by the Labour Department of the Board of Trade. The left-wing press tended to advance a conspiracy theory of government labour policy according to which the Board of Trade's primary aim was to secure a cheap and servile labour force for industrial capitalism.[2] In conjunction with State arbitration and conciliation, labour statistics were designed, it was argued, to perpetuate the false consciousness of old unionism, to alienate public opinion from the more militant leaders and rank and file of the Labour Movement and to legitimise the prevailing structure of income inequality.[3]

Such views were mainly articulated in the Socialist press. The bulk of the Trade Union Movement adopted a more pragmatic attitude to labour statistics. Nonetheless, it did not regard the Labour Bureau and the Labour Department of the Board of Trade as progressive institutions and viewed their statistical activities with the distrust traditionally accorded by labouring men to the bureaucratic controls of the governing classes.[4] During the 1880s and 1890s, the attitude of organised Labour was particularly influenced by a concern that Robert Giffen would manipulate official labour statistics in order to sustain in government circles a complacent view of 'the progress of the working classes', to discredit trade unionist perceptions of the economy and the labour market, and to frustrate the efforts of the Labour Movement to secure advances in working-class incomes and working conditions.[5]

This distrust affected union responses to the whole range of Board of Trade enquiries. For example, in view of the Board of Trade's apparent determination to demonstrate the cost ineffectiveness of industrial militancy, unions were increasingly reluctant to furnish the Department with information on strike benefit and wages foregone during labour disputes. This reluctance was reinforced after 1906 by the belief that information relating to industrial unrest was liable to be '"cooked" in order to bolster up the demand for repressive legislation'.[6] Likewise, union leaders objected to the disclosure of details as to their membership and financial resources for fear that such data would merely strengthen the bargaining position of employers and provide valuable intelligence for any counter-attack on the Trade Union Movement.[7] As the North Yorkshire and Cleveland miners observed to John Burnett: 'Your schedules are of a prying nature and calculated to do the working class more harm than good'.[8]

A similar rationale - of declining 'to enable

the employers to know when to put the screw on' - underlay resistance to the provision of unemployment statistics.[9] John Burns reflected that:

> Trade unions do not respond as they should, and nervously hesitate to give the exact numbers out of work for fear that their position should become known to the employers, who, they assume, would exploit their necessity by reducing wages or by some other encroachments.[10]

Trade unionists reacted with equal sensitivity to the wages and earnings enquiries of the Department. They were concerned that, by ignoring a range of factors such as the irregularity of employment and shifts in work intensity due to technical innovation, such enquiries would present an unduly optimistic picture of labour remuneration and thereby legitimate not only orthodox assumptions as to the 'progress of the working classes' but also the efforts of Edwardian capitalists to counteract Britain's loss of competitiveness in world markets by deflating wage costs of production. In addition, it was argued that the provision of wage data was both misleading and potentially exploitative in the absence of commensurate information on profit margins and production costs.[11]

Resistance also characterised the Board of Trade's enquiries into working-class expenditure patterns and costs of living. Labour leaders were apprehensive that such data would merely provide an excuse for 'middle-class moralising' as to secondary poverty and that this 'stomach policy of the bourgeoisie' would obscure rather than illuminate the fundamental causes of destitution and their implications for welfare policy.[12] They were increasingly concerned at the preoccupation of the Labour Department with the fiscal and commercial significance of labour statistics, and its failure to translate working-class earnings and expenditure data into concrete proposals for statutory measures of income maintenance.[13]

Resistance confronting investigations of female employment, pay and expenditure patterns, appears to have stemmed from a different set of moral and social inhibitions. Married working-class women especially, rarely possessed sufficient identity and social confidence actively to participate in such enquiries. In part, they were resented as an intrusion into family income relationships. There was also clearly felt to be an element of impropriety in male bureaucrats examining the more intimate details of female expenditure. [14]

In contrast, the Conservative and trade press viewed the Labour Department of the Board of Trade as the mouthpiece of New Unionism and Fabian Socialism. [15] In their view, its aim was to 'punish Capitalism'; in particular, to divert profits from productive investment to non-productive working-class consumption, to inflate the labour and social overhead costs of private enterprise, to secure the solidarity and legal immunity of working-class unrest and to discredit the efforts of employers to ensure economic efficiency by means of industrial discipline; thus safeguarding the interests of the Labour Movement rather than the needs of the economy. [16]

Frequently, such allegations were deliberately inspired by militant right-wing organisations such as the Liberty and Property Defence League or the National Free Labour Association. [17] However, it is clear from business and public archives that these views were also shared by many industrialists. While they were prepared to submit statistical returns to administrative departments for the purpose of implementing a familiar range of commercial and industrial regulations, they were unwilling to supply information to 'a purely statistical office in whose machinations they could detect some lurking devilry'. [18] Industrialists feared that the Labour Department, staffed by former trade unionists and middle-class radicals, many of whom had played a prominent part in the rise of New Unionism, would use labour statistics as a means of undermining private enterprise and the existing structure of industry and society. It was alleged that so-called 'impartial intelligence' would be distorted so as to validate Socialist doctrines of surplus value and under-consumption, to erode market criteria of wage determination, and to reinforce left-wing demands for a range of welfare provisions such as contra-cyclical public works and minimum wage legislation, to the lasting impairment of work incentives and business efficiency. [19]

Many employers viewed industrial relations, including wage agreements and the deployment of

their labour force, as a strictly private issue
and regarded the labour market intelligence of the
Board of Trade as a fundamental threat to their
managerial autonomy.[20] They anticipated that the
Trade Union Movement would exploit such
intelligence in order to inflate wage demands and
generally to increase workers' control over the
speed and mode of production. Accordingly, all
the most vital enquiries undertaken by the Labour
Department in the 1880s and 1890s were seriously
impaired by the refusal of employers to disclose
information. *The Times* industrial correspondent
reported in 1902 that there was:

> widespread reluctance on the part of
> employers to give any information whatever to
> the Labour Department. There are employers
> who systematically return with the following
> endorsement the forms sent to them by that
> department: 'Decline to report. Have no
> confidence in the Labour Department of the
> Board of Trade as present constituted.' Some
> firms regard this endorsement as so much a
> matter of routine that they are even said to
> make it with the help of a rubber stamp.[21]

In an effort to offset this lack of
confidence, the Board appointed a staff of fee-
paid employers' correspondents in 1902,[22] but the
'burden of furnishing information' continued to
fall on 'a few sympathetic employers', seriously
biassing official statistics.[23] Indeed, if one
uses the completion rate of schedules as an
indicator, the attitude of employers, if anything,
further deteriorated. The proportion of schedules
completed by employers in the 1906-10 hours and
earnings enquiry was as low as 25 per cent as
compared with 65 per cent in the 1888-94 wage
census.[24]
This pattern of response was, in part, a
reaction to the increasing range of compulsory
returns produced by the extension of workmen's
compensation and the introduction of health and
unemployment insurance.[25] It also reflected the
frustration of provincial traders and
industrialists with the failure of the Board of
Trade to represent their interests in policy-
making circles and with its increasing collusion
after 1905 in radical State intervention in both
social and industrial affairs.[26] Significantly,
the Board of Trade retained as 'characteristic'

the vitriolic response of one industrialist in 1912 to a request for data as to the average wages, hours and regularity of employment of his workforce, to the effect that:

> it was an utterly futile return ... Some idiot is hard up for employment and has hit upon this brilliant idea to give overpaid and underworked officials a chance of wearing out government pens and filling government foolscap with rubbish. Your department is the last refuge of the decrepit trade union official or the out at elbows socialist orator.[27]

In addition to the specific ideological distrust felt by employers towards the Department, there existed the traditional disinclination of manufacturers to reveal details of their methods and costs of production to competitors and tax authorities.[28] This disinclination was inevitably intensified during a period when British industrialists were facing falling profit margins and increased foreign competition in world markets, as well as the prospect of fundamental revisions in the revenue structure.[29]

Such resistance was of course self-reinforcing. The more the Board of Trade was starved of first-hand information, the more it was forced to rely on either indirect or highly selective data. This in turn further reduced the confidence of both sides of industry in its investigations and their willingness to participate. Moreover, as compared with administrators in other industrialised economies such as Germany, the Board was not armed with the investigatory powers of Roman Law by which to compel statistical returns.[30] The protracted debate surrounding the Census of Production of 1907, the extent to which it encompassed fundamental issues of personal liberty and the rights of the State *vis a vis* private enterprise, and the degree to which Lloyd George was forced by industrial opinion to contain the enquiry,[31] testifies to the strength of resistance within Edwardian Britain to any significant extension of bureaucratic powers to obtain information relating to social and economic phenomena. Furthermore, the resistance encountered by the Board of Trade in attempting to obtain a more systematic measure of the 'Labour Problem' no doubt in part reflected the significant element of opposition to scientific thought, methods of inquiry and expertise prevailing, as MacLeod has demonstrated, in all classes of late-Victorian and Edwardian society.[32]

Industrial Resistance

1. *S.C. on Official Publications, Mins. of Ev.*, PP 1906 (279) XI, Q. 1523; P.R.O., T9/44, T. to B.T., 2 Feb. 1914.
2. *Justice*, 17 Aug. 1901, 18 June 1910, 10 Sept. 1910, 29 July 1911, 27 April 1912; *Clarion*, 3 May 1912; *Socialist Review*, VII (1911), p. 248; *New Age*, 22 May 1913; *Labour Leader*, 24 July 1908.
3. *Justice*, 18 June 1898, 16 Nov. 1907, 21 Oct. 1911, 27 July 1912; *Clarion*, 5 Jan. 1912; *Socialist Review*, VIII (1911-12), pp. 246-7; *New Age*, 20 Nov. 1913; *Labour Leader*, 1 Sept. 1900.
4. C. Bradlaugh, 'Labour Statistics: Their Utility to Employers and Employed', *Our Corner*, VII (1886), p. 130; *The Times*, 7 Nov. 1889; T.U.C. Archives, T.U.C. Parliamentary Committee Proceedings, 1 Feb. 1893.
5. *Justice*, 4 Oct. 1884; J.G. Hutchinson, 'Progress and Wages: A Workman's View', *Nineteenth Century*, 26 (1884), pp. 630-2; *Hansard*, 3rd Series, 337, Col. 724. This is certainly how *The Times'* industrial correspondent interpreted Giffen's role. See, *The Times*, 15 Feb. 1890, 5 Dec. 1891.
6. *T.U.C. Annual Report* (1896), p. 51; Ibid. (1912), pp. 139-40.
7. See, e.g., *4th Report on Trade Unions*, PP 1890-91 (C.6475) XCII, p. 1. Similar sentiments had previously been expressed with regard to the registration of trade unions under the Friendly Societies Act. See especially, *T.U.C. Annual Report* (1871), p. 32: 'Registration ... would do that which a traitor in an army could do - tell the weakness of the whole lot. It would let every master in the Kingdom know the extent of their resources and funds'.
8. *2nd Report on Trade Unions*, PP 1888 (C.5505) CVII, p. 3.
9. *T.U.C. Annual Report* (1893), p. 36.
10. J. Burns, 'The Unemployed', *Nineteenth Century*, 32 (1892), p. 851.
11. J. Burns, *The Unemployed* (Fabian Tract No. 47, 1893), p. 8; *T.U.C. Annual Report* (1893), p. 19; Ibid. (1896), p. 51.
12. *Returns of Expenditure by Working Men*, PP 1889 (C.5861) CXXXIV, p. 4; *JRSS*, 56 (1893), pp. 268, 290.
13. *T.U.C. Annual Report* (1908), p. 154; Ibid. (1911), pp. 225-6.
14. *Accounts of Expenditure of Wage-Earning Women and Girls*, PP 1911 (Cd.5963) LXXXIX, p. 96.
15. See, e.g., *The Times*, 9 Dec. 1897; *Liberty Review*, VIII (1899), p. 57; IX (1900), pp. 175-6.
16. *The Times*, 13 Sept. 1897, 16 Jan. 1902; *Liberty Review*, VIII (1899), pp. 37, 57, 62; IX (1900), pp. 104, 176, 206, 242, 260, 289; X (1901), pp. 31, 51, 113; XXII (1907), p. 3.

17. P. Mantoux and M. Alfassa, *La Crise du trade-unionisme* (Paris, 1903), pp. 278, 316.
18. C. Dilke, 'Presidential Address', *JRSS*, LXX (1907), p. 562.
19. See, e.g., Clyde Shipbuilders' Association Archives, C. Connell & Co. to T. Biggart, 16 Dec. 1912.
20. *R.C. on Labour, Mins. of Ev.*, PP 1893-94 (C.7063) XXXIX Pt I, p. 128. This was despite the fact (Q.1813) that there was 'a much better spirit abroad amongst employers, 50 per cent better than it was in the fifties'. See also, P.R.O., LAB41/186, Engineering Employers' Federation to B.T., 13 Dec. 1912.
21. *The Times*, 16 Jan. 1902.
22. P.R.O., T1/9891A/18946, B.T. to T., 10 March 1902.
23. A.L. Bowley, 'The Improvement of Official Statistics', *JRSS*, LXXI (1908), p. 477.
24. P.R.O., LAB41/161/L1070/1908, memo. on 'The Progress of the Census of Wages' by F.H. MacLeod, 3 April 1908.
25. P.R.O., LAB41/186, Monks Hall & Co. to B.T., 7 Feb. 1913.
26. J. Melling, 'The "Servile State" Revisited: Employers, Workplace Conflict and State Intervention in Britain 1914-16', unpublished paper, University of Glasgow (1982), pp. 29-30. Recent research by Dr Terry Rodgers would suggest that the behaviour of employers' organisations varied. Local associations were usually the most reluctant to divulge information. The main concern of the national organisations, such as the Engineering Employers' Federation, was to ensure that all information about the industry was supplied to the Board of Trade *through* the Federation, and not direct.
27. P.R.O., LAB41/186, Day, Summers & Co. to B.T., 20 Dec. 1912.
28. *Statist*, 65 (1910), pp. 157-8.
29. P.R.O., BT11/2/C6378/1906, Transcript of Conference between Lloyd George and Industrialists regarding Census of Production Bill, 25 Oct. 1906.
30. A.W.Flux, 'The Census of Production', *JRSS*, 87 (1924), p. 355.
31. See especially, the debate on the second reading of the Census of Production Bill, *Hansard*, 4th Series, 162, cols. 1171-5. T.M. Healy: 'They were merely sacrificing their liberty to a gang of clerks in Downing Street'.
32. R.M. MacLeod, 'Law, medicine and public opinion: the resistance to compulsory health legislation 1870-1907', *Public Law* (1967), pp. 210-11.

Chapter 10

THE TECHNICAL STRUCTURE OF LABOUR STATISTICS

INNOVATIVE ASPECTS

In many respects, the quantitative techniques
adopted by the Board of Trade in collating and
interpreting labour statistics were markedly in
advance of those employed by other departments of
social administration.[1] The pattern of
recruitment, the motivation and the operational
philosophy of the Board's statisticians and
investigators rendered them peculiarly receptive
to more scientific methods of quantification. In
many instances, a formal training in economics or
first-hand experience of the labour market had
been supplemented by extensive exposure to the
practical application and limitations of empirical
methods of social enquiry on the Booth Survey, on
the Royal Commission on Labour, and on the surveys
of working-class mobility and consumption patterns
undertaken by Toynbee Hall and the London Economic
Club. Attendance at the statistical classes run
by Bowley at the L.S.E. and by Foxwell and Yule at
University College, London, and regular, informal
contact with leading theoreticians, such as
Edgeworth and Karl Pearson, provided additional
stimuli.[2]

Furthermore, as has been demonstrated (see
Chapter 4), senior posts linking the Board's
investigators and statisticians with policy-making
circles were occupied by officials who appreciated
the importance of more reliable and rigorous
methods of data accumulation, processing and
analysis for the fulfillment of the Board's
intelligence function. In particular, Llewellyn
Smith was, on his own admission, 'unlikely either
by taste or training to underrate the value of
mathematical methods in elucidating economic

problems'.[3]   As early as 1890, his University
Extension lectures on 'Methods of Social Enquiry'
had revealed an awareness of the value of theories
of association and probability in advancing the
'scientific   treatment   of   social   problems'.[4]
Moreover,   he   appears   to   have   maintained   an
innovative attitude towards statistical method in
the course of his subsequent career at the Board
of Trade.   As he observed as Permanent Secretary
in 1910, when reflecting upon the scientific study
of statistics:

> I   do   not   know   whether   statistical
> investigation has been conceived as forming
> one or more toes of both or either of the two
> now famous feet on which political economy is
> said to rest, but it certainly seems to be an
> indispensable   adjunct   to   both   ...
> Quantitative measurement is the backbone of
> science, and whenever the quantities handled
> are   in   any   way   indeterminate   or   inexact,
> either   in   regard   to   their   definition   or
> enumeration,   we   need   the   assistance   of
> scientific rules and criteria to enable us to
> correct, or neglect, or at least to limit the
> error   introduced   into   our   results   by   the
> faulty nature of the data.   The mere direct
> measurement,   counting,   or   weighing   of
> quantities is scarcely worthy of being called
> a   statistical   operation.   The   essentially
> mathematical   conception   of   functions   and
> mutually   dependent   variables   offers
> incomparably   the   most   powerful   and
> appropriate   method   of   expressing   the
> interrelations among such economic phenomena
> as rent, interest, price, wages, product and
> capital.   Moreover,   the   apparatus   of   the
> infinitesimal   calculus   affords   the   only
> satisfactory   mode   of   representing   and
> analysing continuous economic changes.[5]

His   recruitment   of   leading   statisticians   such   as
Bowley   and   Yule   as   technical   advisers   to   the
series   of   enquiries   into   Edwardian   working-class
earnings,   consumption   and   costs   of   living
undertaken by the Board was symptomatic of such an
outlook.
      The more innovative aspects of the technical
structure of the Board's labour statistics can be
reviewed   most   effectively   under   four   main
categories; time series analysis, the measurement

of the relationship between variables, measures of central tendency and dispersion, and the use of imperfect data.

The Board of Trade was closely associated with developments in the theory and use of index numbers as a means of time series analysis. In the late 1880s, Robert Giffen played a leading role in the proceedings of the committee of the British Association for the Advancement of Science established to investigate the value of index numbers in the measurement and explanation of economic and social phenomena.[6] At the International Statistical Institute in 1887 he 'originated the idea' of using them to identify movements in working-class earnings and purchasing power,[7] and thereafter, Board of Trade officials remained thoroughly conversant with theoretical advances in the field, and especially with the contributions of Edgeworth, Sauerbeck, Marshall, and Bowley to the development of scientifically weighted index numbers.[8]

This awareness was reflected in the growing sophistication with which the Board's statisticians utilised time series. During the 1890s, the Labour Department had increasing recourse to this type of data matrix as a means of identifying shifts in the level of industrial unrest and unionisation.[9] In the evidence of Llewellyn Smith to the Select Committee on Distress from Want of Employment, time series were deployed for the first time as a means of differentiating *statistically* between the effects of seasonal and cyclical factors on the labour market.[10] However, the most dramatic advances in the Board of Trade's statistical approach were associated with its series of memoranda on working-class income and consumption patterns incorporated within the celebrated Fiscal Blue Books on British trade and industry. In these memoranda, 'the powerful method' of index numbers was 'freely utilised' for the first time in order to identify long-term movements in money wages, working-class expenditure and costs of living, and to provide a rough indication of their relationship to similar movements in other industrialised economies.[11] During the latter part of the Edwardian period, under pressure to furnish more precise and composite measures of trends and fluctuations in real wages, consumption and employment, such indexes became increasingly refined, with the partial assimilation of advances in weighting theory.[12]

Another significant aspect of the Board's shift from descriptive to explanatory statistics, from aggregate accounts of social phenomena (which continued to characterise the data of the Home Office and the Local Government Board) to statistics of social causation, was its use of cross-tabulation to examine the relationship between economic and social variables. For example, the Labour Department increasingly employed cross-tabulation in order to expose the dynamics of industrial unrest; classifying the incidence of strikes and lockouts against a wide range of variables including causation, duration, occupation, outcome, economic activity, and mode of settlement.[13] The same focus on analytical statistics and interpretative techniques characterised the Department's reports on trade unionisation, employment, and changes in money wage rates. Moreover, after 1902, the Board of Trade began to construct composite indexes in order to establish a clearer relationship between variables such as working-class earnings and costs of living, where the problems of quantification required a more sophisticated statistical approach.[14]

A third, distinctive feature of the Board's labour statistical output, indicative of its emphasis upon interpretative data rather than mere social accounting, was its extensive use of summary measures of central tendency and dispersion. A comparison between the techniques adopted in the 1886 wage census and the 1906 earnings enquiry is instructive. It reveals an increasing refinement in statistical methodology, from the use of rather crude averages and ranges as perceived by employers to obtain an estimate of the frequency distribution of wage rates, to the intensive employment of the arithmetic mean, median and quartiles of the *raw data* as precise measures of the central tendency and dispersion of working-class earnings.[15] By 1906, the Labour Department's intelligence regarding workforce remuneration was widely regarded by social scientists as incorporating the most technically advanced data of Britain's official statistics.[16] Such techniques also played a crucial role in the Board's cost of living enquiries in providing statistical measures by means of which levels of working-class expenditure and costs of living might be summarised and rendered more readily comparable.[17]

Perhaps the most innovative aspect of the Board's labour statistics was its treatment of imperfect data. From its earliest enquiries, the Labour Department was forced, faux de mieux, to rely upon non-random samples to estimate the general tendency of a range of labour market variables. For example, although its wages census covered merely 25 per cent of the workforces of the trades examined, the Board submitted in 1892 'that with all drawbacks' such a return 'not selected in any way, but taken promiscuously from each district, appear[ed] to supply a most ample statistical basis as to the average wages in those trades'.[18] Similarly, a grab sample from trade-union unemployment benefit schemes was held to be 'sufficiently representative' to provide an accurate reflection of changes in the state of employment as a whole.[19]

As the fiscal and national efficiency debates after 1900 created statistical demands of unprecedented complexity, relating to the measurement of social phenomena such as working-class living standards, the Department had increasing recourse to sampling techniques. Llewellyn Smith summed up the dilemma facing labour statisticians of the period:

> Statistical enquiries oscillate habitually between the two dangers as between Scylla and Charybdis - the danger on the one hand that overinsistence on elaborate precision of data may so narrow the field that the results obtained from the sample may be unrepresentative of the whole, and the danger on the other hand that the 'common statistics' which alone cover the whole field are necessarily obtained not only for one but for many diverse purposes, and are therefore unlikely to be entirely appropriate to any particular inquiry. Between these characteristic dangers of the intensive and extensive methods respectively, we have to steer our difficult course as best we may.[20]

However, his overriding conviction was that it was the 'besetting error of the public to exaggerate the defects of the intensive method' and to underestimate how few samples if underpinned by 'the powerful engine of the mathematical theory of probability' and 'if honestly chosen at random' sufficed 'to give a good approximation of the truth'.[21] To a certain, though limited extent, it was this attitude which informed the Board's investigations into the Edwardian labour market.

TECHNICAL CONSTRAINTS

Yet, if in comparison with other departments of social administration the Board of Trade's labour statistics were technically advanced, there still remained a significant shortfall not only between such data and the statistical demands of contemporary economic and social debate, but also and more seriously between the quantitative techniques of the Board and those made available by advances in the mathematical theory of statistics.[22]

During the 1880s and 1890s, the level of time series analysis undertaken by the Board was extremely modest. Chronological series on labour unrest and unionisation were used more as the basis for 'impressions' or 'indications' rather than the statistical measurement of the impact of long and short-term factors. Likewise, the Board's decomposition of unemployment time series was only partial with little systematic differentiation between trend, cyclical, and residual influences. Its use of index numbers displayed similar constraints, being constructed primarily 'as a means of consolidating data'[23] rather than of isolating and evaluating the main components determining temporal shifts in economic and social phenomena. There was a noticeable lag between Giffen's advocacy of the use of index numbers to monitor working-class income and expenditure patterns and its implementation after the Boer War.

Even then, as the deficiencies of the Board's statistics outlined above (Chapter 6) bear witness, the Department's methodology lacked scientific precision and the full assimilation of new techniques. Departmental and private archives reveal not infrequent resistance from generalist statisticians such as MacLeod and even Llewellyn Smith to the more innovative proposals of advisers such as Bowley and Yule.[24] These proposals included the application of more sophisticated methods of averaging and standard deviation to refine the weighting, chain-linking, and base period of indexes, the more rigorous and extensive use of sampling to provide a more statistically valid and measurable data base, and the employment of mathematical techniques such as regression analysis to identify the structural implications of time series and to generate more composite indexes; above all, a real wage index measuring the movement of wages directly in terms of commodity prices, with which the more contentious issues relating to the labour market and the 'social efficiency' of the economy might be addressed.

The shortfall between the quantitative techniques of the Board and contemporary developments in statistical theory was even more marked in the application of measures of association to labour statistics. This was the more surprising in that the Board's statistical officers were acquainted with the major advances in the theory and application of correlation and regression analysis. Some of the leading innovators such as Bowley and Yule were, after 1900, employed by the Board of Trade on its major enquiries. The memoirs of labour officials and surviving inventories of their departmental library also reveal that they were conversant with the statistical work of biometricians such as Francis Galton and Karl Pearson in the field of correlation analysis.[25]

Nonetheless, despite its extensive use of cross-tabulation, the methodology adopted by the Labour Department in its analysis of the relationship between social and economic variables remained theoretically under-developed before the First World War. For example, in the early 1890s the Department drew increasing attention to the relationship between the incidence of industrial unrest and the level of economic activity. Yet, its report on strikes and lockouts for 1893 was content to observe that:

It is often difficult to trace any direct connection between the state of the labour market and the frequency or otherwise of trade disputes, and though it is perhaps impossible to lay down any general principle as to the relation between the two, there can be no doubt that such a relation does exist. Very often this may but be the relation of cause and effect, but even this cannot always be asserted with confidence.[26]

Subsequent reports maintained this defeatist attitude rather than incorporating regression analysis to identify statistically the nature and strength of the relationship.

Likewise, the Labour Department's reports on the causes of unemployment lacked statistical rigour. Their objective was 'to break up into their elements the congeries of industrial and social problems' generating the 'multiform and complex disease' of unemployment.[27] Their achievement was merely to establish a set of descriptive categories of unemployment rather than to specify the relationship between its various determinants. Such a statistically simplistic approach with its readiness to settle for a rough 'indication of general connection' was symptomatic of the whole range of labour intelligence furnished by the Board of Trade.

The absence of correlation and regression analysis to test the interdependence of social and economic phenomena also characterised the Board's Edwardian investigations into working-class standards of living. Efforts to measure the relationship between the Department's main indexes of wages, employment, rents and commodity prices were tentative and ineffectual. Its family budget survey adopted the synthetic procedure of the Booth Survey of combining expenditure data to form types, rather than undertaking multi-variate analysis of the relationships between, for example, items of expenditure, total income, occupational status, and family structure.[28]

It is significant that the application of advanced statistical methods to the Board's data was delayed until its most 'technically progressive' statisticians had severed any formal connection with the Department. Yule's plea to the Royal Statistical Society in 1909 for the application of correlation analysis to social and industrial statistics, and his deployment of Board of Trade data at the International Statistical Institute the same year to measure the correlation between unemployment and economic activity, testified to the lag in the technical refinement of official statistics,[29] as did Bowley and Wood's subsequent application of measures of standard deviation and correlation to movements in the level of wages and retail prices.[30]

The Board's use of measures of central tendency and of absolute or relative dispersion also lacked conviction. Until the earnings and hours enquiry of 1906, median and quartile measures were not systematically employed as summary measures by the Labour Department. Even the Board's use of the arithmetic mean lacked statistical precision. Many of its more quantitative reports on the late-Victorian labour market lacked an exact definition of the 'average'. In many investigations, such as the first wage census, the mean of a non-random sample was represented as providing a trustworthy 'average' for entire trades without any proper statistical substantiation,[31] and the continued reliance of the Department upon simple averages for measuring composite data relating to large groups of workmen rendered much of its summary findings 'statistically valueless' in the eyes of many social scientists.[32]

Despite the methodological advances in official labour statistics after 1900, their use of summary measures remained tentative and vulnerable to theoretical criticism. For example, in producing weighted averages for its indexes on wage rates and living costs, the process of averaging was often based upon 'personal estimation' by the Board's investigators. Bowley and Yule protested that if the Board's data was to command any credibility the 'mean had to be derived by objective quantification. The use of judgement in guessing the mean', they argued, 'only added to, instead of lessening the uncertainty of defining the "typical" housing and consumption patterns of the "average" working man'.[33] As the Department's findings were dependent on the interpretation of the general average of various composite budgets, it was, they insisted, all the more imperative to apply mathematical theory to estimate its precision.

In addition, the Board's weighted averages lacked sufficient statistical finesse to produce indexes which revealed the degree of variation in working-class incomes and expenditure outwith London and in the impact upon living standards of specific types of rent and commodity prices.[34] Finally, a failure to deploy the full repertoire of available summary measures in conjunction with sampling techniques, impaired the potential of such measures. It is arguable that by applying theories of probability and distribution to the average and median values derived from limited investigations, the Board could have extrapolated fairly precise estimates as to the aggregate level of Edwardian wage costs, employment, and working-class purchasing power, and obtained a more economical and statistically significant measure of international variations in wage earnings and costs of living.[35]

Meanwhile, Edwardian labour statistics also failed to incorporate advances in the measurement of dispersion. Measures such as the standard and quartile deviations, the coefficient of variation, or Bowley's coefficient of skewness, were not employed. Indeed, such was the concern of Bowley and Yule at the conservatism of the Board in this area of methodology that they urged the Department to publish the entire frequency distribution of its data 'so that the reader might judge the value and meaning of the average'.[36] Moreover, they were increasingly concerned at the use by the Board of Trade in its major social enquiries of the mode and predominant range. As Yule minuted to MacLeod, the Superintendent of Statistics, the mode lacked any associated measure of dispersion and was therefore of 'low utility value', while the predominant range possessed a variety of weaknesses. It was an extremely vague and impressionistic measure and consequently highly vulnerable to bias and 'provided no indication of the overall distribution of variable data'. The adoption of such techniques without the aid of more scientific measures of dispersion meant that it was often impossible for social commentators and scientists to determine whether deviations in official labour statistics were accidents of observation or statistically significant.[37] As Bowley observed with typical astringency to the British Association in 1906, the consequence was that erroneous conclusions were inevitably drawn about the nature and extent of the 'Labour Problem':

> The growth of popular interest, and of a certain blind and misguided confidence in statistical statements has resulted in the printing of cautions that the statistics did not mean what they appeared to mean; and thus boards were erected to the effect that this table was dangerous to statisticians, and newspaper writers should drive with caution; but it did not for long occur to those responsible that it was their business to put the public roads in good order for the convenience of travellers.[38]

However, the most notable shortfall in the
quantitative methods of the Board of Trade was its
failure to assimilate systematic sampling
techniques by means of which to process and to
interpret the mass of imperfect data relating to
Labour. It was not that the Board's statisticians
were unfamiliar with contemporary developments in
the theory of sampling. Representatives of the
Department regularly attended the International
Statistical Institute, British Association and
Royal Statistical Society at which its relevance
to the measurement of social and economic
phenomena was discussed, and many labour officials
were introduced to the mathematical principles and
practical application of sampling at the
statistical classes run by Bowley and Foxwell at
the L.S.E. and University College, London.[39]
Moreover, a leading innovator in the field
(specifically, in the theory relating to the
validation and probable error of random samples)
and leading advocate of the use of scientific
sampling in official statistics, A.L. Bowley, was
employed as senior technical adviser to the Board
during many of its most significant social
enquiries.[40]

Nonetheless, prior to 1914, no labour
investigation undertaken by the Board fully
incorporated random sampling techniques. They
either aimed at a complete coverage of the
workforce or at a partial coverage possessing some
unspecified degree of typicality. Implicit within
many of the Labour Department's reports was the
assumption that the available data was a
sufficiently 'representative' sample to provide a
reliable basis for general estimates. In practice,
however, the basic principles of randomness were
invariably violated. Very often, the selection of
data was seriously biased by the subjective
'judgement' of investigators or simply by the
incidence of apathy or resistance to the provision
of labour statistics (see Chapter 9). As Bowley
objected, the alleged 'promiscuity' of the Board's
data base was no substitute for independent random
sampling.[41] As a result, although the Board often
used non-random samples to make estimates of the
aggregate characteristics of labour market
phenomena, it was unable to provide a statistical
measure as to the accuracy of such estimates.
Still less could it utilise its limited
information on certain variables such as earnings
and output as a means of calculating the values of

missing variables such as labour productivity.

Such deficiencies in the labour statistical output of the Board of Trade may readily be illustrated. Its earliest reports on trade unions subscribed to the view that 'irrespective of how representative' the information might be, it was still invaluable to contemporary debate.[42] Subsequently, the detailed analysis of 100 so-called 'principal unions' was employed by the Labour Department as a 'reliable indicator' of the nature of trades unionisation as a whole, but without any measure as to the degree of reliability.[43] More surprisingly, sampling techniques were not adopted to establish the level of unionisation within the workforce nor to guage the likely differential between the income, employment, and welfare characteristics of unionised and non-unionised labour.

Similar constraints characterised the measurement of labour remuneration. No measure of precision was attached to the Board's estimates of the distribution of wage rates of the late-Victorian manual working classes, and its assertion in 1894 that 'although there might be a considerable margin of error', the data supplied by selected unions and employers relating to wage shifts 'might be fairly taken as reflecting the general effect of the wage movements of the year upon the trades of the nation at large',[44] typified the primitive methodology of the Department. Furthermore, despite its use of more sophisticated measures of central tendency and dispersion, and despite the protests of Bowley and Wood, the Board of Trade failed to incorporate random sampling techniques into its survey of Edwardian wage earnings. Not only did this deny to its average, median and quartile values a *declared* measure of accuracy, but also a means of adjustment for variations in the regularity and intensity of employment as well as in other significant variables.[45]

Likewise, while in the period 1886-1904 the Department persistently stressed 'the lack of available means by which the extent of demand for labour [could] be accurately ascertained' and the inability of available information to produce more than a 'tolerably accurate reflection' or 'general indicator of the condition of the national labour market',[46] it ignored random sampling techniques in refining its employment index. Admittedly, by 1905, it could claim that its data base constituted a 'very sensitive barometer' of the state of the labour market in that it focussed 'upon those trades which propagated waves of inflation and depression', and that:

> although membership of unions keeping [benefit] records included but a comparatively small minority of the total industrial population ... it formed as a whole a *sufficiently representative sample* of that population to justify the conclusion that changes in the state of employment for the workpeople included, reflect[ed] corresponding changes in the state of employment as a whole.[47]

Nonetheless, there still remained a growing gap between such data and the demand for precise intelligence on the level, duration, incidence, and causation of unemployment, generated by the debates over tariff reform and economic efficiency as well as by the welfare imperatives of New Liberalism. In confronting this gap, the Board's labour officials were again resistant to the use of random sampling,[48] and ultimately the shortfall in such data was only bridged by the statistical output consequent upon the introduction of a national system of Labour Exchanges and Unemployment Insurance.[49] Clara Collet's application of random sampling techniques, using Census material, in her spasmodic studies of female employment patterns, was exceptional.[50] Her investigations were not encouraged within the Department and indeed created considerable friction within the office. Significantly, her diaries reveal that this may well have been as much a function of statistical outlook as of male chauvinism.[51]

The conservatism of the Department in its use of sampling is perhaps best exemplified by its investigations into the standard of consumption and cost of living of the working classes, for it was in this area of empiricism that the method had most potential for the quantification of factors central to late-Victorian and Edwardian social politics. The Board of Trade's statistical approach to such investigations remained under-developed compared with the techniques adopted in America, Australasia, and Germany and compared with private surveys undertaken within the United Kingdom.[52] Its 1889 report on working-class

expenditure was defeatist. While it viewed the
issue as 'a wide and instructive field of
enquiry', it concluded that the problems of
obtaining a 'true statistical basis were enormous
and were perhaps properly speaking insuperable'.[53]
The Labour Correspondent, John Burnett, did not
discuss the possible application of sampling
techniques, and despite the relevance of
expenditure data to the poverty debates of the
1890s there was no further attempt by the Labour
Department to monitor working-class consumption
patterns prior to the Boer War.

Moreover, as we have seen, the budget surveys
of 1903-4 were not based on a scientifically
designed sample. The preliminary survey of 1903
was mainly derived from a miscellany of secondary
sources. Under the guidance of Bowley, the 1904
enquiry was conducted more systematically, but
again the selection of data was heavily biased,
being obtained primarily through the auspices of
voluntary societies and thrift agencies. No
attempt was made to represent accurately various
occupational and status groups, nor variations in
family size. No measure of probable error could
be provided for the Board's summary findings and
the Department was content to stress the
'considerable conjectural element' in its
estimates.[54]

Similar weaknesses in methodology
characterised the Board of Trade's subsequent
efforts to compare urban working-class living
standards in a range of industrialised societies.
Only the systematic use of random sampling could
have ensured the production of worthwhile and
comparable data. Instead, the Board relied upon
highly selective non-random samples determined
ostensibly by standardised investigative
procedures but, in reality, mainly by the value
judgements of local employers, trade unionists and
civic leaders.[55] In the circumstances, the
Board's admission that for the purposes of
comparative analysis its summary data could only
be treated as 'approximate truths' was less than
candid.[56] It possessed no measure as to their
margin of error and it is evident from official
archives that many labour administrators not only
resisted the extension of the Board's wage and
cost of living enquiries abroad but were also
extremely reluctant to use their conclusions as a
basis for policy-briefings.[57]

Nor were they disposed to exploit the

pressure of demand created by the tariff reform campaign for information on the proportion of the workforce at or below the subsistence level, in order to initiate official surveys based on sampling techniques of the extent of urban poverty in Edwardian Britain. On a number of occasions, public and parliamentary concern over the social effects of fiscal reform presented the Board with the opportunity to test the validity of the findings of Booth and Rowntree as a measure of the level of aggregate destitution, but the Department's senior labour officials were reluctant to respond.[58] It was left to the private initiative of Bowley to take up the mantle of Booth and Rowntree and to utilise sampling techniques as a means of surveying national trends in living standards.

Several explanations can be advanced for this shortfall in the technical sophistication of official labour statistics. Firstly, although committed to the more rigorous measurement of the 'Labour Problem', many of the Board's more influential officials held serious reservations as to how far advances in statistical theory might safely be applied to the processing and analysis of government information.

Robert Giffen, whose statistical philosophy dominated the late-Victorian Board of Trade, possessed a 'strong arithmetical sense' but 'appears to have had little or no knowledge of the modern mathematical theory of statistics'. His 'feeling' for the significance of data, for the probable error of the factors used and for their susceptibility to meaningful measurement was primarily 'intuitive'; 'a matter of judgement, not of scientific analysis'.[59] In his reaction to the innovations in statistical methodology of the 1880s and 1890s, Giffen displayed the characteristic reserve of the skilled practician towards theory. As he warned in 1888, when surveying the potential of governmental labour statistics:

> There is no notion more foolish than that a statistical investigation is a sort of mill into which all sorts of material may be cast and ground up into percentages and averages which will have a virtue that the original figures have not. You might as well throw

sawdust into a flouring-mill and expect to get flour out of it.[60]

As already noted, to a significant extent, Giffen's statistical outlook was perpetuated by his protégé within the Labour Department, F.H. MacLeod, in his capacity as Superintendent of Statistics.[61]

Moreover, more 'progressive' investigators within the Department were also concerned that reliance upon new quantitative techniques might be overdone. In many respects, officials such as Schloss and Wilson Fox were nearer to Le Play in their statistical philosophy than to modern procedures of translating a concept into a well-defined system of indexes, as was evidenced in the contrast between their contributions to the International Statistical Institute and those of professional statisticians such as Bowley and Yule.[62] Even Llewellyn Smith adopted a cautious stance towards some innovative techniques. 'It is', he argued:

> clearly possible to lean on statistical investigation more heavily than it will bear, and it is not only possible but probable that the public demand for quantitative information will ... outrun the available means of supply. Certainly, the pressure for more and better statistics is increasing very rapidly at the present time and not always with due regard to the limitations of what is practicable. In order to form a sound and sober judgement of the true possibilities of advance along this line, it is necessary to recognise frankly the chasm which separates the crude and primitive means of measurement, or rather of quantitative estimate, which alone are open to the economist, from the relatively perfect apparatus and methods which are available to the physicist.[63]

Furthermore, he was concerned that while, in principle, more sophisticated techniques were desirable, they might render official statistics unintelligible to policy-makers, to public debate, to industry, and to social scientists. As a result, both the credibility and practical utility of labour statistics would be seriously impaired. Too much technicism would, he argued, merely lead to labour intelligence being dismissed as the 'monopoly of a professional clique', having no relation to practical life; and 'being elaborated in the closet by statistical experts, it [was] quite certain to suffer in balance, and proportion and reality and in all that [gave] it value to the world'.[64]

Administrative statisticians such as Llewellyn Smith were highly problem-orientated and more interested in the practical implications than the methodology of government investigations. Indeed, evidence would suggest that their conversance with contemporary statistical theory was often, in reality, very limited. It is noteworthy that professional statisticians such as Yule and Karl Pearson vigorously opposed Llewellyn Smith's appointment in 1903 to the Examinership in Statistics at London University as 'a retrograde step' on the grounds that, although he possessed a working knowledge of the extent and possible deployment of economic and social intelligence for administrative purposes, he lacked 'a proper acquaintance' with recent advances in the theory and application of statistics.[65]

In explaining the somewhat defensive response of labour officials to advances in quantitative techniques, one must also remember that, as in other areas of late-Victorian and Edwardian scientific enquiry, such as criminology or epidemiology, no 'professional' consensus existed as to the validity and application of the mathematical theory of statistics.[66] In his illuminating study of the social construction of scientific knowledge, MacKenzie has clearly revealed the intensity, not only of the celebrated debate between the Biometric School and Mendelism over the value of mathematical statistics to the determination of biological issues relating to heredity and evolution, but also of the controversy between the Eugenists and theorists affiliated to the Royal Statistical Society over measures of association between variables.[67] More generally, many leading economists were sceptical about the value of such measures. Marshall's remarks in a letter to Bowley in 1901 provide a typical example of such scepticism:

In my view, every economic fact, whether or not it is of such a nature as to be expressed in numbers, stands in relation as cause and effect to many other facts: and since it *never* happens that all of these can be expressed in numbers, the application of exact mathematical methods to those which can is nearly always a waste of time; while in the large majority of cases it is positively misleading: and the world would have been further on its way forwards if the work had never been done at all ... Surely *the* thing to do is to build the basis of our economic structure soundly and not to put a varnish of mathematical accuracy to many places of decimals on results the precisions of which are not established within 20 or 50 per cent.[68]

A range of practical constraints also operated upon the technical structure of the Board of Trade's statistical output. As we have observed (see Chapter 8), weaknesses in the data produced by other departments of social administration and by the Census inhibited the ability of the Board to obtain statistics of sufficient quality and homogeneity for the application of more sophisticated quantitative techniques. Similarly, Treasury control militated against new methods. They were resisted by the Treasury as being cost-ineffective, and as involving both the appointment of senior personnel to supervise the design and interpretation of enquiries, and the creation of an additional field of expertise by which the Board of Trade might seek to evade the principle of open competition.[69] It has also to be remembered that, in a period when the Civil Service possessed few mechanical aids for information gathering and processing, new techniques such as cross-tabulation and indexing were highly labour-intensive and necessitated the employment of an extensive, clerical support staff.[70]

There were, in addition, more structural aspects of statistical conservatism relating to the operational philosophy of the Board of Trade's labour officials and the incompatibility of bureaucratic imperatives with the priorities of the 'technical innovators' amongst the Department's statisticians. While senior officials such as Wilson Fox, Llewellyn Smith and George Askwith were anxious to improve the scope and accuracy of official labour statistics, they were more concerned with the relevance and coherence of information as an input into policy-briefings than with its methodological rigour and statistical refinement, the more so as after 1905 they became increasingly preoccupied with an intensive programme of industrial and welfare legislation. As Llewellyn Smith observed in 1910, 'when men of action have important work on hand they have no time or use for elaborate polemics as to the proper tools and apparatus to employ'.[71] Reflecting in 1914 upon his past association with the Board of Trade, Yule presented the viewpoint of the professional statistician:

> They are wearying things are Government departments. They will never turn out and cannot turn out work really of the first class ... simply because they must work more or less to order and on assigned problems and have one eye only on their work and the other on their chief and the party in power and what it is intended to DO (God help us!).[72]

Furthermore, similar tensions manifested themselves, especially after 1900, between established statisticians and investigators within the Board of Trade and statistical advisers in the temporary employ of the Department. This friction was primarily due to the ambivalent effect on the role of expertise of the growth and differentiation of the Civil Service after 1870. It reflected what MacLeod has identified as the emergence of the 'administrative expert' who rather than 'playing the heroic role at the leading edge of policy' became 'merely another part of the administrative system defending group or professional interests' and adopting a defensive stance towards innovation.[73] In this respect, late-Victorian and Edwardian official statisticians can be viewed as subject to the same processes of bureaucratisation as characterised other specialists within Whitehall such as lawyers, doctors, and engineers. In the case of statisticians, these processes would have been reinforced by the fact that they tended to work in closer contact with administrators than most other professional staff and were therefore particularly susceptible to goal reorientation and to the assimilation of an 'administrative philosophy'.[74] Ironically, the provision of a separate pay and promotion structure for labour investigators within the Board of Trade, designed to sustain their motivation, probably facilitated their shift from a problem-orientated to a career-orientated approach to labour statistics.

Certainly, there is ample evidence that career statisticians resented the employment of 'technical zealots' on the Board's enquiries as undermining the credibility of their own specialist status and as devaluing by implication the existing statistical skills within the Department. Moreover, then as now, technical zeal was viewed as a threat to overriding administrative priorities; those of rationalising procedures, minimising the vulnerability of the Department to public and parliamentary criticism, and sustaining, as far as possible, belief in the 'infallibility' of government statistics.[75] Thus, 'administrative experts' were ill-disposed towards quantitative techniques such as random sampling, correlation analysis and significance testing involving margins (or as they perceived them 'admissions') of error, even where they would have facilitated more ambitious social and economic enquiries or the more rigorous interpretation of existing data.[76]

As a result, as Bowley protested, many labour market phenomena were needlessly ignored and 'a vast amount of data suppressed which would [have] convey[ed] a correct impression but [did] not satisfy the false sense of accuracy' of existing departmental policy.[77] Moreover, statistical administrators were extremely reluctant to reveal the inadequacies of their data base or to modify existing series in the light of more complete information or more sophisticated techniques. For example, during the Board's cost of living enquiries, MacLeod stubbornly resisted Yule's recommendation that the narrowness of the Department's data base and the degree to which its investigators' impressions had been allowed to influence the values chosen as representative should be openly admitted.[78] There was similar resistance after 1906 to pressure from Bowley and Wood for the revision of the Board's major wage indexes, despite a general awareness within the Department of their inadequacies.[79] In 1910, embittered by the failure of the Board to utilise his massive archive of wage data to generate a fresh index with which to inform economic and social debate as to the progress of the working classes, Wood drew the attention of *The Times* readership to 'the obtuseness of the official statistician' and 'the perpetuation of obvious errors because of the assumption that a Government

Department can do no wrong, and if it does, it must not acknowledge its error'.[80] In the event, only mounting criticism from social scientists and professional statisticians in the press, and the threat in 1912 of a parliamentary campaign, orchestrated by Wood, sufficed to overcome this inertia.[81] As Clara Collet, herself fighting a losing battle to initiate 'a more comprehensive and scientific appraisal of the female labour market', confided to her diary: 'The prevailing concern of my superiors appears to be with departmental reputation rather than the truth'.[82]

Furthermore, to a significant extent, this constraining effect of Whitehall upon statistical innovation appears to have been self-reinforcing in that university curricula were often tailored to meet the needs of a bureaucratic environment. As Alfred Marshall observed to A.L. Bowley in 1901, the statistical courses at the L.S.E., at which many of the Board of Trade's labour statisticians received their formal training, failed to provide a proper insight into the real potential of recent innovations in statistical theory and quantitative methods. They were, he revealed, 'designed for officials in public employment whose province is the faithful execution of orders rather than a profound investigation of the principles on which those orders should be based'. Accordingly:

> The training emphasises mechanical methods of investigation, i.e. those in which highly specialised calculating machines - whether made of cog-wheels or of torpid flesh and blood can be set to tunes based on formulae to grind out results which are officially pure and above reproach.[83]

Bowley subscribed to a similar viewpoint. In his opinion, the application of 'advanced analysis' to economics and statistics was seriously neglected both in university curricula and the First Division Civil Service exams. As a result, in a period of unprecedented demand for social and industrial intelligence, there was no mechanism for ensuring that the Civil Service:

> was staffed by competent statisticians able to handle statistics expertly, to follow the rapid mathematical developments which alone can get the full significance of records, and

to inform the public with reasoned knowledge of the measurable phenomena of national life.[84]

Sociologists have identified a range of conditions conducive to the diffusion and adoption of new statistical techniques; in particular, the existence of effective channels of communication, of 'value consonance' which ensures that 'potential adopters' perceive new techniques as legitimate and useful, and of a supportive social structure which not only secures innovators a recognised professional status but also provides established practitioners with the incentive to alter their methodology.[85]

This framework of analysis furnishes valuable insights into the broader social determinants of the technical lag in official labour statistics between 1886 and 1914. During the period, British empirical social research continued to lack the unified professional identity, institutional setting and theoretical consensus necessary for the sustained diffusion of ideas and techniques. 'Ease of entry' meant that the investigation of the 'Labour Problem' within social science organisations such as the Royal Statistical Society remained dominated by generalists. As a result, the 'discipline' of statistical investigation remained eclectic and fragmented, and its links with the machinery of government *ad hoc* and often informal, thus reducing the impact and status of new techniques.[86] In addition, the prevailing norms and imperatives of social administration within late-Victorian and Edwardian Whitehall further militated against any speedy or systematic adoption of new methods of statistical analysis.[87]

NOTES

1. A.L. Bowley, 'Address to the Economic Section of the British Association', *JRSS*, 69 (1906), pp. 542-3.

2. R. Davidson and R. Lowe, 'Bureaucracy and Innovation in British Welfare Policy', in W.J. Mommsen (ed.), *The Emergence of the Welfare State in Britain and Germany* (1981), pp. 265-7; P.R.O., T1/9397B/6885; *JRSS*, 103 (1940), pp. 548-61.

3. *Report of the B(ritish) A(ssociation) for the A(dvancement) of S(cience)*, (1910), p. 668.

4. H. Llewellyn Smith, *Methods of Social Enquiry* (Oxford, 1890), pp. 4-6.

5. *Report of the B.A.A.S.*, (1910), pp. 666-8

6. *Report of the B.A.A.S.*, (1887), p. 247; Ibid., (1888), p. 100; *JRSS*, 53 (1890), pp. 686-8.

7. *Bulletin of the International Statistical Institute*, Vol. 2 Pt I (1887), pp. 130-1.

8. See memo. by H. Fountain on 'The Construction of Index Numbers', *Report on Wholesale and Retail Prices*, PP 1903 (321) LXVIII, pp. 429-42.

9. *9th Report on Trade Unions*, PP 1897 (C.8644) XCIX, pp. xiii-xiv; *9th Report on Strikes and Lockouts*, PP 1897 (C.8643) LXXXIV, pp. x-xiv.

10. *S.C. on Distress from Want of Employment*, *Mins. of Ev.*, PP 1895 (365) IX, pp. 48-9.

11. PP 1903 (Cd.1761) LXVII, p. vii; 1905 (Cd.2337) LXXXIV, p. vii.

12. See generally, P.R.O, LAB41, Statistics Branch, selected working papers.

13. See, e.g., *19th Report on Strikes and Lockouts*, PP 1907 (Cd.3711) LXXX.

14. See especially, P.R.O., LAB41/213.

15. P.R.O., LAB41/150, memo. by F.H. MacLeod, 26 Feb. 1906.

16. *JRSS*, 69 (1906), p. 542.

17. See, e.g., *Report on Earnings and Hours of Labour*, PP 1910 (Cd.5196) LXXXIV, p. 184; *Report on the Cost of Living of the Working Classes*, PP 1908 (Cd.3864) CVII, pp. vi, xxv.

18. *Return of Rates of Wages in Principal Textile Trades in the United Kingdom*, PP 1889 (C.5807) LXX, p. vii.

19. *Report on British and Foreign Trade and Industry*, PP 1905 (Cd.2337), LXXXIV, p. 80.

20. *Report of B.A.A.S.* (1910), p. 669.

21. Ibid., pp. 669-70.

22. *JRSS*, 69 (1906), pp. 546-50.

23. See, e.g., *Report on the Cost of Living of the Working Classes*, PP 1908 (Cd.3864) CVII, p. vi.

24. See, e.g., Yule Papers, R.S.S. Archives, Box 15, MacLeod to Yule, 11 Sept. 1907; G.H. Wood Papers, 1A/80, draft Letter to *The Times*, 6 Jan. 1910; P.R.O., LAB41/213.

25. *JRSS*, III (Pt 3, 1948), p. 254; Clara Collet Diary, 20 Aug. 1904, 2 July 1905; Wood Papers, 1A/77; PA/12.
26. PP 1894 (C.7566) LXXXI Pt 1, p. 10.
27. *Report on Agencies and Methods of Dealing with the Unemployed*, PP 1893-4 (C.7182) LXXXII, p. 6.
28. See PP 1908 (Cd.3864) CVII, p. xxv.
29. *JRSS*, 72 (1909), pp. 721-30; *Bulletin of the International Statistical Institute*, 19 (1909), pp. 91-7.
30. *Report of the B.A.A.S.*, (1913), p. 578.
31. *General Report on the Wages of the Manual Labour Classes*, PP 1893-4 (C.6889) LXXXIII Pt 2, p. xii.
32. Wood Papers, 1A/78, Bowley to Wood, 2 Aug. 1910; P.R.O., LAB41/213, memo. by Wood, 25 Jan. 1906; *JRSS*, 69 (1906), p. 589.
33. Yule Papers, R.S.S. Archives, Box 15, Report to Board of Trade on 'Processes of Averaging and Index-Numbers', p. 4; Wood Papers, 1A, Bowley to Wood, 2 Aug. 1910.
34. See review by Bowley of *2nd Report on British and Foreign Trade and Industry*, in *JRSS*, 68 (1905), pp. 177-9.
35. A.L. Bowley, 'A Suggestion for the International Comparison of Wages by the use of the Median', *Bulletin of the International Statistical Institute*, 19 (1909) p. 553.
36. *Report of B.A.A.S.* (1906), pp. 631-42, Presidential Address to Section F. by A.L. Bowley.
37. Ibid., p. 634; Yule Papers, R.S.S. Archives, Box 15, memo. on 'Processes of Averaging', p. 3.
38. *Report of B.A.A.S.*, (1906), p. 630.
39. See Clara Collet's memoirs of the Labour Department, *JRSS*, 103 (1940), pp. 548-61; 108 (1945), pp. 480-5; Bowley Papers, R.S.S. Archives, Foxwell to Bowley, 7 Feb. 1901.
40. For Bowley's contribution to sampling theory, see R. Kent, *A History of British Empirical Sociology* (1981), pp. 80-4. For his advocacy of sampling in official statistics, see especially, *JRSS*, 69 (1906), pp. 553-4; *S.C. on Income Tax*, Mins. of Ev., PP 1906 (365) IX, pp. 82-3.
41. *JRSS*, 69 (1906), pp. 546-9.
42. PP 1887 (C.5104) LXXXIX, p. 6.
43. PP 1899 (C.9443) XCII, p. xiv.
44. *Report on Changes in Rates of Wages and Hours of Labour*, PP 1894 (C.7567) LXXXI, p. xii.
45. G.H. Wood Papers, 1A/78, Bowley to Wood, 2 Aug. 1910; 1A/77, Bowley MSS on Statistical Techniques and Official Enquiries.
46. *Report on Strikes and Lockouts*, PP 1894 (C.7403) LXXXI, p. 7; P.R.O., CAB37/38, memo. on 'The Unemployed' by H. Llewellyn Smith, 23 Jan. 1895.
47. *Report on British and Foreign Trade and Industry*, PP 1905 (Cd.2337) LXXXIV, p. 80. My italics.
48. P.R.O., LAB2/1555/L1099/1903, memo. by A. Wilson Fox, 14 July 1903.
49. W.R. Garside, *The Measurement of Unemployment:*

Methods and Sources in Great Britain (1981), p. 27.

50. *Report on the Statistics of Employment of Women and Girls*, PP 1894 (C.7564) LXXXI Pt 2.

51. Clara Collet Diary, 5 March 1905.

52. R.S.S. Archives, Box 3, File 19, memo. to Minister of Labour on 'Earnings and Cost of Living', 21 Jan. 1936; *Bulletin of the International Statistical Institute*, 15 (1905), p. 102, 'Rapports, Communications et Memoires: Theorie et methodologie de la statistique 1885-1905'.

53. PP 1889 (C.5861) LXXXIV, p.3.

54. PP 1903 (Cd.1761) LXVII, pp. vi-vii, 209-10; PP 1905 (Cd.2337) LXXXIV, pp. vi-vii, 3; *JRSS*, 71 (1908), p. 476.

55. See P.R.O., LAB2/1598/L549/1907, Foreign Towns Enquiry: Instructions to Investigators.

56. *Report on the Cost of Living of the Working Classes in American Towns*, PP 1911 (Cd.5814) LXXXVIII, p. lvi.

57. See, P.R.O., LAB2/1598/L263/1904, C.P. Sanger to H. Llewellyn Smith, 3 Feb. 1904; T1/10562/22706, minute by Sir George Murray, 31 Dec. 1906.

58. P.R.O., LAB2/1555/L1099/1903, minutes by Llewellyn Smith and C.E. Collet, 14 and 18 July 1903.

59. See *JRSS*, 73 (1910), p. 532; *Economic Bulletin*, 3 (1910), pp. 140-2; *Economic Journal*, XXIV (1914), p. 92-4; P.J. Fitzpatrick, 'Leading British Statisticians of the Nineteenth Century' in M.G. Kendall and R.L. Plackett (eds.), *Studies in the History of Statistics and Probability* (1977), p. 63.

60. *Memorandum explaining the progress made in carrying out the arrangements for collecting and publishing statistics relating to Labour*, PP 1888 (433) CVII, p. 13.

61. See especially, Yule Papers, Box 15, MacLeod to Yule, 11 Sept. 1907.

62. See *Bulletin of the International Statistical Institute* (1906), pp. 87-92, 292-3, 310-13; (1909), pp. 54-60, 91-7, 537-48, 552-5.

63. *Report of B.A.A.S.* (1910), p. 669.

64. Ibid., p. 668. The existence of a trade-off between the technical refinement of official information and its value to public debate also concerned commercial statisticians within the Board of Trade. See, e.g., Observations of A.W. Flux in *JRSS*, 71 (1908), pp. 490-1.

65. Karl Pearson Papers, U.C.L., File 931.

66. See H.C. Selvin, 'Durkheim, Booth and Yule: the non-diffusion of an intellectual innovation', *Archives of European Sociology*, XVII (1976), p. 47; Kent, *British Empirical Sociology*, p. 197.

67. D.A. MacKenzie, *Statistics in Britain: 1865-1930* (Edinburgh, 1981), Chs. 6-7.

68. Bowley Papers, R.S.S. Archives, Marshall to Bowley, 3 March 1901. It should be noted that many of the Board of Trade's First Division statisticians, such as Henry Fountain,

A.W. Flux and Sydney Chapman had been recruited from a generation of Cambridge economists and mathematicians deeply influenced by Marshall's philosophy of social science. See especially, Sydney Chapman Papers, L.S.E. Coll. Misc. 640, Autobiography, pp. 18-27.

69. The Treasury was equally resistant to innovations in the presentation of data, and the increasing use of graphs, pie charts, and histograms by the Labour Department after 1903 was only sanctioned after protracted negotiations. See P.R.O., T9/34, T. to B.T., 6 Feb. 1904.

70. See P.R.O., RG29/4, papers relating to the mechanization of official statistics, 1907-1912.

71. *Report of the B.A.A.S.* (1910), p. 666.

72. Yule-Greenwood Letters, Yule to Greenwood, 5 Jan. 1914.

73. R.M. MacLeod, 'Statesmen Undisguised', *American Historical Review*, 78 (1973), p. 1403.

74. J. Irvine *et al.*, *Demystifying Social Statistics*, p. 132.

75. P.R.O., LAB41/213, Wood to MacLeod, 4 April 1912.

76. See, e.g., Clara Collet Diary, 17 May 1908; P.R.O., LAB41/213, MacLeod to Bryce, 18 Sept. 1906; *JRSS*, 69 (1906), p. 543; 71 (1908), pp. 469, 475.

77. *JRSS*, 71 (1908), p. 476.

78. Yule Papers, Box 15, MacLeod to Yule, 11 Sept. 1907.

79. P.R.O., LAB41/213, memo. on 'Mr Wood's Index Number (Wages)', by H.L. Trachtenberg, 10 June 1912; Wood Papers, CB/95, Wood to MacLeod, 10 April 1905; Ibid., 1A/69, Interview with Wood in *Factory Times* (1908), 'A Talk with a Statistician'.

80. Wood Papers, 1A/80, draft letter, Wood to *The Times*, 6 Jan. 1910.

81. P.R.O., LAB41/213, Wood to MacLeod, 11 April 1912; minute by MacLeod, 15 April 1912.

82. Clara Collet Diary, 20 Aug. 1904.

83. Bowley Papers, R.S.S. Archives, Marshall to Bowley, 3 March 1901.

84. *JRSS*, 69 (1906), pp. 544-5.

85. Selvin, 'The non-diffusion of an intellectual innovation', pp. 45-6.

86. S. Cole, 'Continuity and Institutionalization in Science: A Case Study in Failure' in A. Oberschall (ed.), *The Establishment of Empirical Sociology: Studies in Continuity, Discontinuity and Institutionalization* (New York, 1972), pp. 73-129.

87. G. Sutherland, (ed.), *Studies in the Growth of Nineteenth-Century Government* (1972), pp. 8-10.

Chapter 11

THE IDEOLOGY OF LABOUR ADMINISTRATION

External constraints upon the Board of Trade's
statistical output were strongly reinforced by the
social and economic ideology of the Department
itself. Its statisticians and investigators
viewed the labour market from the standpoint of
the labour aristocracy and middle classes, and to
a significant extent their social status
conditioned their attitude to the Board's
intelligence role. While they believed that the
provision of better labour statistics might
facilitate the erosion of the worst forms of
labour exploitation, they were equally concerned
to construct an 'impartial' information system
with which to discredit idealistic schemes of
social reconstruction.[1] Hence, the Board of
Trade's effort to identify and measure the defects
of the labour market was motivated as much by the
fear that public ignorance and uncertainty as to
their extent might exacerbate social conflict and
industrial unrest, as by a positive commitment to
social equity.

The statistical policy adopted by the Board
was also influenced by the economic philosophy of
the Department. Its overriding objectives were
the preservation of free enterprise, the security
of capital, and the continuity and cost
competitiveness of industrial production.[2] While
its more 'progressive' statisticians rejected the
wage-fund theory and orthodox economic
assumptions, they did not espouse Socialist views
of the economic system and still considered that
economic viability and investment in capital
assets should remain the prime determinants of
wage levels and labour utilisation. It was
anticipated that the Board's labour market
intelligence would refute 'statistically the

alleged principles upon which the idea of surplus
value and Socialist doctrines were based';[3] that
it would perpetuate consensus theories of capital-
labour inter-dependence with their deference to
the security of the profits fund and for the need
for unit labour costs and the level of
unemployment to vary accordingly. Furthermore, by
means of information brokerage, it was intended to
undermine the destructive potential of
'irresponsible' data and to generate an
authoritative intelligence bank with respect to
the economy and the labour market which unions,
employers and governmental institutions would
combine to produce and use in common.[4]

The aim of the Department's statistical work
was therefore perceived as pre-eminently one of
'crisis avoidance'. The range and depth of its
investigations and the categories of its
statistical analyses were not objectively
determined but were, on the contrary, the product
of a series of value judgements within Whitehall
as to the proper function of social and economic
statistics.

For example, the Board was concerned to
identify marginal dysfunctions in the system of
industrial relations rather than the structural
conflict inherent within the social relationships
of production. Its data on industrial unrest were
therefore collated within traditional, economistic
categories relating to wage levels, hours and
working conditions; i.e. to the conventional norms
and remit of collective bargaining. There was a
reluctance to measure unrest as a dependant
variable of economic growth and to identify its
relationship to national income distribution and
to shifts in the organisational and technical
structure of industry. To render such linkages
explicit might generate yet further alienation of
the workforce from the existing industrial system
and serve merely to validate left-wing proposals
for the government regulation of private
enterprise and the market economy.[5]

Similar ideological constraints operated upon
the Board's trade union statistics. In monitoring
the factors conducing to labour solidarity, the
Department focussed upon economic factors at the
point of production rather than upon more
structural economic and societal determinants.
Thus, its data on labour combination concentrated
on the conciliatory role of industrial organisations and their potential as welfare agencies

rather than their relationship to shifts in the concentration and inter-dependence of industry and in the scope and ideology of labour militancy.[6] With the failure of trade unionism to fulfil the stabilising role accorded to it in the 1880s and 1890s by the consensus idealism of Liberal and Tory progressives, there was an increasing reluctance in Whitehall to furnish for public consumption a full analysis of the activities and objectives of labour organisations. This was reflected in the growing disparity after 1904 between the conventional focus of the Board of Trade's annual reports on trade unionism and the detailed appraisal of the structure of authority within union hierarchies, including the motivation and strength of shop steward and syndicalist organisations, contained in its confidential memoranda.

The Board of Trade was equally ambivalent in its attitude to the provision of data on the pattern of working-class income, expenditure and standards of living. Although it wished to identify such patterns, and to relate them to a range of contentious social and economic issues, such as the productivity and cost effectiveness of Britain's labour force and the extent of 'urban degeneration', the Department was highly sensitive to the danger that such data might also fuel industrial unrest and Socialist propaganda. As Sidney Webb observed:

> What they really feel is that the ascertained statistical facts lend themselves so easily to the support of what they think injurious proposals, that they dislike their wide circulation among uncritical people.[7]

For example, the marked discontinuity in the Board's investigations into the relationship of wage costs to total costs of production partly reflected its awareness that questions of 'technical' economic distribution and of social distribution were intimately linked, and that this type of information might serve not merely to identify specific reasons for the deterioration in Britain's cost competitiveness, but also to highlight the differential return to Capital and Labour within national income, and thereby appear to validate Socialist theories of surplus value.[8] Similarly, the absence of statistical analysis of the significance of working-class earnings as a cause of a range of contemporary social problems reflected a reluctance to shift the focus of welfare debate from the conventional areas of housing, health and Poor Law administration to more drastic policy options, such as statutory income maintenance, which implied a fundamental reappraisal of the relationship of government to the market economy. The Board's reluctance to relate its working-class earnings, consumption and cost of living data to the poverty debate also stemmed as much from ideological inhibitions as from logistical constraints. In terms of labour remuneration, the Department subscribed to as minimalist a programme of State intervention as was consistent with the reduction of urban destitution and with the competitive needs of British industry.[9] It explicitly rejected the 'abuse' of its labour statistics as a data base for any system of 'national minimum earnings defined and imposed by the State' and addressed its standard of living data to the question of tariff reform, where the majority of industrial and union organisations were in broad agreement, rather than towards the more divisive issues of low-income destitution and the adequacy of conventional criteria of wage determination.[10]

This fundamental conservatism of the Board of Trade's statistical philosophy was most clearly reflected in its analysis of unemployment. As J.A. Hobson noted in 1895, 'the miserably defective character' of unemployment statistics provided a convenient 'basis of ignorance upon which to base discreet official answers to awkward questions'.[11] The cyclical pattern of the Board's data output with respect to unemployment reveals its reactive rather than innovative motivation, while its focus upon supply as opposed to demand factors reflects the continuing pre-occupation of even social radicals within the Labour Department with micro-economic explanations of unemployment which might, at most, justify minor adjustments in the relationship of the State to the labour market. Official statisticians were clearly convinced that attempts to obtain a comprehensive census of the unemployed would be interpreted by the media as an entrée to Socialist schemes of public works and as an admission on the part of Whitehall of the 'Right to Work'.[12] They were also concerned that more innovative, causal analysis might produce simplistic, environmental explanations of labour displacement as being a

function of technical innovation and economic
growth, which might endorse policies that aimed to
eliminate unemployment through revolutionary
changes in the organisation and control of
industry.[13]

Moreover, it is arguable that the social and
economic ideology of the Labour Department was a
major cause of the methodological conservatism of
the Board's labour statistics. As recent studies
by MacKenzie, Ackroyd and Hughes have demonstrated, statistical techniques are not neutral
atheoretical tools:

> Statistical theory has evolved in historical
> interaction with conceptual change in other
> sciences, with the needs of production and
> with theological, political and ideological
> developments. It is a social, historical and
> ideological product and not merely a
> collection of neutral techniques.[14]

The 'social context' therefore determines the
content as well as the pace of theoretical
advances in statistical methodology. Such
advances are goal-orientated and the choice of
quantitative techniques is conditioned to a
significant extent by the culture and ideology of
dominant groups within society, and in particular
by the economic and social philosophy (in
MacKenzie's terms, the social or 'cognitive
interests'; as Ackroyd and Hughes express it, 'the
instrumental presuppositions') of the
statisticians and social scientists involved.[15]

Thus, the partial shift by the Board of Trade
after 1880 from aggregative accounting of social
and economic phenomena relating to the labour
market to interpretative statistics of causation
was closely related to its perception of the
'urban crisis' and of the desirable policy options
needed to confront it. As Levitt rightly
observes:

> In an era when traditional policies were fast
> crumbling, there had to be some 'modus
> operandi' to enable a debate about future
> policy to occur. 'Accounts' were by
> themselves, little short of meaningless,
> because they did not offer interpretations.
> If existing strategies could no longer be
> relied upon, then the whole rationale that
> underpinned 'Blue-Book' publications was

destroyed. The electors, the ratepayers, the public were beginning to have their conceptions shattered. They needed to be informed, educated, advised and even persuaded, if administrators were to 'manage' and 'contain' the new social problems ... Administrators discovered the production of a social relationship to be worth more than a thousand words. The validity of zero sum relationships had become questionable, while in their place probabilistic or conditional relationships reflected the mood of uncertainty.[16]

It is within this context that the more innovative aspects of the Board of Trade's statistical methodology, as outlined above (Chapter 10), have to be viewed.

At the same time, however, its labour administrators were acutely aware that 'statistical relationships, because of their calculability, had acquired a new authoritative acceptance' and that, as official data now defined to a significant extent the terms and parameters of welfare debate, they had ceased to be mere clerks in a subordinate social role and now fulfilled a highly contentious role of mediating between the public and social issues.[17] As the bulk of the Board's statisticians became bureaucratised, the political sensitivity of such a function became increasingly inhibiting. Hence their reluctance to apply new statistical techniques such as sampling and regression analysis for fear that the data might serve to fragment rather than modify the existing social policy paradigm; to generate social conflict rather than legitimate welfare strategies of crisis avoidance.[18]

A comparison with the statistical philosophy of the Eugenics Movement is especially instructive in revealing the degree to which the Board of Trade's economic and social ideology constrained its propensity to innovate. MacKenzie has clearly identified the degree to which eugenists developed a range of statistical concepts after 1880 as a means of providing a scientific (i.e. quantitative) basis for a systematic programme of Social Darwinism designed to secure racial progress.[19] Thus, theoretical advances in the biometric mathematics of association, such as the refinement by Galton and Pearson of the concepts

of regression and correlation, were specifically
related to the 'social interests' of the Eugenics
Movement. To move from prediction to potential
control over evolutionary processes required
powerful and accurate predictive tools. Precise
measures of statistical dependence and variation
were essential in validating eugenic claims as to
the relationship between heredity, 'civic worth'
and social evolution, and in establishing the
viability of systematic social engineering.
Similarly, measures of standard deviation and
multivariate distribution were vital in the
prediction of inherited characteristics and the
'objective' identification of social 'deviants'
such as the unemployable residuum, destined to be
segregated from the labour market and eliminated
by measures of negative eugenics.

Senior labour statisticians and investigators
within Whitehall shared the same professional
middle-class background which characterised the
membership of the Eugenics Society, adopted a
similar stance of enlightened paternalism towards
the working classes, and identified with some of
the basic objectives of Social Darwinism such as
improved workforce efficiency and the scientific
treatment of 'urban degeneracy'. Nonetheless,
Board of Trade officials firmly rejected eugenics
as a solution to the 'Labour Problem'.

Two main explanations for this rejection may
be advanced. Firstly, as social administrators,
they articulated 'the major systematic pole of
opposition to eugenics - environmentalism'.[20] In
contrast to a number of liberal ideologists, they
were not disposed to view environmental and
hereditary approaches to social reform as
complementary - as 'another synthesis which
accommodated the ethical base of the new
liberalism to scientific developments'.[21] They
regarded eugenic ideas as a fundamental threat to
constructive measures of social amelioration
designed to eliminate the worst welfare
dysfunctions of the capitalist system.[22]

Secondly, the Board of Trade viewed the
policy options of Social Darwinism as socially
divisive and provocative, as measures which might
seriously compromise governmental efforts at
crisis avoidance.[23] The thrust of the Board's
measures in dealing with Labour was the
'reattachment of marginal or disaffected groups to
the social order rather than their segregation'.
As environmentalists, their strategy for social

control was 'integration' in contrast to that of 'exclusion and the tightening of boundaries' advocated by eugenics.[24] Moreover, while the Labour Department also subscribed to a meritocratic social theory, they were opposed to the degree of compulsion and social intervention posited by eugenics. Its aggressive 'scientism' offended not only their liberal sensibilities but also, and more importantly, their perception of the extent to which legislation might regiment social groups without producing confrontation between Labour and the State.

This variance between what MacKenzie would term the 'cognitive interests' of the Eugenics Movement and of social administrators within Whitehall was duly reflected in their statistical techniques. To a limited extent, as we have seen, in their efforts to gain new insights into the dynamics of the labour market and the environmental determinants of the 'Labour Problem', Board of Trade statisticians shared the eugenic concern for measures of statistical variation and dependence. Nevertheless, they were generally resistant to eugenic statistical techniques in so far as they reflected the values and objectives of Social Darwinism.

While the latter required a unitary statistical theory and sophisticated mathematical techniques, such as multi-variate analysis, with which to validate and implement a programme of eugenics, the Board of Trade's more limited environmentalist strategy did not require such rigorous predictive measures. Indeed, the Department feared that too liberal an application of such measures to an environmental analysis of the 'Labour Problem' might prove as provocative and socially divisive as eugenic statistics; that labour statistics would cease to fulfil their intended functions of monitoring the more overtly exploitative features of the employment structure and of 'educating' dissident groups within the workforce as to the identity of interest between Capital and Labour.

For example, labour officials were apprehensive that measures of deviation, if applied too explicitly to existing data on earnings and consumption, might engender social discontent, and that the deployment of the full technology of correlation analysis as developed by Galton and Pearson to the evaluation of unemployment and low-income destitution might

strengthen the credibility of welfare strategies
incorporating drastic changes in the structure of
industry and society.[25] Similarly, quite apart
from other logistical and bureaucratic
reservations, Board of Trade officials feared
that, while the use of systematic sampling
techniques might increase the range and
significance of their data output, it might also
encourage aggregate schemes of government
intervention involving serious and counter-
productive distortions of the relationship between
factor costs and the market environment.[26]
Moreover, to statisticians, many of whom had
served their apprenticeship on the intensive
community enquiries undertaken by Booth, the
Charity Organisation Society and other relief
agencies in the 1880s and early 1890s, the
technique of random sampling was seriously lacking
in potential 'as a means of social contact and
control'.[27]

Thus, although the Board of Trade was
markedly more progressive than other departments
of social administration in its statistical
methodology, its 'cognitive interests' ensured its
primary adherence to the conventional empiricism
of Victorian social research. Its labour
statistics were designed primarily to provide a
data bank for refining the efficiency of existing
agencies of social administration rather than the
quantitative basis for a sociology of the labour
market. In line with other areas of British
empirical research, their wider implications for
social theorising were neglected in favour of the
clever manipulation of ecological data.[28] It is
significant that even Udny Yule, who was
technically the most advanced of the Board's
statistical advisers and a former associate of
Karl Pearson, reacted against the more radical
concepts of eugenic statistical methodology; that
he used the Royal Statistical Society with its
conservative 'statistical sub-culture' as the
forum for his theoretical research, and that,
although incorporating advanced mathematical
theories of statistics, his approach to social
quantification was also constrained by 'an
ameliorative orientation' which focused on
pragmatic issues of social administration rather
than the more fundamental relationships within
Britain's social and economic structure.[29]

The Ideology of Labour Administration

NOTES

1. R. Davidson, 'Llewellyn Smith, the Labour Department and government growth 1886-1909' in G. Sutherland (ed.), *Studies in the growth of nineteenth century government* (1972), pp. 239-50.

2. R. Davidson, 'The Board of Trade and Industrial Relations', *Historical Journal*, 21 (1978), p. 584.

3. See Hicks Beach Papers, PC/PP/60, memo. by R. Giffen on 'Labour Statistics', 16 April 1891.

4. *Labour Gazette*, Vol. 1, No 1 (May 1893), p. 1. On the issue of information brokerage, see R. Davidson, 'Corporatism - A Pre-History', unpublished paper to S.S.R.C. workshop on Corporatism and Accountability (Canterbury, 1981), pp. 5-6.

5. See, e.g., *1st Report on Strikes and Lockouts*, PP 1887 (C.5104) LXXXIX, pp. 7-9; *8th Report on Strikes and Lockouts*, PP 1896 (C.8232) XCIII, pp. xv-xvi.

6. G.H. Wood Papers, 1A/69, *Factory Times* (1908), 'A talk with a statistician'.

7. Passfield Papers, S. Webb to B. Potter, 26 Oct. 1891.

8. *Memorandum on the progress in collecting and publishing statistics relating to Labour*, PP 1888 (433) CVII, p. 9; *Statist*, LIII (1904), pp. 1194-5.

9. See Davidson, 'Board of Trade', pp. 581-5. For an explicit statement of its philosophy of labour remuneration, see PP 1913 (268) XIII, Appendices, p. 11.

10. For its refusal to be drawn into the poverty debate, see especially *S.C. on Post Office Servants, Mins. of Ev.*, PP 1913 (268) XIII, pp. 1432-8.

11. Cited in W.R. Garside, *The Measurement of Unemployment: Methods and Sources in Great Britain* (1981), p. 9.

12. P.R.O., CAB37/38, memo. by Llewellyn Smith on 'The Unemployed', 23 Jan. 1895, pp. 8-9.

13. See, e.g., P.R.O., LAB2/1480/L303/1897, memo. by Llewellyn Smith, 16 Nov. 1897 re representations from the S.T.U.C. for a 'Government enquiry into the relationship of unemployment to the ownership of capital and fluctuations in business activity'.

14. D.A. MacKenzie, 'Eugenics and the Rise of Mathematical Statistics in Britain' in J. Irvine *et al.* (eds.), *Demystifying Social Statistics*, (1979), p. 48. See also E.M. Yeo, 'Social Science and Social Change: Some Aspects of Social Science and Social Investigation in Britain 1830-1890', unpublished D. Phil. thesis, Sussex University, 1972.

15. S. Ackroyd and J.A. Hughes, *Data Collection in Context* (1981), p. 139.

16. I. Levitt, 'The Use of Official Statistics', *Quantitative Sociology Newsletter*, 22 (1979), p. 72.

17. Ibid., p. 73.

18. For the links between statistics and crisis avoidance, see R. Davidson, 'Economic Crisis and Welfare Empiricism: A Case Study', Paper presented to 8th International Economic History Congress (Budapest, 1982).

19. D.A. MacKenzie, *Statistics in Britain: The Social Construction of Scientific Knowledge* (Edinburgh, 1981), Chs. 3-4.

20. Ibid., p. 48.

21. M. Freeden, *The New Liberalism: An Ideology of Social Reform* (1978), p. 188.

22. See Wilson Fox Papers, undated satirical poem: 'The Strength of the Race'.

23. Ibid., Rider Haggard to Wilson Fox, 11 Aug. 1905; *Report on Agricultural Settlements in British Colonies*, PP 1906 (Cd.2978) LXXVI, note of dissent by Wilson Fox, pp. 26-7.

24. MacKenzie, *Statistics in Britain*, p. 50.

25. Clara Collet Diary, 20 Aug. 1904; G.H. Wood Papers, CB/95, F.H. MacLeod to Wood, 3 Sept. 1906.

26. Wilson Fox Papers, Bowley to Wilson Fox, 4 Aug. 1906.

27. E. Yeo, 'The early years of social science'. Paper read to Sociology Workshop Conference, City University (1976).

28. R. Kent, *A History of British Empirical Sociology* (1981), pp. 6, 74, 83; A. Oberschall (ed.), *The Establishment of Empirical Sociology: Studies in Continuity, Discontinuity and Institutionalization* (New York, 1972), pp. 115-20.

29. MacKenzie, *Statistics in Britain*, pp. 111, 174.

Part Five

THE   IMPLICATIONS

Chapter 12

LABOUR STATISTICS AND SOCIAL POLICY

It is evident that, both for logistical and
ideological reasons, welfare debate and policy
formation during the period 1886-1914 lacked the
informational and statistical basis for systematic
social engineering consistent with the more
coercive strategies of social control. Nor does
this study of the production structure and output
of official statistics support a simple conspiracy
theory of social legislation as purely a function
of the values and perceptions of the financial and
industrial elite within market capitalism. The
ambivalence or active resistance of this elite
towards governmental enquiries has been amply
demonstrated, reflecting a policy-making process
which incorporated a range of competing elites,
including bureaucratic and professional groups
whose status and aspirations were less directly
and less critically dependent on the imperatives
of the market. Nonetheless, an analysis of the
rationale and scope of official statistics
relating to the late-Victorian and Edwardian
'Labour Problem' clearly sustains an
interpretation of social reform as primarily a
means of social control.

Firstly, the *ad hoc*, fragmented pattern of
investigation and its lack of focus upon the
structural causes and context of labour problems
were inconsistent with any progressive programme
of social reconstruction designed to modify the
structure of industry and society. The data base
of policy making was not designed to address the
systemic problems of exploitation and deprivation
produced by the social relationships of capitalist
production. Instead, it reflected the overriding
concern of late-Victorian and Edwardian policy-
makers to contain social unrest, to re-establish

industrial consensus and to secure a stable environment within which the vitality of the British economy might be restored. The limited scope and rigour of government statistics and their focus upon the horizontal rather than vertical distribution of income and consumption were strongly indicative of a desire either to disguise or to legitimate the more provocative inequalities in British society; to pacify or discredit alienated groups by cosmetic adjustments to the content and machinery of social administration rather than by any fundamental re-evaluation of policy options and reformulation of the social and economic theory underpinning welfare measures. Thus, the empirical basis of legislative initiatives was more compatible with a static, restorative concept of reform than with a dynamic, regenerative ideology of State intervention. It was essentially a reactive and reactionary empiricism engendered by the 'crisis' perceptions of the governing classes.

Secondly, official labour intelligence did not conform to a progressive model of social reform in that the issues addressed, the phenomena and relationships monitored, and the categories of statistical analysis adopted, were primarily market rather than welfare-orientated. They reflected a concern with the competitive needs of industry rather than the social needs of the working classes; a concern with the cost and efficiency of Labour as a factor of production rather than its welfare rights of citizenship. Labour statistics mirrored a governmental perception of the 'Labour Problem' as pre-eminently a problem of market imperfections rather than of social deprivation, and intellectual and welfare historians have signally ignored the degree to which, throughout most of the late-Victorian and Edwardian period, official investigations subordinated social politics to industrial and commercial issues. That the most advanced labour statistics should have been incorporated within the Fiscal Blue Books is indicative of this subordination of welfare to economic priorities.

Even where official statistics did confront the distributional aspects of the 'Labour Problem', they evaded the more contentious welfare issues of income inequality, focussing instead upon the industrial and fiscal implications of the pattern and elasticities of working-class demand.

Investigations were clearly not designed to establish any normative welfare values of income and consumption with which existing levels of working-class remuneration and expenditure might be compared. Data on wage earnings and costs of living were symptomatic of governmental concern with the physical and cost-efficiency of human capital stock rather than any programmatic commitment to the 'Minimum' as an exercise in redistributive justice.

This focus of labour statistics upon economic rather than welfare concerns was also indicative of the disciplinary and regulatory intent of social reform. Many investigations, such as those relating to labour unrest and unemployment, mirrored less a commitment to monitor areas of social distress and destitution than to identify groups within the workforce for whom the normal controls of the work ethic and industrial discipline were either unacceptable or inoperative. Similarly, considerations of productive efficiency rather than of social amelioration appear to have underpinned government enquiries into the problems of under-employment and 'sweating', reflecting an overriding concern of policy-makers with the impact of the residuum upon the equilibrium of the urban labour market and hence the earnings potential and motivation of the regular, skilled and semi-skilled workforce. To the extent that attention *was* directed at the social rather than economic repercussions of idleness and low-income destitution, the categories of analysis retained strong overtones of conventional middle-class individualism, echoing Whitehall's intention to preserve within welfare measures the moral and economic sanctions of 'less-eligibility'.

Furthermore, the rationale and scope of labour statistics did not indicate a pluralist structure of social policy-making, incorporating the popular demands and aspirations of organised Labour. While the conspiracy theory of government labour policy propounded by the Socialist press lacks credibility, this study suggests that the distrust displayed in Labour circles was amply justified. Official labour intelligence clearly reflected the paternalism of pre-war social administration in which Labour was perceived and treated as a problem amenable to administrative solution imposed unilaterally from above, rather than as a 'class' whose aspirations required a fundamental shift in the ideology and personnel of social policy-making, and in which Whitehall remained relatively uninhibited by the need to consult and to compromise with the welfare perspectives of the working classes.

The employment of former trade unionists as statisticians and investigators well illustrates the incorporative aspects of late-Victorian and Edwardian social reform. They were clearly recruited not as zealots articulating a cause, still less the interests of a class, but as experts deployed to clarify social problems (or deviances) as defined by the ruling elite. As representatives of the Labour Movement, their role was conceived as legitimating governmental perceptions and diagnoses of the 'Labour Problem' rather than as securing for Labour fuller participation in the policy-making process and a shift in the social objectives of bureaucracy. In so far as the data base of debate and policy formation revealed the motivation and social significance of welfare measures, this study therefore endorses a view of late-Victorian and Edwardian social reform not as a stepping stone to Socialism but as a buttress to Capitalism.

Official statistics did not merely *reflect* the control functions of social reform, they actively sustained them. This study clearly demonstrates that the process of monitoring the 'Labour Problem' within Whitehall not only constrained the terms of reference of late-Victorian and Edwardian debate but also the scope of industrial and welfare provisions relating to the labour market - in particular, those measures designed to alleviate unemployment, low-income destitution and industrial strife.

INDUSTRIAL RELATIONS POLICY

In confronting the problem of industrial relations, Whitehall viewed labour statistics as a means by which consensus policies and perceptions might be legitimated and conflict strategies either discredited or starved of an empirical base. This function was fulfilled in three main ways. Firstly, during the period 1886-96, when the role of the State in industrial relations was at the forefront of public debate, official statistics with regard to the labour market were deployed to undermine the credibility of Socialist measures designed to modify the ownership and control of production. As noted above (see Chapters 5 and 11), the Board of Trade sought to demonstrate the fundamental identity of interest between Capital and Labour, and the degree to which industrial unrest stemmed from a simple lack of awareness of the market forces operating upon the level and stability of all factor incomes rather than from any sinister and structural process of exploitation. Similarly, it endeavoured to show the extent to which the dominant issues in contention were traditional economistic issues at the point of production and not broader ideological conflicts over the legitimacy of free enterprise and the structure of industrial power. The central message enshrined within the annual reports of the Labour Statistical Bureau and Labour Department was that strikes and lockouts should be perceived as temporary deviances from the conventional norms of collective bargaining rather than systemic confrontations between the competing values and interests of the managerial and labouring classes.

The policy implications of such statistics were clear-cut; that any drastic interference by the State in the social relationships of production was unmerited, and would, by eroding managerial and work incentives and by fracturing the links between economic performance and factor costs, prove counterproductive; and that the only legitimate area of State intervention compatible with the security of capital and with the continuity and cost competitiveness of British industry was the provision of statutory conciliation and arbitration machinery designed to complement existing dispute procedures. Moreover, in defining its terms of reference and in shaping its empirical brief, Board of Trade statisticians and investigators ensured that these policy implications were duly incorporated within the recommendations of the celebrated Royal Commission on Labour, and subsequently embodied in the Conciliation Act of 1896.[1]

The second major function of labour statistics in the development of industrial relations policy was to provide the intelligence for government conciliation and arbitration procedures after 1896.[2] Although the Conciliation Act prescribed no formal code of intervention comparable to the statutory regulations that characterised other areas of social administration, such intelligence enabled the Board of Trade to pursue a coherent and vigorous strategy of positive voluntarism designed to contain labour unrest, to stabilise industrial relations and to protect a capitalist employment structure, by the institutionalisation of industrial conflict and the confinement of collective bargaining within the bounds of existing wage relativities and orthodox market criteria.

An accurate and intensive system of labour intelligence was vital to the process whereby, contrary to the intention of the Conciliation Act, Whitehall took the initiative in activating State arbitration and conciliation machinery. In each labour dispute, its strategy was based upon a detailed assessment of the factors likely to determine industrial response to State intervention, from economic variables such as the cost structure and profit margins of the firm and the financial resources of the union involved, to social and bureaucratic determinants such as the previous history of labour relations and bargaining procedures within the trade and the structure of authority within management and union hierarchies. Moreover, when an industrial stoppage was exceptionally bitter and prolonged, involving severe social hardship, economic dislocation, or civil strife, the Labour Department interpreted its investigative powers as a mandate to exert public pressure upon management and workforce to resolve their differences; labour intelligence being either formally or informally deployed to educate public opinion as to the (officially perceived) merits of the dispute.

In practice, as recent research into the administration of industrial relations under the Conciliation Act demonstrates, such intervention invariably operated against the interests of Labour. It is evident that, after the turn of the century, the aim of these quasi-public enquiries undertaken by the Labour Department during serious and protracted disputes was less to erode the more dictatorial and provocative forms of industrial management than to discredit rank and file militancy within the Trade Union Movement. More significantly, although the Board of Trade never imposed any formal wages policy upon its umpires, in briefing its arbitrators, the Labour Department ensured that the traditional criteria of wage determination were broadly adhered to, by focussing upon the state of trade, the competitive needs of the district, or changes in the selling price of the product involved. After 1906, umpires were occasionally supplied with additional data on local variations in rents and commodity prices but these constituted little more than a token gesture to welfare criteria and were rarely incorporated within arbitration proceedings and awards. Arbitrators were denied information concerning the profit margins and cost structure of firms involved in disputes, despite the fact that it would have provided the most accurate indicator of their ability to sustain pay advances. The data base of State collective bargaining procedures clearly placed labour negotiators at a distinct disadvantage. While they were starved of vital information on production costs and industrial profits, the labour statistics published by the Board of Trade provided employers with data on comparative wage rates and the financial reserves of trade unions. Thus, in sustaining the strictly commercial criteria of wage determination under the Conciliation Act, official statistics inevitably hampered the efforts of the union movement to secure a more equitable distribution of income between Capital and Labour.

In the context of industrial relations policy, perhaps the most vital contribution of labour statistics to the process of social control was in furnishing the empirical basis for the rejection by late-Victorian and Edwardian government of successive measures designed to endow the machinery of collective bargaining with legal sanctions. Schemes involving compulsory conciliation with a statutory cooling-off period and/or compulsory arbitration with legally binding awards had been widely canvassed since the early 1890s. At Westminster, a sizeable group of Conservative backbenchers representing 'villa Toryism' and fearful of the threat to property and dividends from industrial stoppages had persistently advocated legal coercion to control trade disputes. In addition, a small but vocal group of Liberal businessmen and even some elder statesmen of craft unionism had sought to contain rank-and-file militancy by investing existing voluntary collective bargaining machinery with powers to enforce wage agreements. The Board of Trade firmly resisted such proposals both in Cabinet and before the Royal Commission on Labour.

Citing evidence on relative factor costs of
production and the price elasticity of demand for
British exports, the Department argued that
compulsory intervention in the process of wage
determination would distort the labour market,
dislocate the cost structure of British industry,
and render it vulnerable to foreign competition.
In addition, on the basis of a series of opinion
polls, the Labour Department was able convincingly
to demonstrate that the consensus of industrial
opinion favoured permissive legislation and that
any dispute procedures involving overt compulsion
would prove unacceptable to the majority of
industrialists and trade unionists and would be
certain to produce a confrontation between Labour
and the State.[3] In short, such measures would
constitute an exercise in social disruption rather
than social control.

After 1896, however liberal its interpretation of the Conciliation Act, the Board of Trade
retained its essentially voluntarist view of
industrial relations. To protect the community
against the more serious economic and social
repercussions of industrial conflict, the Board
was prepared to exercise a considerable degree of
bureaucratic license in implementing its powers.
In an effort to ensure that voluntary dispute procedures were fully utilised and the merits of
protracted stoppages fully investigated and publi-
cised, it was also prepared to endorse the various
schemes for a National Conciliation Board
advocated by the General Federation of Trade
Unions, the Trades Union Congress and the Industrial Co-operation Movement between 1898 and 1904.
Nonetheless, the Board of Trade vigorously opposed
a fresh campaign for compulsory arbitration with
legal sanctions initiated by an 'unholy alliance'
of right-wing politicians obsessed with the impact
of strikes and restrictive practices upon national
efficiency, trade union leaders in the engineering
and transport sectors seeking legal sanctuary from
the counter-attack of the employers' associations,
and middle-class social engineers infatuated with
Australasian collectivism.

Whitehall was concerned that any attempt to
impose legal coercion upon collective bargaining
would only exacerbate class conflict and foster
the growth of revolutionary Socialism. The
statistics of industrial unrest and the soundings
of industrial opinion regularly taken by the
Labour Department clearly indicated that the

frontal attack on the legal status of trade unionism culminating in the Taff Vale Judgement had not served to stabilise labour relations but further to alienate the workforce from the machinery of government, and seriously erode the ability of trade union leaders in strategic sectors of the economy to control rank and file militancy and pursue conciliatory tactics. Official intelligence predicted that compulsory arbitration would merely reinforce this trend, discredit the existing system of voluntary collective bargaining and render the Conciliation Act a 'dead letter'. Furthermore, detailed analyses by the Labour Department of the rationale and impact of statutory conciliation and arbitration procedures in the Dominions served to strengthen resistance to compulsory measures within British policy-making circles. Their apparent success in New Zealand was shown to be dependent on factors peculiar to the nature of its economy and labour market; in particular, the existence of a weak and highly fragmented trade union movement and the ability of employers within a temporarily buoyant and relatively isolated economy to sustain compulsory wage advances at the expense of the consumer.[4]

With the escalation in industrial conflict after 1909, the Board of Trade was once again confronted with demands for more stringent legislation. While the Department now wished to incorporate a statutory 'cooling-off' period as part of dispute procedure in major stoppages and to legalise the community's right to investigate the merits of such disputes, its overriding concern in advising government on the prevention of industrial strife remained that of dissuading it from policy options that involved compulsion. In the view of senior labour officials within Whitehall, the evidence from routine intelligence reports of industrial opinion and from specially commissioned investigations into overseas legislation, such as the Canadian Lemieux Act, was unambiguous. Repressive measures entailing penal or military sanctions and threatening to curtail the right of the workforce to withhold its labour would prove 'practically inoperative' and merely strengthen the influence of Socialist agitators over the Labour Movement, thereby increasing the likelihood of industrial violence.[5]

In contrast, in its administration of industrial relations, the Board of Trade sought to

disseminate the view that consensus strategies
towards labour unrest, such as voluntary
arbitration and selective social investment,
constituted the most effective antidote to
Socialism and preservative of industrial
capitalism. The Board was ideally equipped for
the task. With its fund of labour statistics and
extensive knowledge of the Labour Movement, its
Labour Department could readily advise its
political chiefs and the Cabinet as to which
policy options would most effectively exploit
divisions within trade unionism, reinforce the
status of moderate leaders, and neutralize the
influence of extremists. Similarly, the Board's
permanent officials could provide an informed and
realistic assessment of the threat of revolutionary movements such as Syndicalism, thereby
preventing the government from over-reacting to
minority groups with measures that could have
precipitated bitter conflict between Labour and
the State. In a period which witnessed a
significant shift in the emphasis of social
control from overt confrontation with the Trade
Union Movement to more subtle methods of
containment, it therefore seems peculiarly
appropriate that the most prominent agency of
official labour intelligence - the Labour
Department of the Board of Trade - was housed
precisely where Collison's strike-breaking Free
Labour Organisation had formerly been sited.[6]

UNEMPLOYMENT POLICY

The precise linkages between labour statistics and
unemployment policy during the late-Victorian and
Edwardian period are less readily discerned.
Harris has argued that:

> although social inquiries were undoubtedly
> important in forming public opinion and in
> reinforcing political argument, many of the
> administrative remedies devised to deal with
> unemployment were based on very inadequate
> statistical knowledge, and to a large extent
> new information about the state of the labour
> market was not the cause but the product of
> experiments in social reform.[7]

She contends that for most of the period, the
discussion of unemployment and the theories on

which reforms were based, were derived as much
from highly conjectural preconceptions about the
nature of the labour market and the characteristics of the unemployed, as from the very limited
statistical data available.[8]

Moreover, serious methodological problems
arise in any attempt to monitor the flow of
statistical information through the decision-
making hierarchy and to evaluate its impact upon
unemployment policy.[9] Information was only one of
several resources which policy makers used in
reaching a decision. There is the additional
problem that the use of information tended to take
place in clusters. Single reports regarding
unemployment were typically not used or applied in
themselves. Officials accumulated evidence
concerning a particular aspect of the problem,
summarised it, and sent a report based on the
compiled evidence to a policy maker. Rarely did a
Cabinet memorandum, a legislative proposal or
administrative guidelines *directly* draw upon and
quote an empirical study. The process of
information procurement and utilization within
late-Victorian and Edwardian government therefore
makes it especially difficult to trace the
influence of a particular piece of statistical
data.

Nonetheless, the difficulties are not
insuperable. The sequence of minuting upon
departmental files furnishes an excellent
indicator of the extent to which statistical
reports relating to the unemployment problem
penetrated policy-making circles. The registration and preservation procedures of the Board of
Trade also provide an invaluable insight into the
subsequent use of this information, briefing
papers relating to policy issues being docketed
together in sequence. Where their original data
base is absent, its identity can often be
extrapolated from policy memoranda. Such evidence
reveals that, despite the lacunae in official
unemployment statistics, they fulfilled a
formative role in defining policy options and that
this role was fundamentally conservative.

During the period 1886-1906, the primary
impact of official unemployment statistics upon
political debate was to discredit a range of
measures advocated by Socialist, labour, and
radical groups. Labour intelligence furnished by
the Board of Trade to policy-makers and the press
was designed to counteract the 'crisis perception'

of unemployment fostered by such groups as a means of legitimating the State regulation of employment. Official statistics were regularly deployed to discredit left-wing estimates of the level of unemployment and the extent of its associated distress.[10] Moreover, in briefing ministers and the Cabinet, information was often 'massaged' in order to present the most optimistic view of the state of the labour market.[11] The explicatory role of the Board of Trade in the major official enquiries of the 1890s served to fulfil a similar function. Rather than furnishing the data base for a range of innovative, preventative measures, its causal analyses underlined the normality of cyclical unemployment in a maturing economy and resisted the logic of structural reforms contingent upon a pathological interpretation of such fluctuations.[12]

In particular, official statistics seriously eroded the credibility of proposals for a legislative eight-hours day and for the provision of public employment, advanced by the Labour Movement as remedies for the unemployment problem. Reports of the Labour Department clearly revealed the lack of consensus among trade unionists over the issue of the statutory regulation of the adult working day, and the degree to which their views diverged according to variations in the pattern of industrial employment and remuneration, and in their economic and political ideology. More seriously, by demonstrating empirically that shorter hours typically led to increased per capita output and labour productivity, the Department helped to undermine the central thrust of the eight-hours movement as an antidote to unemployment. Finally, in interpreting the available evidence for the Royal Commission on Labour, the Board of Trade injected into the debate a decisive consideration that, if the cost competitiveness of British exports was to be maintained, any unilateral initiative by British government in regulating the working hours of its adult labour force would, in all probability, have to be accompanied by a reduction in wages and a consequent reduction in consumer demand and employment.[13]

Meanwhile, the Board's labour intelligence underpinned governmental resistance to the campaign for public employment or the 'Right to Work'. The campaign advanced a variety of proposals ranging from the simple extension of the existing powers of local authorities under the Poor Law to initiate temporary relief works for the unemployed during periods of acute distress, to a co-ordinated programme of public investment designed to counter cyclical unemployment.

The majority of such measures were revealed by the Labour Department either to be irrelevant to the paramount needs of the 'competent victims of trade fluctuations', or to be positively counter-productive. British and overseas relief schemes were shown to be patronised predominantly by chronically irregular workmen, to be thoroughly cost-ineffective and a potential source of pauperisation. Meanwhile, evidence derived from monitoring public investment programmes in New Zealand and New South Wales clearly indicated their minimal impact upon the labour market and their propensity to erode work incentives and industrial discipline within the private sector.[14] Although the Board of Trade's investigations did much to reveal the economic determinants of unemployment, implicit within its evaluation of demand-orientated strategies, such as counter-depressive public works, was the fear that they would endanger the investment fund and destabilise the capital market for private enterprise. Basic inhibitions in its philosophy of prevention towards the unemployment problem were thus firmly embedded in its role as an information broker to late-Victorian government.

Contemporaneously, the Board's intelligence served to discredit the more provocative and coercive schemes advocated by right-wing authoritarian ideologies aimed at segregating the unemployed from the normal labour market. Indeed, Arnold White, the celebrated ideologue of Social Imperialism and the National Efficiency Movement, was moved to condemn the Labour Department's analysis of the unemployment problem as 'obsequious to Demos'.[15] Its findings on the causes of unemployment and the efficiency of existing agencies for dealing with the unemployed indicated that schemes, such as regimented labour colonies, could have at best only a peripheral effect upon the level of employment and could not provide any permanent solution to the aggregate problem of urban redundancy.[16] In particular, their rationale was shown to assume a degree of social engineering that lacked a sufficient empirical base. In briefing public opinion and parliamentary debate, the Department was unequivocal that, in the absence of systematic data on the social incidence of unemployment and the industrial history of the unemployed, it was impossible either to establish the existence and parameters of an unemployed 'class', or to differentiate between the so-called 'residuum' or the congenitally unfit and the respectable unemployed. Without such a distinction, evidence suggested that there was a real danger of imposing upon the 'reputable unemployed' repressive agencies which, from continental experience, were only appropriate to the suppression of vagabondage and vagrancy, which would further politicise the unemployed as a movement, and precipitate social unrest.[17]

Within the context of unemployment policy-making, official statistics during the period 1886-1906 therefore underlined the need, in the short term, to evade drastic and contentious measures, in favour of marginal innovations designed to widen the repertoire of relief provisions in the dispensation of local authorities; a strategy broadly adopted in the Chamberlain and Fowler Circulars of 1886 and 1892, the 1902 Labour Bureaux (London) Act, and the Unemployed Workmen Act of 1905. However, official intelligence also indicated that in the long run, the overriding aims of economic efficiency and social consensus would best be served by a policy option in which both the regimentation *and* the welfare of the unemployed might be conflated.

Furthermore, labour statistics played a vital role in realising this option after 1906. Previous investigations by the Labour Department had served to redefine the role of labour bureaux in unemployment policy. Official reports and ministerial briefings had consistently dismissed their potential for job creation. Detailed analyses of the performance of existing bureaux in Britain and overseas indicated that their net impact upon unemployment during periods of generalised cyclical depression was minimal and that, given the immobility of the labour force due to factors such as social and cultural ties, skill-specificity, and the inter-dependence of family income, their ability to alleviate local pockets of structural unemployment was also slight.[18] In contrast, the potential of labour registries for manpower surveillance and for providing systematic intelligence concerning the composition and level of unemployment, otherwise lacking in official statistics, and upon which selective social investment might 'safely' be based, was increasingly identified both in Whitehall and by a growing body of managerial opinion.[19] A national network of labour exchanges was explicitly viewed as an extension of the statistical functions of Edwardian government by means of which the deserving, bona fide unemployed might be distinguished from the voluntarily idle and unemployable, and the supportive and coercive elements of welfare measures varied appropriately.

In particular, bureaucrats of the New Liberalism, such as Llewellyn Smith and Beveridge, viewed the data generated under the Labour Exchanges Act of 1909 as critical in regulating statutory measures of social insurance in accordance with the need for industrial discipline and efficiency.[20] By monitoring the demand for labour and the industrial record of welfare recipients, such data was designed to ensure that work incentives and motivation were sustained despite the increasing security of working-class incomes provided by unemployment insurance, that inefficient and disruptive patterns of industrial behaviour or engagement were identified and penalised, and that the desert and eligibility of beneficiaries were calculated by reference, not to any criterion of social need nor to any welfare right of citizenship, but to their conformity to the work ethic and the traditional controls of capitalist production.

MINIMUM WAGE POLICY

Official statistics fulfilled a similarly conservative role in defining the scope of minimum wage policy during the late-Victorian and Edwardian period. Firstly, they greatly under-stated the extent of low-income destitution. The problem was identified as an anomaly of certain 'diseased' and 'parasitic' trades rather than as a general feature of the unskilled and secondary labour market. For both ideological and logistical reasons, the real parameters of the mass of urban destitution consequent upon low and irregular earnings remained uncharted, despite the constant demands from Socialist and social radical groups for more detailed information. In collating wage and earnings data, Whitehall assiduously adhered to the traditional focus upon occupational wage relativities at the mean rather than a measure of the extremes within the social distribution of remuneration, central to the informational needs of the minimum wage debate.

Minimum wage campaigners viewed the limitations of official data as both sinister and inhibiting. Beatrice Webb noted with ill-disguised frustration the unwillingness of the Board of Trade to use the *Labour Gazette* as a vehicle for advancing the issue,[21] while at the height of the campaign for wage board legislation in 1907, Charles Dilke significantly devoted his presidential address to the Royal Statistical Society to the lack of an empirical basis for British welfare debate.[22] As the Anti-Sweating League pointed out, this omission had a vital impact upon policy making. By identifying low-income destitution as a problem specific to certain sweated occupations that were characterised by home work, female employment and outdated technology, and that were atypical of the general labour market, the Board of Trade's intelligence effectively restricted the application of minimum wage legislation before 1914 to a few isolated trades, and diverted public policy from the general demand for a statutory minimum applicable to the workforce as a whole.[23] Furthermore, by demonstrating the abnormality of the labour market within such trades, Whitehall was able to dissociate the introduction of selective measures such as the 1909 Trade Boards Act from more general demands for a National Minimum.[24] In the context of minimum wage policy, empirical and ideological constraints were therefore integrally linked.

The scope of minimum wage policy was also confined by the Board of Trade's analysis of the *causes* of 'sweated' labour. Rather than evaluating it as part of the broader exploitative relationships inherent within the production structure of British industry, the Board's investigations interpreted it as primarily a function of localised imperfections in the machinery of collective bargaining which generated abnormal levels of exploitation inimical to the efficiency of the specific workforce concerned and to the general cost equilibrium of the urban labour market. The logic of such an approach was that the remedy for 'sweating' lay in identifying and filling the more acute or overt lacunae in industrial organisation rather than any fundamental innovation in the criteria of wage determination, and it was precisely this order of priorities which informed British minimum wage legislation of the period.[25] Minimum wage measures were explicitly designed to constrain State intervention in the normal mechanisms of wage determination. The overriding objective was to underpin working-class associative effort either (as in the implementation of the Fair Wage Resolutions) by furnishing the Trade Union Movement with data relating to traditional areas of low pay such as public sector employment,[26] or (as in the formulation of the 1909 Trade Boards Act) by providing 'surrogate' collective bargaining machinery for trades in which the structure of production or the composition of the workforce militated against its spontaneous evolution.[27]

In its provision of commercial and social intelligence, the Board of Trade was clearly concerned to resist any broader remit for government intervention in labour costs. This it achieved by discrediting the concept of statutory minima as an alternative means of wage determination, reinforced with a critical appraisal of overseas legislation, and by denying welfare debate any rigorous assessment of wage norms necessary to ensure the physical efficiency and the subsistence of the workforce. While official enquiries often exposed the diseconomies of sweated labour, they did not sustain a radical critique of market forces. The central thrust of the Board of Trade's more interpretative labour statistics was that, as far as possible, factor costs should remain flexible if profit margins and investment incentives were to be sustained, and that any attempt to impose social rather than commercial criteria upon wage determination might seriously undermine the viability of British enterprise. Broader considerations, such as fluctuations in the cost of living, might legitimately play a role in wage regulation only if they did not significantly disturb the vital nexus between wage levels and the value of output and were not permitted to exert a ratchet effect upon labour costs.[28] According to the Board's evaluation of overseas labour legislation, it was precisely these conditions that Australasian minimum wage measures failed to observe. Indeed, British official welfare intelligence was in marked contrast to the mainstream of contemporary welfare literature, typified by the works of Pember Reeves, in focussing upon the deficiencies rather than the virtues of Dominion measures.[29]

Meanwhile, in addressing issues of industrial remuneration, official labour statisticians refused to provide any official poverty line or to establish a data base upon which national or regional minima might be constructed. To a limited extent, they were prepared to furnish a profile of existing working-class income and consumption patterns but not to extend their analysis to identify a subsistence or living wage that might form the basis of statutory regulations. Indeed, they remained remarkably resistant to constructing *any* authoritative index of real wages with which to illuminate the minimum wage debate. The evidence of the Director of Labour Statistics, F.H. MacLeod, to the Select Committee on Post Office Pay in 1913 admirably reveals the ideological constraints operating within Whitehall:

> They (the Board of Trade) have never thought it worth while to get out a model budget upon which they consider a man could maintain himself and his family in a state of physical efficiency? - No, I do not think any useful end would be attained. What we want to ascertain is what the facts are. It would be no use our getting out a model budget if no one followed it.
>
> But if the Board of Trade got out a budget which showed the amount of food stuff which a family ought to have to maintain themselves in a state of physical efficiency, if it did no further service it would be a sign-post? - You mean a model budget which would be a measure of the minimum that a man could live on?
>
> Yes, an indication to a man and his employer of what a man and his family ought to have to maintain themselves in a state of physical efficiency? - No, I think we do a greater service by telling you what in fact people are living on. I do not think any advice from the Board of Trade as to what people ought to live on would be accepted.
>
> You take the amount that people are forced to

work upon as the basis of your calculations?
- No, I think you must not use the word
"forced". Our duty is only to give you the
existing facts.

I am not disputing them, but you will admit
that the amounts some families are receiving
are too little to maintain them in a state of
physical efficiency? - I should not think
there is any doubt about it, but I do not
feel it my business to say it.[30]

It is therefore apparent that, in so far as
the Liberal welfare reforms incorporated minimum
wage legislation, it was very much in spite of,
rather than because of the welfare intelligence
generated within Whitehall. Its function was
essentially to contain the process of reform and
to render it compatible with the existing norms of
British industrial relations; to identify for
policy-makers the most contentious areas of public
disquiet without radically altering the
conventional relationship of the State to the
process of labour valuation within market
capitalism.

NOTES

1. See especially, Hicks Beach Papers, PC/PP/60, memoranda by R. Giffen and J. Burnett for the Royal Commission on Labour, 16 April 1891; P.R.O., HO73/34, Working Papers and Minutes of Labour Commission.

2. Unless otherwise stated, the following section is based upon R. Davidson, 'The Board of Trade and Industrial Relations 1896-1914', *Historical Journal*, 21 (1978), pp. 571-91; *idem*, 'Social Conflict and Social Administration: The Conciliation Act in British Industrial Relations' in T.C. Smout (ed.), *The Search for Wealth and Stability* (1979), Ch. 9.

3. P.R.O., BT13/26/E12293/1896, memoranda by R. Giffen and H.L. Smith on 'Conciliation in Trade Disputes', early 1893; *Annual Report on Strikes and Lockouts*, PP 1894 (C.7403) LXXXI Pt 1, p. 37.

4. P.R.O., LAB2/936/L416/1908, memoranda by A.W. Fox and J. Burnett on the Conciliation and Arbitration (Amendment) Bill (1904) and Trade Disputes (Arbitration) Bill (1908).

5. See P.R.O., CAB37/107/70 and 98; CAB37/110/62-3; CAB37/118/14.

6. *Liberty Review*, 15 May 1899.

7. J. Harris, *Unemployment and Politics: A Study in English Social Policy 1886-1914* (Oxford, 1972), p. 362.

8. Ibid., p. 47.

9. For a general discussion of the methodological problems involved, see R.F. Rich, *Social Science Information and Public Policy Making* (1981), pp. 111-28.

10. See, e.g., P.R.O., CAB37/38, memo. on 'The Unemployed', by H.L. Smith, 23 Jan. 1895; P.R.O., LAB2/1478/L210/1903.

11. See, e.g., P.R.O., LAB2/1597/L117/1905.

12. See especially, the evidence of H.L. Smith to the *Select Committee on Distress from Want of Employment*, PP 1895 (365) IX, pp. 47-84.

13. See, *Annual Reports on Changes in Wages and the Hours of Labour*, PP 1896 (C.8075) LXXX Pt 1, p. xxv; 1897 (C.8444) LXXXIII, p. xxiv; Harris, *Unemployment*, p. 72.

14. See, e.g., *Report on Agencies and Methods for Dealing with the Unemployed* PP 1893-94 (C.7182) LXXXII, pp. 407-9; P.R.O., LAB2/213/L156/1904, memo. by J.J. Wills on 'The Public Provision of Work for the Unemployed', 5 Feb. 1904.

15. A. White, *The English Democracy: Its Promises and Perils* (1894), pp. 33-4.

16. PP 1893-94 (C.7182) LXXXII, p. 407; PP 1895 (365) IX, QQ.4977-8, 4992.

17. See, e.g., P.R.O., LAB2/1555/L1099/1903, memo. by H.L. Smith, 18 July 1903.

18. PP 1893-94 (C.7182) LXXXII, p. 406; P.R.O., LAB2/1477/L1294/1894, H.L. Smith to Courtenay Boyle, 8 Aug.

Labour Statistics and Social Policy

1894; PP 1895 (365) IX, pp. 63-4.

19. See Churchill Papers, C/11/2, memo. on 'Labour Exchanges' by A.W. Fox, 21 July 1908, p. 2; C/11/11, memo. on 'The Intelligence Bureau' by H.L. Smith, 19 May 1909; J.R. Hay, 'Employers and Social Policy in Britain: the Evolution of Welfare Legislation 1905-14', *Social History*, 3 (1977), p. 443.

20. This role of statistics in welfare measures is most explicitly formulated in Llewellyn Smith's Presidential Address to Section F of the British Association for the Advancement of Science. See *Transactions* (1910), pp. 9-17.

21. Beatrice Webb Diary, Vol. 19, 24 Aug. 1898.

22. *JRSS*, LXX (1907), pp. 553-82.

23. Tuckwell Papers, File 200 I, 'Sweating and Wages Boards', Leaflet by National Anti-Sweating League, 1909; P.R.O., LAB2/19/TB2677/1914, memo. by S.L. Besso on Labour (Minimum Conditions) Bill, 8 April 1914.

24. For a more general treatment of these issues, see R. Davidson, 'Sir Hubert Llewellyn Smith and Labour Policy 1886-1916', unpublished Cambridge PhD (1971), pp. 197-224.

25. P. Ford, *Social Theory and Social Practice*, (Shannon, 1968), p. 139.

26. P.R.O., LAB2/1479/L2343/1893, memo. by J.J. Wills on 'Labour Statistics and the Fair Wages Resolution', 19 Dec. 1904.

27. H.A. Clegg, A. Fox and A.F. Thompson, *A History of British Trade Unions since 1889: Vol. I 1889-1910* (Oxford, 1964), p. 404.

28. See especially, Board of Trade Memorandum on 'Proposals for Regulating Wages', PP 1913 (268) XIII, p. 11; Davidson, 'The Board of Trade and Industrial Relations', pp. 584-7.

29. P.R.O., CAB37/91/27, memo. by H.J. Gladstone on 'The Wages Board System in Victoria'; *Report on the Wage Board and Industrial Conciliation and Arbitration Acts of Australia and New Zealand*, PP 1908 (Cd.4167) LXXI; J. Rickard, 'The Anti-Sweating Movement in Britain and Victoria: The Politics of Empire and Social Reform', *Historical Studies*, 18 (1979), pp. 582-97.

30. PP 1913 (268) XII, p. 1437.

EPILOGUE

Since 1914, this conservative impact of official statistics upon government labour policy has remained a continuing source of frustration and concern to social reformers. In recent years, in particular, the issue has assumed increasing prominence within British social politics, and the rationale and scope of government statistics relating to the labour market have become the subjects of vigorous debate. A growing number of social commentators and activists have subscribed to a conspiracy theory of official labour intelligence, viewing it as a means of stigmatising problem ('deviant') groups within the workforce and of justifying social and industrial controls. It is alleged that the data base of labour policy-making is persistently massaged and manipulated so as to validate elitist and reactionary perceptions of dysfunctions within the labour market, consistent with the 'requirements of capital', and to evade, obscure or discredit structural diagnoses relating to income and welfare inequalities.[1] Within this framework of analysis, official statisticians stand condemned as 'quislings of the ruling class'.[2]

To a varying degree, radical criticism has been levelled at all the major areas of government labour intelligence. Official dispute statistics have been vigorously criticised for distorting the public image of the extent and legitimacy of labour unrest and hence the desirability of additional legal constraints upon the conduct of British industrial relations. The relative strike propensity of British industry has, it is alleged, been greatly exaggerated. Moreover, it is argued that official intelligence on the causation and character of stoppages has been unduly simplistic and biased against Labour; that it has failed to account for the role of fluctuating demand,

Epilogue

production problems and mismanagement in
initiating or sustaining industrial stoppages and
for disruption created by shifts in the conditions
or context of employment consequent upon
productivity-incentive schemes. It is also
contended that the incidence of unofficial and so-
called 'unconstitutional' strikes has been
inflated by official statistics in the pursuit of
statutory controls over rank and file militancy,
and that in locating the rationale behind
industrial disputes, government data has focussed
almost exclusively upon the conventional
categories of the terms and conditions of employment and assiduously ignored the broader
ideological roots of confrontation. Finally, it
is argued that, by uncritically equating strike
costs with the aggregate number of working days
lost and with the value of scheduled output as
assessed by employers, Whitehall has grossly
inflated the costs of industrial disputes to the
British economy. In particular, it is emphasised
that such estimates ignore pre-existing levels of
under-employment and overcapacity, the savings in
wages and materials during stoppages, and the
ability of large-scale enterprises to sustain
plant-level disputes with only a marginal impact
upon final output.[3]

Official unemployment statistics have also
encountered extensive criticism. The extent and
severity of the unemployment problem have, it is
claimed, been considerably deflated by a cynical
manipulation of the published returns. According
to this school of thought, by a series of cosmetic
devices, latterly characterised in *New Society* as
'statistical Tebbitry',[4] Whitehall has continued
to conceal the true dimensions of the problem, as
a means of preserving existing economic and
welfare policy options. As a result, the
efficiency of government measures has been
assessed in relation to a very unreliable index of
the state of the labour market. Critics have
contended that, by subtle adjustments in the
administrative definition of the unemployed and in
the techniques of accounting adopted, a significant proportion of British unemployment is
discounted in the official statistics. The
propensity of government statisticians to exclude
so-called marginal workers, such as married women,
from the returns, despite the fact that their
'marginality' is often a function of the severity
of the unemployment problem, has generated

---

particular concern, as being a mechanism for self-sustained public delusion. The narrow focus of unemployment enquiries undertaken by the statistical intelligence services has also received hostile press coverage; in particular, their determination to monitor 'scrounging' and abuse of the benefit systems rather than to gain greater insight into the social and economic costs and repercussions of unemployment.[5]

However, some of the severest strictures have been reserved for government statistics relating to working-class standards of living. Official earnings surveys have been censured for facilitating wage controls rather than identifying variations in disposable income and the real dimensions of low-income destitution within British industry. Meanwhile, the scope and composition of official cost of living indicators, and of the expenditure surveys upon which their weighting is based, have been criticised for failing to monitor the adequacy of wage earnings and, in particular, the disproportionate impact of inflation upon the purchasing-power of low-income households and the erosive effects of shifts in fiscal policy upon the social wage. The adoption of new price indexes has, in the view of poverty-action groups, constituted 'no more than an attempt to ask working people to wear officially provided rose-tinted spectacles', and served merely as a 'policy apologia' for economic and welfare strategies fundamentally inimical to the standard of living of large areas of the workforce.[6]

More generally, Whitehall's adherence to a statist, elitist definition of poverty based upon a narrow physical conception of need, and its failure to monitor the cause and extent of 'relative deprivation' have attracted vigorous criticism. Indeed, this is viewed by many social commentators as a deliberate ploy by the establishment to divert public attention away from the underlying but potentially divisive issues of income distribution and resource allocation within British society, and to restrict welfare intelligence to those aspects of the labour market most directly relevant to the 'needs' of the capitalist economy.[7] Moreover, it is contended that, in a period of financial retrenchment, this strategy has effectively discredited pressure upon social administrators and policy-makers to broaden their data base relating to low-income destitution as 'statistical scrounging'.[8]

Whatever the precise merits of such arguments, this study would suggest that, in general, radical concern for the role of official statistics in formulating labour policy is amply justified; that much of the investigatory response of government to labour problems is a cosmetic exercise and does not incorporate a genuine shift in the scope and rigour of enquiry. Partly, this is seen to be a function of logistical and institutional constraints; for example, problems associated with financial accountability or with bureaucratic resistance to the refinement and centralisation of official data. In part, it is also a function of broader societal resistance to the provision of information and to the inquisitorial role of the State.

Yet, this study clearly identifies the overriding constraint as being the social and operational philosophy of policy-makers and of their statistical advisers. It indicates that during a period of economic and social crisis, or perceived crisis, welfare intelligence is viewed as fulfilling a fundamentally conservative function; to retrieve and justify the consensus upon which existing policy options are founded rather than to provide the data base for their critique and re-appraisal, and to present crisis phenomena as 'manageable' within the existing framework of social theory and administration. As a result, official labour statistics fail to address the more structural issues underlying welfare debate, and government intelligence relating to the labour market becomes not only a very powerful constraint upon the content and outcome of social politics but also a decisive weapon in the armoury of social controls deployed by modern British government.

Epilogue

NOTES

1. See, e.g., R. Hyman and B. Price, 'Labour Statistics' in J. Irvine *et al.*, *Demystifying Social Statistics* (1979), pp. 222-36.
2. D. Triesman, 'The Radical Use of Official Data' in N. Armistead (ed.), *Reconstructing Social Psychology* (1974), p. 296.
3. M. Silver, 'Recent Strike Trends: A Factual Analysis', *British Journal of Industrial Relations*, 11 (1973), pp. 66-104; R. Hyman, *Strikes* (1975 edition), pp. 18, 25, 35, 47-8, 140-3, 151; H.A. Turner, *Is Britain really strike-prone? A Review of the Incidence, Character and Costs of Industrial Conflict* (Cambridge, 1969).
4. C. Pond, 'First you see it', *New Society*, 16 Dec. 1982.
5. See, e.g., F. Field (ed.), *The Conscript Army: A Study of Britain's Unemployed* (1977), Chs. 1,4,6;*Radical Statistics*, 16 (1979), p. 4; 25 (1982), pp. 2-4; 'The Rise and Rise of Unemployment', *The Economist*, 20 Feb. 1982; M. Wilkinson, 'The Controversial Computer Count of the Unemployed', *Financial Times*, 2 Dec. 1982; F. Field, 'Scroungers: Crushing the Invisible', *New Statesman*, 16 Nov. 1979; *Observer*, 24 July, 1983, p. 17.
6. *New Society*, 19 July 1979, p. 119; 23 Aug. 1979, p. 403; 20 Dec. 1979, p. 657; 9 April 1981, pp. 56-7; *New Statesman*, 24 Aug. 1979, p. 261; 26 Feb. 1982, p. 4; *Radical Statistics*, 12 (1978), p. 3; *Low Pay Unit Bulletin*, 28 (1979), pp. 4-8; *Low Pay Review*, 9 (1982), pp. 1-6.
7. See especially, P. Townsend, 'Politics and the Statistics of Poverty', in P. Townsend (ed.), *Sociology and Social Policy* (1976); *New Society*, 17 Sept. 1981, pp. 477-8; 1 April 1982, p. 13; 7 Oct. 1982, p. 22.
8. *New Society*, 7 May 1981, pp. 228-9.

MANUSCRIPT SOURCES

DEPARTMENTAL ARCHIVES (Public Record Office)

Board of Trade:

B.T.11 Commercial Department: Correspondence and Papers
B.T.12 Commercial Department: Out-Letters
B.T.13 Establishment Department: Correspondence and Papers
B.T.14 Establishment Department: Registers of Correspondence
LAB.2   Labour Department: Correspondence and Papers
LAB.7   Labour Department: Nominal and Subject Indexes
LAB.41 Statistics Branch: Selected Working Papers
M.T.9   Marine Department: Correspondence and Papers

Cabinet:

CAB.37 Photographic Copies of Cabinet Papers 1880-1916

Development Commission:

D.4   Correspondence and Papers

General Register Office:

R.G.19 Census Returns: Correspondence and Papers
R.G.20 Establishment and Accounts: Correspondence and Papers
R.G.29 Census Letter Books

Home Office:

H.O.45 Registered Papers
H.O.73 Various Commissions
H.O.82 Accounts and Estimates Entry Books
LAB.14 Safety, Health and Welfare: General
LAB.15 H.M. Factory Inspectorate

Manuscript Sources

Local Government Board:

M.H.10   Circular Letters and Returns
M.H.15   Registers of Papers and Correspondence
M.H.19   Correspondence and Papers
M.H.25   Miscellaneous Correspondence and Papers
M.H.78   Establishment and Organization Files

Ministry of Labour:

LAB.17   Statistics Department Files

Treasury:

T.1   Treasury Board Papers
T.3   Skeleton Registers
T.9   Out-Letters to Board of Trade
T.13   Out-Letters to Home Office
T.108   Subject Registers
T.171   Chancellor of the Exchequer's Office:
         Budget and Finance Bill Papers

OTHER INSTITUTIONAL ARCHIVES

Royal Statistical Society:

Council Minutes
Correspondence and Papers

Trades Union Congress

Minutes of the T.U.C. Parliamentary
Committee

PRIVATE MANUSCRIPTS

Civil Servants and Statisticians:

William Beveridge Papers (British Library of
Political and Economic Science)
Charles Booth Papers (B.L.P.E.S.)
A.L. Bowley Papers (Royal Statistical Society
Archives)
Sydney Chapman Papers (B.L.P.E.S.)

Manuscript Sources

Clara Collet Papers (in the possession of Mr. W.R. Collet)
W.H. Dawson Papers (Birmingham University Library)
Francis Galton Papers (University College London)
Robert Giffen Papers (B.L.P.E.S.)
Walter Layton Papers (in the possession of Lord Layton)
H. Llewellyn Smith Papers (in the possession of Dr S. Llewellyn Smith)
Alfred Marshall Papers (Marshall Library, Cambridge)
Passfield Papers (B.L.P.E.S.)
Karl Pearson Papers (University College London)
Gertrude Tuckwell Papers (Trades Union Congress Library)
Beatrice Webb Diary (B.L.P.E.S.)
A. Wilson Fox Papers (in the possession of Captain R.D. Raikes)
G.H. Wood Papers (Huddersfield Polytechnic Library)
G.U. Yule Papers (Royal Statistical Society Archives)
Yule-Greenwood Letters (in the possession of Mr. George B. Greenwood)

Politicians:

A.H.D. Acland Papers (in the possession of Sir Richard Acland)
A.J. Balfour Papers (Whittinghame Archive)
G.W. Balfour Papers (Public Record Office)
Sydney Buxton Papers (in the possession of Mrs. Elizabeth Clay)
Winston Churchill Papers (Churchill College, Cambridge)
Charles Dilke Papers (British Library)
Herbert Gladstone Papers (British Library)
W.E. Gladstone Papers (British Library)
Hicks Beach Papers (County Record Office, Gloucester)
Lloyd George Papers (House of Lords Record Office)
A.J. Mundella Papers (Sheffield University Library)
Rosebery Papers (National Library of Scotland)
Walter Runciman Papers (Newcastle University Library)

Full references to all the Parliamentary Papers, published works and learned articles, upon which I have drawn in this book or to which I have alluded, are contained in the footnotes to the text.

In the references given in the footnotes, it is to be assumed that the place of publication is London, unless it is stated otherwise.

Index

Index

Index

12 *passim*
and Treasury control
Ch. 7 *passim*
ideology of Ch. 11
passim
industrial resistance
to Ch. 9 *passim*
origins Ch. 3 *passim*
personnel and funding
Ch. 4 *passim*
statistical methods
Ch. 10 *passim*
Labour Exchanges
(bureaux, registries)
96, 142-3, 159-60,
162-3, 227, 268-9
Labour Gazette 98, 141-
2, 144, 182, 206, 270
labour mobility 186,
196, 215
Labour Movement
and labour statistics
89, 189, 206-8, 257-8,
264
and social reform 9-
11, 20-1
'Labour Problem'
crisis perceptions of
51-69
incidence of debate on
34-5
nature of 35-51
labour productivity 136,
141, 150, 154-5, 163,
181, 184, 186, 225-6,
243, 256-7, 266
Labour, R.C. on 39, 68,
95, 116, 118, 133,
172, 195, 215, 259,
262, 266
Labour Statistics
and social policy, Ch.
12
and Treasury control,
Ch. 7
content and rationale
Chs. 5, 11
deficiencies of Chs.
6,8
industrial resistance
to Ch. 9

production structure
Ch. 4
technical structure
Ch. 10
see also consumption,
cost of living,
earnings, employment,
expenditure, family
budgets, female
labour, home work,
hours, immigration,
industrial unrest,
Labour Exchanges,
labour mobility,
Labour Movement,
labour productivity,
low-income
destitution,
purchasing power,
savings, standard of
living, trade union
statistics, under-
employment,
unemployment, wage
costs, wage data,
working-class incomes,
working conditions
land reform 143, 162
Lavollée, R. 157
Lemieux Act 145, 263
Le Play, F. 156, 230
Levitt, I. 245
Liberty and Property
Defence League 209
Llewellyn Smith, H.
and Home Office 181,
183
and Treasury control
173-4, 176
background and
motivation 113-7, 126
statistical philosophy
109, 119-20, 146, 215-
20, 230-3, 269
Lloyd George, D. 15,
175, 178, 211
Local Authorities 18,
192-3
Local Correspondents 98,
113, 171
Local Government Board

289

Index

Index